Date Due

ROMANTICISM IN AMERICA

ROMANTICISM IN AMERICA

PAPERS CONTRIBUTED TO A SYMPOSIUM

HELD AT

THE BALTIMORE MUSEUM OF ART

MAY 13, 14, 15, 1940

EDITED BY GEORGE BOAS

New York

RUSSELL & RUSSELL

1961

810. 91
B 63 n

The publication of these papers is part of a Community Art Project made possible by a grant to the Johns Hopkins University by the Carnegie Corporation of New York.

42,602

March, 1962

PREFACE

For now three years there have been held at the Baltimore Museum of Art symposia on what may be called the history of taste. The purpose of these symposia has been twofold: to discuss in a series of papers the spread of aesthetic doctrine throughout the arts and culture in general, and to illustrate it as far as possible in painting, music, and the theatre. To do more than suggest the pervasiveness of certain ideas would have been impracticable, not only because of the financial and other material obstacles but also because of the problem's magnitude. To carry out such a program adequately would require the resources of a wealthy museum whose collections would embrace every period and style, the works of minor as well as major arts, a staff with leisure and knowledge to investigate remote corners of western culture, galleries which could be transformed into gardens and city squares if desired, a theatre with a troop of versatile actors, a ballet, an orchestra, and above all several years of free time during which the presentation could be prepared. It seems hardly likely that even were the material necessities at one's disposal, anyone would have the enthusiasm and energy to see such a plan through. What the editor of this volume and his collaborators have attempted to do is merely to indicate, to suggest, leaving it to the imagination of others to fill in the gaps.

In previous years the symposia have had as their subjects, Naturalism and the Greek Tradition. The former was chosen because it illustrated so clearly the lateral spread of an aesthetic doctrine during a given period, the latter because it illustrated the longitudinal spread. This year we return to a movement whose age is not great. One hundred and fifty years ago no one knew the word " romanticism " and the idea it named was only beginning to be felt. But, though the thing itself is new, its influence has been deep. As Professor Lovejoy has said, " There have, in the entire history of thought, been few changes in standards of value more profound and more momentous." [1] Two hundred years ago few critics, if any, would have judged a picture good because of its originality, its internal variety, its revelation of a human personality—the artist's, its difference. Whereas a few generations ago it was obvious that conformity to a universal rule was a mark of greatness, to-day most people call such conformity "unoriginality." Whereas a few generations ago a German, a Frenchman, an Italian, an Englishman would have sought to make works of art comprehensible and delightful to all men regardless of race and nation, to-day each strives to bring to fruition in his works those qualities which he feels to be potential in something called his "national (or racial) genius."

The romantic movement was, as everyone knows, international in its effects. But its teachings emphasized the desirability of difference. A German, for instance, was not only admittedly different from a Frenchman, but it was his duty to accentuate his difference, to be as German as possible. If God made different kinds of things, it was argued, He approved of variety; He wished things to be different from one another. The man, therefore, who would smooth out differences, who would strive for universal standards of goodness and beauty—and indeed even of truth—was acting counter to Divine Command.

In effect the demand for national and consequently cultural differences was a demand for liberation from Mediterranean civilization. For the civilization of the Mediterranean basin, Christianity in its Roman form, Greek and Latin letters and science and philosophy and law, was the one culture which had succeeded in spreading beyond narrow geographical limits to become the civilization of the western world. For sixteen hundred years after the birth of Christ no one thought of his local customs and superstitions as more than quaint survivals of barbarism. Greece, Rome, and Judea were accepted as the homes of ideas whose values were really universal, good for all men insofar as they were men. Religion was no longer the magic ritual of clan or tribe or nation; it

[1] *The Great Chain of Being*, Cambridge, 1936, p. 293.

[vi]

was the belief in a God who was the god of all men alike, whose laws were valid for all alike, whose love was equally distributed to all alike. The importance of the word " Catholic " lay in that; the Catholic church was neither national nor tribal, it was universal. Even when the authority of its terrestrial rulers was denied, the men who denied it asserted the fundamental tenet of one of its founders, Saint Paul. But by the eighteenth century nations arose whose people seemed to feel that their self-respect demanded a recognition of their own peculiar values. Classicism, if that is the proper name—what we have called " the Greek Tradition "—became merely another national culture; why was the Latin language inherently better than the German or French or English? That it was instrumentally valuable to have a universal tongue must have been obvious, but after all if one can have national churches, one can also have national languages. Again, in what sense of the word are the myths of Jupiter and Juno and the other Olympian gods inherently any more interesting than those of Odin and Thor and Freya and Loki? That art for two thousand years had used them to symbolize even Christian morality might have been expected to give them at least the value of habitual symbols. But, again, if each language has as much right to be spoken and read as every other, then the literatures expressed in each language are of equal value.

But since all nations in the seventeenth and eighteenth centuries had acquired certain common habits of thought, the only way left to discover the national genius of a people was to go back to a time before it was in contact with the civilization of the Mediterranean. The savage Saxon or Celt or Gaul or German alone could reveal the national soul in its purity. The folklore of these savages, their rude arts and laws, their rudimentary religious ideals, must be disinterred and revitalized, for in them alone could the *Volksseele* be found untouched by civilization. There was nothing surprising then in a new kind of primitivism, not now the cult of all primitive men, a Golden Race in the words of Hesiod, but the specific savages living in specific countries from whom a given nation might imagine itself to have sprung. Their ignorance could be called innocence; their barbarism childlike simplicity; their savagery primeval strength.

The forest primeval had disappeared from the Mediterranean basin generations before Homer. But in North Europe it still survived. Its darkness and its beasts, its wildness and mystery, were accessible to all who care to investigate them. They were the home of the forebears of Germans and Englishmen; they provided the *décor* for their rites. Consequently if the men were to be admired, so was their home. If they lived close to a state of nature, then nature must not be the nature of Vergil and Theocritus, the smiling Sicilian fields; it must be the nature of north Germany, of Wales, of Scotland, the nature of rocky crag and tumultuous cumulus clouds, of great waterfalls; untamed by human art, raw, terrible, sublime.

Such a setting for man's life held within it neither clarity nor even intelligibility. It was dark, forbidding, mysterious. It was a setting in which obscure forces were at work which could not be explained by the ordinary processes of reason. It was a world in which only the Magician, the Medicine Man, would feel at home. It was the world of Merlin, of Morgana, of the Wierd Sisters. To understand such a world rationally was impossible. Hence one must cease to make the effort and recognize the mysteries at the heart of reality. Magic, from the dark forms of Satanism to the more polite forms of table tipping, became logical consequences of such beliefs. Ghosts, maleficent spirits, vampires, became the natural subject for poets and novelists. Ruined castles took on the aspect of mountain crags; the ghosts who dragged their clanking chains over the wet stone floors replaced the nymphs and fauns who provided the supernatural elements in Vergil.

Could one find human beings in whom reason was either undeveloped, or entirely lacking, or subordinated to some psychic power attuned to mystery, one would have appropriate heroes for one's fiction. Such beings were children, fools, and women. Children had existed in literature from an early epoch but they had to wait for the Romantic Movement to become idealized. They are of course nothing more—and nothing less—than immature adults, but being more savage, and hence more "natural," than adults they were to be preferred to them by poets and other artists. They were held to have unspoiled, simple and innocent characters, all of which was true. A wolf likewise is unspoiled, simple, and innocent. And we have seen how in recent times man has been urged to develop his lupine nature. If one substituted for the word "unspoiled" the word "untrained," and made similar substitutions further on, the characterization of children would be equally true if not so attractive.

Fools, too, were unspoiled. That they had a kind of innate holiness had always been maintained, it seems probable, by folklore. The Wise Fool had the kind of wit that appears without training. He is inspired like the poet in Plato's *Ion*. God may be said to speak directly through him, as Zeus spoke through the oracle at Dodona. The fact that he does not know what he is saying makes his wisdom all the more wonderful. He is as close to Nature as a man can get without turning into an animal. The Fool in romantic literature becomes the rural clown or the simple peasant, the unlettered friar, the village cobbler, or sometimes the more polite Pierrot, who, after Victor Hugo and the romantic revolution of 1830, turns into the Bohemian. The poet as Bohemian is above all law and custom. He must have none of the bourgeois virtues. He must turn his back on schooling, relying on his spontaneous and instinctive ability to take its place. He must "live his own life," a procedure which invariably causes suffering, suffering which it is his glory to proclaim and other people's duty to share. If he is a drunkard, like Poe, or an opium eater, like De Quincey, a vagabond, like Verlaine, that is because the artist cannot live within the restrictions acceptable to other men. There is no making "sense" out of such a life, for sense lies within the realm of reason and the artist is the captain of the modern *Narrenschiff*. Is it any wonder that Freud thinks of art as the release of hidden fears and shames?

But the artist and the child were not alone in presenting to modern man the inarticulate wisdom of the ancient folk-soul.

Even more mysterious than the infant's babble and the artist's wail was the "enigma of woman." Whether German women were essentially different from English and Latin women, it is clear to anyone who reads that Goethe's announcement of the eternal lure of women was the cue for the *femme fatale* to enter the literary stage. From early Christian times—in fact from the time of Pandora—women had been the cause of many human ailments. But men knew only too well what it was in women that tormented them. There was no mystery, no puzzle, in the lure of Eve. It was just one of those terrible or comical facts that made up the complexity of human life. Priests and other moralists might warn their fellow men against the temptations of the flesh; Horace might point out that women were the most dreadful cause of war; Saint Bernard might thunder and denounce; Villon might describe the aged courtesan in the most revolting details; but the most vehement of them never felt that there was any enigma in the situation. When, however, a philosopher like Schelling began equating the female with the passive, dark, negative, yet fertile womb of Nature, every Gretchen, Corinne, and Molly could stretch, sigh, sink into a sofa and wait for the male with arachnid patience. Baltimore, which saw the birth of the most celebrated of these dark mysteries, in Annabel Lee, in Lenore, in Ulalume, must feel a certain fraternal interest in their history. Most of these languid women have died; if their race survives, it is probably in the more remote corners of Hollywood. Their last great representative, Theda Bara, whose surname in reverse suggests how the Orient colored the legend, was greeted not with hushed awe, but with howls of derision, when she recently appeared upon this city's screen.

Woman as a mystery had to have surroundings in keeping with her nature. The classic façade, which did well enough for the daughters of the revolution, was too clear and logical. Something dim, shadowy, with a faint touch of the religious, must be created. An architecture which had been developed out of the religious aspirations of the twelfth and thirteenth centuries, was turned to domestic use, and the Lucindas of the United States could—if

[x]

their husbands had the money required—move about in the stained glass light of Gothic drawing rooms. That the pointed arch and stained glass window were not inherently symbolical of domestic felicity was no more obvious to romantic architects than that Doric porticoes and Egyptian façades were not appropriate to banks and prisons. One had the best of precedent in Sir Walter Scott's Abbotsford.

It is easy to ridicule the Romanticists with their sentimental archaeology and spiritualistic metaphysics, but at the same time they were our direct ancestors. It is to them that we owe our sense of tolerance for individualism, our interest in primitive men, our love of rural nature, probably our kindness to children and animals. They could with plausibility be presented as the authors of the Woman's Movement and Progressive Education. When one stops to think of the future of America, with its medley of races and religions, one begins to see that Romanticism as a philosophy was much more useful to the country than the more traditional classicism. The Greeks and Romans, the French, the English, might with reason plead for convention, for over-individual standards, for tradition, for *genres tranchés*; when Americans attempted to so plead, they were bound to be following a blind alley. There was no American tradition in the arts and philosophy, and, what is more, there was never any American people in a racial sense of the word. The very founding of the United States was brought about by people of various national origins and the strength of American culture made itself felt at the very moment when American thinkers built on this varied foundation instead of denying it. It was the spirit of Romanticism which gave us Emerson, Poe, Bronson Alcott, Cooper, Melville, Thoreau, to name only a few outstanding names of that early period. All of these men and many whom they influenced had ridiculous traits, but if there is such a thing as American culture distinct from European culture, it is to such men that we must give thanks. There are those who think that no thanks are due for this doubtful gift. It is they especially who may benefit by reading this volume.

G. B.

CONTENTS

DEMOCRATIC BIFOCALISM:
A ROMANTIC IDEA AND AMERICAN HISTORIOGRAPHY

by

Eric F. Goldman

ON Christmas Day, 1832, the *Brig Jasper* sailed from Boston with tons of lumber, tobacco, sugar, beeswax, cheese, and young Ralph Waldo Emerson. For days a storm rocked the ship, and Emerson, between spells of seasickness and meditations about the bottom of the ocean, noted in his *Journal* what splendid men the sailors were. He noted, too, the words of the captain who believed that Americans, whether they were sailors or not, could show Europeans how to run things. Emerson did not disagree, nor would most of his countrymen have disagreed. To an American of the thirties, America was achievement and America was expectations.

In a Bostonian the national exuberance took a Boston form, for to him the United States was a vast and wonderful place centering in his city. And little wonder. No other community was more America's past incarnate; if the future did not belong to Boston, there was much in the city to permit Bostonians to think that it would. In the harbor floated scores of *Brig Jaspers*, ships that even Nelson's countrymen envied, ships that had sped American tobacco to Continental snuffboxes or put the Wong merchants on Boston ledger-books or introduced to far-off Calcutta the custom of using ice in table-drinks. In eastern Massachusetts and surrounding states, factories were multiplying, and Boston was their banker and their tie to markets scattered over the seas. "Where are your poor?" Lafayette wanted to know. On the Cambridge side of Beacon Hill he might have found a slum, but the dominant impression was one of prosperity, where the poor were comfortable and the rich had Chinese butlers serving Madeira in handsomely furnished libraries.

Libraries were important. People read and write adventurously in eras filled with a sense of emancipation, and the men who owned the ships and built the factories felt they were freeing themselves—freeing themselves from the village conservatism of John Adams, freeing themselves from England's condescension, freeing themselves from John Calvin's pitchfork. Boston, of course, was still Boston, and freedom was not permitted to dance unchaperoned. Unitarianism became what the wags called a cult of the arrived, village Federalism was replaced by industrial Whiggism, and speakers appeared in London-tailored suits to hail American superiority. There was something symbolical in Daniel Webster as he rose above his brandy tumblers and unpaid debts to summon others to respectability and the rights of property. Yet this huge, elemental thunderer, reveling in the lusciousness of words as of living, spoke for a good deal more than hypocrisy. His was the pride of people who had done things and knew it, of men delighting in their individual appetites and their individual ways of satisfying them.

Such rugged exuberance provoked its sharpest Boston reaction not so much from the unarrived but from those who wanted to go in a different direction. "Strange," Emerson remarked as the *Brig Jasper* tossed him about, "that because one of my neighbours had some trumpery logs and notions which would sell for a few cents more here than there, he should thrust forth this company of his poor countrymen to the tender mercies of the northwest wind." Strange, worse than strange to men like Emerson was the whole grapple-and-grab of an industrializing civilization. In particular they hated the hawk individualism of business, which they felt ended in everyone's pursuing the same bad ends in the same bad ways. Their appeal was for the individual to follow an inner self whom they, in their intimacy with the ways of the divine, declared to be an emanation of God. "Whoso would be a man," Emerson was sure, "must be a nonconformist." Webster, too, was an individualist but his was the anarchic individualism of men on the make. (The philosophy of Emerson not only made the individual everything; it also made him nothing except as he was part of a brotherhood of God-illumined men.) In writers of this school there was an emotional tendency to raise the cobbler and Daniel Webster to the same level as emanations of the Over-Soul, to exalt a mystical something called man or the people. (American Romanticism has meant many different things to many different critics.) But (the tendency to glorify the individual and an abstract people in a certain way was a unit-idea common to figures of the New England Renaissance and to writers like Walt Whitman who have come to be known as Romantics.)

(The certain way took form as part of the reconciliation the Boston Romantics made with their society.) Massachusetts in the thirties was full not only of brash money-making but of brash democracy, of agitation for social reform, of men with Utopias in their pockets, of fervent votes for Andrew Jackson. In important respects the Boston Romantics were closer to the Websterians than they were to the men for whom democracy meant food and clothing and money for a canal boat ride. They suspected, were sometimes even afraid of majorities. " Any man more right than his neighbours," Thoreau insisted, " constitutes a majority of one already." They had little enthusiasm for that liquor-drinking, hard-cursing, duel-fighting hero of mechanics and farmers, Andrew Jackson. Social reform interested them more if it concerned some other region's back yard. "The unmixed malignity, the withering selfishness, the impudent vulgarity" of a democracy in action— the words are Emerson's applied to a caucus of Jackson's followers—repelled these men. Yet the Boston Romantics were too much a part of the general exuberance, too interested in humanitarian tamperings with the status quo to isolate themselves completely from popular movements of the day. Exalting an abstract people and the individual simultaneously permitted them to float with these currents without being submerged in them. Glorifying man—the abstract people—gave the Romantics a sense of emotional oneness with the democratic whirl. When popular action took a form repellent to them, when men and women made money

[3]

by compromises with a harsh world, or staged strikes, or ruined the White House furniture in their enthusiasm for Old Hickory, then the abstract people was not talked about. The people became persons, persons whom the Romantic was inclined to call money-grubbers or the mob. The concept of the individual aided the Romantic further in expressing his dislike of such persons, for their action could always be called an infringement of the liberties of the individual. The people and the individual—these ideas, potentially useful in the most thoroughgoing democratic philosophy, contained in their Romantic combination little Lincolnian feeling for ordinary men.

In historical writing this democratic bifocalism is expressed most completely in a Bostonian of the Romantic era, George Bancroft. A protégé of the Harvard circle, Bancroft went further than most of his friends by actually campaigning for the party of Jackson, but his activity seems to have been motivated primarily by shrewd ambition. Certainly Bancroft gained politically, to use his phrase, by pulling his chair "close up" to the powers in Washington; certainly in him there was little sense of identity with the men and women he passed on the street. "I love to observe the bustle of the world," Bancroft wrote, "but I detest mixing in it. I like to watch the shouts of the multitude but had rather not scream with them."

There is a great deal of screaming for the multitude in Bancroft's *History of the United States.*

The declaration of independence [he declared in a typical passage] was silently but steadily prepared in the conviction of all the people; just as every spire of grass is impearled by the dews of heaven, and assists to reflect the morning sun. The many are more sagacious, more disinterested, more courageous, than the few. Language was their spontaneous creation; the science of ethics, as the word implies, is deduced from the inspirations of their conscience; the greatest jurists have perceived that law itself is necessarily moulded and developed from their inward nature; the poet embodies in words their oracles and their litanies; the philosopher draws ideal thought from the storehouse of their mind; the national heart is the great reservoir of noble resolutions and of high, enduring designs. It was the common people, whose craving for the recognition of the unity

[4]

of the universe and for a perfect mediator between themselves and the Infinite, bore the Christian religion to its triumph over every worldly influence; it was the public faith, that, in the days of the reformation, sought abstract truth behind forms that had been abused, and outward acts that had lost their significance; and now the popular desire was once more the voice of the harbinger, crying in the wilderness.

Much as Bancroft exalted the people, he was equally rapturous about the individual. Indeed, he attacked Rousseau because the French philosopher

lost out of sight the personal and individual freedom of mind. . . . Rousseau claimed power for the public mind over the mind of each member of the state, which would make of democracy a homicidal tyranny. He did not teach . . . that the sovereignty of the people presupposes the entire personal freedom of each citizen.

Entire personal freedom and the people—Bancroft, a Romantic in this as in other matters, glorified both and solved his dichotomy by hailing an abstract people. The abstraction was put into action only in historical incidents of which he approved. Bancroft delighted in the American Revolution; the people had made it. He considered the Constitution of unexcelled excellence; the people, by "meditation and friendly councils," had prepared it. The kind of popular action Bancroft disapproved is suggested by a line in which he glorified the American people because they "so thoroughly represented the middling class of the civilized world." When the people acted in a way that he considered unrepresentative of the middle class, the people became persons, persons violating the rights of the individual. Bancroft disliked the violence and the attack on property of the paper money movement which immediately preceded the writing of the Constitution. Though a majority in more than half the states at one time or another supported the inflationists, this majority, in Bancroft's *History*, is not the people but debtors or malcontents or insurgents. Indeed, the anti-inflation party was equated with "the mind of the country." In his opposition to the paper money movement the historian appealed further to the sacred individual, to "the security of private rights."

[5]

Bancroft's approach is emphasized by comparison with that of a contemporary Boston historian, Richard Hildreth. This man, an important Whig journalist, wrote history that was considered in its day the Websterian story of the past. Certainly Hildreth's *History* was in the Federalist tradition of not exalting an abstract people; the author, a conscious anti-Romantic, expressed his conservatism by having persons do things, and by praising and blaming persons. Hildreth liked the paper money rebellion in Massachusetts no more than Bancroft, but his account is a matter-of-fact one of struggling factions. Even when writing of the American Revolution, Hildreth frequently broke the people into persons in sentences like, " The old Committee of Correspondence at New York was composed principally of ' Sons of Liberty ' of the middle class, headed by M'Dougall, Sears, Willett, and Lamb, upon whose discretion the more wealthy citizens did not entirely rely." Partly as a result of this approach, Hildreth attached to himself the reputation of being out of sympathy with the more democratic trends of his day. Bancroft, who clung just as tightly to the fundamentals of the status quo, expressed himself in terms of a Romantic people and came to be regarded as the radical of early American historiography.

After the Civil War the people and the individual lived on as part of an essentially conservative terminology, but the concepts changed somewhat in a changing intellectual environment. By the time William McKinley entered the White House, American conservative thinking was hardening along Websterian lines. Emerson was dead, even the nonagenarian Bancroft was dead now, and with them had died other things. There was less exuberance over America as a spiritual force remaking the world and more thrill in the spectacular upward lines of wheat and steel on statistical tables. How the pages of Emerson's *Journal* would have sizzled had he heard Andrew Carnegie exclaiming, " The sixty-five million Americans of today could buy up the one hundred and forty millions of Russians, Austrians, and Spaniards; or, after purchasing wealthy France, would have pocket money to acquire Denmark, Norway, Switzerland, and Greece "! Conservative talk about democracy was shot through with the realization that politics, too, was business, and with apprehension that the business fabric would be torn apart by movements swirling among farmers and factory hands. The people, yes, but after all the country was overrun with income tax advocates, and "socialistic Slavs," and William Jennings Bryan. The individual, of course, but only in pulpits was there much demand that he be God-illumined.

Historiography, always a weathervane in the climate of opinion, swung toward a Websterian conservatism, but it did not adopt the terminology of Hildreth. Instead, historians continued to express their satisfaction with the fundamentals of the status quo through a concept of the people and of the individual. One school, counting among its members many of the men who made the writing of history a profession in the United States, provided an approach that fitted in with the growing fear of "socialistic Slavs." The older Romantic conception of the people, created before thousands of Russians, and Slovaks, and Carpatho-Ruthenians were tumbling into the melting pot, had not excluded newcomers as newcomers. Now the ships taking wheat and steel to Europe brought back immigrants who seemed to the old stock, as one scholar said, "the exact opposite of genuine Americans in everything which goes to make up folk characteristics." Such historians glorified a limited people—the Americans whom they made a part of a Teutonic or Aryan race. In addition to excluding the new migration, the Teutophiles also removed from their concept of the people groups who could be called immigrants only if an overwhelming proportion of the American population were to 'be called immigrants. In 1881, Edward Freeman, the English pontiff of the international Teutophile school, visited the United States and received the plaudits of his cardinals scattered in history professorships and other positions of influence. "Very many approved," Freeman found, "when I suggested that the best remedy for whatever was amiss would be if every Irishman should kill a negro and be hanged for it."

Transfixed by their abstract Anglo-Saxon people, the Teutophiles made their concept work for their conservation. The established institutions of the United States, they found, were the work of the Teutonic people; strikes, social legislation, socialism—in short, everything they disliked—were associated with mere persons, persons whose ancestors had not roamed the Anglo-Saxon forests. Anglo-Saxons did not do such things, Teutophiles were sure, because of that " principle of individual personality [which] lies deep down at the bottom of our characters." The individual and a people—again the ideas were a two-edged sword that was used to cut one way.

Teutophilism is plain in the favorite historian of McKinley's generation, John Bach McMaster.

The revolution by which we shook off the rule of England [McMaster wrote] was a Saxon revolution, and conducted with the sobriety, with the dignity, with the love of law and order that has ever marked the national uprisings of the Saxon race. The French Revolution was a Celtic revolution, and accompanied with the violence, the wanton destruction of property, the wilful waste of life, that has ever disgraced the movements toward liberty among the Celts.

In more ways than Teutophilism McMaster epitomized the approach of the new conservatism. His *History of the People of the United States* is known, and justly so, as the work which put ordinary persons into American history. In the eight bulky volumes we see different groups eating differently, dressing differently, and reacting differently to their political and social environment. Yet McMaster, too, had an abstract people—" that great tribunal," he wrote, " . . . before which in our country all public issues sooner or later must be tried "—and his abstraction served his conservatism. " The great middle class," Jefferson " saturated with democracy in its rankest form," " the [Jeffersonian] Republicans . . . the party of violence, of disorder, of mob rule," " the ignorant rabble . . . loudly declaiming against the evils of trade and manufacturing "—phrases like these scattered through McMaster's *History* indicate the kind of men he admitted to his abstract people and the type of instance when he implicitly invoked the individual to criticize the action of persons. McMaster's *History*, like McMaster, voted for McKinley, and nothing showed this more than the way he used the people-individual concept.

While McMaster was turning out his stout volumes, Frederick Jackson Turner exploded into the historical firmament. Turner, a son of Wisconsin, emphasized the West in a way that the predominantly Eastern historiography had never done. Not to the Anglo-Saxon race, not even to New England, Turner challenged, but to the frontier did Americans owe many of their most important habits. By running a vertical line through the United States, by dividing the country into an East and a frontier, Turner sharply divided the people. Yet Turner did not abandon an abstract people and the individual as a means of expressing his satisfaction with the fundamentals of the status quo. Far from destroying the people, Turner's work gave tremendous impetus to talk about American political habits, American individualism, the American mind—in short, the ways of a people. The difference was chiefly that this Westerner had desirable habits of the abstract people coming from an abstract section of the people—the frontier. The best known passage of Turner's famous essay argued

that to the frontier the American intellect owes its striking characteristics. That coarseness and strength combined with acuteness and inquisitiveness; that practical, inventive turn of mind, quick to find expedients; that masterful grasp of material things, lacking in the artistic but powerful to effect great ends; that restless, nervous energy; that dominant individualism, working for good and for evil, and withal that buoyancy and exuberance which comes with freedom—these are traits of the frontier, or traits called out elsewhere because of the existence of the frontier.

This glorified conception of the frontier and of a people profoundly influenced by the frontier gave Turner a way of expressing his apprehensions about the leadership of the Populist Movement and the socialistic stirrings in the cities. The West Turner liked was the one about which he could write, " This land of farm owners, this land trained in proven ideals, has a dry conservatism, at bottom, in spite of its social and political pioneering. It may yet make new contributions to America, by its union of democratic faith and innovation with a conservative subconsciousness." When the West acted with the approbation of Turner, the West was a people. " The West believed in the rule of the majority. . . .

The West demanded cheap or free lands. . . . The West as a whole developed ideals of the future of the common man, and of the grandeur and expansion of the nation," and so forth. When Turner disapproved, the West atomized into persons. In the bitter struggle over Kentucky's statehood, we read of the " Kentucky radicals " and settlers of " self-restraint." Many aspects of the agrarian movement after the seventies disturbed Turner, and we learn that " there never was in these fifty years a united Western movement." No historian has found the individual more useful to his purposes than did Turner. Social movements of which he disapproved worked to the destruction of those splendid " pioneer ideas of individualism and free competition." Bancroft, the Teutophiles, McMaster, and Turner—different as they were, these historians were alike in accepting the underlying premises of their society and all of them expressed this acceptance by a symbiosis of the people and the individual.

It is not surprising to find that an interpretation consistently splitting the people was adopted by an historian eager for basic change. As a young man Charles A. Beard was a case-study in dissidence. He worked with Socialists in England, helped found the Rand School of Social Science in New York, and wrote an account of the Industrial Revolution that reads like a popularization of *Das Kapital*. Many things Beard disapproved were supported by the prevailing idea that the people had created them. The Constitution, a natural subject of attack by men interested in drastic changes, received part of its sanctity from the popular assumption that it had sprung from the people, and Beard's first important book was *An Economic Interpretation of the Constitution*. Challenging the Bancroft and the Teutonic schools, making a bow to Hildreth, approving Turner as far as Turner went but going far beyond, Beard argued that the Constitution was the product not of the people but of factions struggling primarily over economic ends. An interpretation based upon the way men make a living has no room for the people or the individual in a Romantic or a pseudo-Romantic sense, for a horizontal line drawn across society pushes aside everything except persons. The people were split into economic groups; the individual manufacturer and the individual factory hand were no longer interchangeable units. In order to defend what he considered the interests of ordinary men and women, Beard attacked the people and re-defined the individual. The historical philosophy behind *An Economic Interpretation of the Constitution* has not been accepted by many American historians or, indeed, continued in its extreme form by Beard himself. But economic interpretations, sweetened by qualifications and, often, by other names, are steadily atomizing the people and socializing the individual.

Whatever changes may be coming over the concepts among professional historians, they linger in many an American mind in their early form and must be given a place with the ideas that have influenced thought and action in this country. The people and the individual were in existence as concepts before the Romantic Movement and had been used, either singly or jointly, by both conservatives and reformers. The ideas would have proved significant had Romanticism never touched this country. But that movement spread them and drove them in more deeply. Because American Romanticism was basically conservative, it helped shape the combination of ideas into a means of expression for democratic thought that was not entirely democratic. The people and the individual, used in this way, did much to put the Tory in our history; and Mr. Beard's method of attack on these ideas may do much to make history the hissing of Tories. No more curious scene presents itself in the history of ideas than that of a fervent democrat who, in his eagerness to protect and broaden the concept of democracy, felt it necessary to rescue individuals from the individual and persons from the people.

NEW PATTERNS OF GREATNESS[1]

by

Eleanor Patterson Spencer

THERE is a bookish taste to all American art of the early nineteenth century. Pedimented Doric porticos and Hudson River Bracketed have at least this in common, that both represent the fruits of the library quite as much as of the native genius of the artist. The demand for painted and sculptured portraits was surely fostered by universal respect for the literary portraits of the heroes of early classical education as well as by the works of art which perpetuated the features of ancestors. Art in its deeper sense meant to the patron of the day a canvas depicting one of the sublimer episodes from the Old Testament, or a tragic motif from the history of ancient times. These could be counted upon to demonstrate good taste and to elevate morals.

To draw a line between Neo-classic and Romantic art of this period becomes impossible if one insists upon a broad definition of Romanticism. There is much in common in the points of view of such artists as Powers and Greenough, who have been labelled neo-classicists, and Washington Allston and Thomas Cole who are generally taken as American romanticists. The aspirations of these four men who are fairly characteristic of American artists of the first half of the century confirm this wider concept of Romantic art.

The whole generation of the 1830's and 1840's seems to have longed desperately to be great. The self-conscious expression of this is of the very fabric of Romanticism, to be linked with the

[1] The writer of this essay is so deeply indebted to the *Flowering of New England* that an appreciative acknowledgment cannot be limited to a mere footnote. If any flavor of Van Wyck Brooks' writing be perceptible in these pages, may the reader accept it as a tribute to that master and an expression of the writer's admiration.

wholehearted recognition of the individual, including oneself, the high values set upon human experiences, and the consequent tolerance of opposites practised by true Romanticists.[2] The idea of greatness is not to be confused with that of Fame, which implies the significance of the applause of the world rather than the strong inner conviction of achievement. In the dreams of a romantic youth *to be great* is the sole justification for the drudgeries of living—until he discovers that life may be made more than endurable by love, with or without greatness. The young Italian Leopardi was already aware of this when he wrote " Mediocrity frightens me; my wish is to love and to become great by genius and by study." [3] Willing to work, conscious of power and fearful of failure, the Italian poet wanted then only a pattern of greatness on which to focus his genius and his ambition. Four Latin words, *per aspera ad astra*, inscribed in the diaries of young and restless Americans voiced this ambition more tersely.

The yearning for fresh modes of greatness came naturally a century ago to the sons and daughters and grandchildren of the American Revolution. The world seemed secure. There were no heroic deeds of battle to be repeated, unless one could go to the aid of the Greeks as today's youth enlists in foreign legions. Frontier life was almost too remote to interest young men in Boston, Philadelphia and Baltimore. The realization that achievement in the world of learning and the arts might lead to greatness rose like a rocket to light up those young minds. " Great writing is only an inevitable substitute for great action " remarked Tuckerman, explaining Leopardi's choice of a literary career. With a sudden perception of the real heroes of America Jared Sparks focused his energies upon the editing of a *Library of American Biography* in twenty-five volumes. The portraits by Gilbert Stuart and Chester Harding record a public that was equally well worth painting.

These men were not afraid to work. Tall tales of fourteen,

[2] JACQUES BARZUN, " To the Rescue of Romanticism," *The American Scholar,* Spring 1940.
[3] H. T. TUCKERMAN, *Mental Portraits,* 1853, p. 152.

sixteen or even eighteen hours at the desk and the easel may be verified in letters and diaries, for the Romantic generation accepted without question that two-fold recipe for becoming great "by genius and by study." If the light of genius flicker now and then, it could be taken for granted that the moral value of work, "which alone will get intellectual bread," [4] would, in the darker hours, steady the seeker after literary and artistic greatness.

"Those who have in their minds the pattern of greatness recognize this pattern wherever they find it" writes Brooks,[5] elaborating Channing's notes upon the need for greatness in the learner as well as in the lessons if there is to be any profit therefrom. The Romanticist, being a pluralist, would have taken this to mean that there would be more than one pattern from which to choose, in order to avoid the limitations of the single model conceived by the classicist for imitation and repetition. The American men of 1830, taking genius and study as the formula for achievement, sought their several patterns at home and abroad, in the ancient, ever-new search for the infinity of God, in a passion for the sublime, and in wonder at the supernatural. Transcendentalism resolved the conflicts in some minds and hearts. "Not a reading man but has a draft of a new Community in his waistcoat pocket," remarked Emerson to Carlyle in 1840. Brook Farm, Oneida and the phalansteries of the Fourierists demonstrated more or less briefly the beauty and the impracticality of the communal life as a pattern for society. The younger generation had reason enough to doubt the efficacy of Noyes' perfectionism, the genuineness of Millerism, whose second Advent was twice dated and twice unfulfilled, or even the doctrines of Transcendentalism. With unusual sharpness, Lowell dismissed the case of these Apostles of Newness, as they were called in New England. "Everybody had a mission (with a capital M) to attend to everybody else's business. . . . Communities were established where everything was to be common but common sense." [6] In the long run it was easier for

[4] JAMES RUSSELL LOWELL, *Collected Works*, v. I, p. 93.
[5] VAN WYCK BROOKS, *Flowering of New England*, p. 92, note.
[6] JAMES RUSSELL LOWELL, *Thoreau*, 1865.

the Romantic mind to " find the light shining through the works of nature and her poets." [7] Painter, poet, lecturer or preacher, they all turned to nature, not in the hope of finding more than was really there, but out of that burning need to reconcile diverse experiences of the heart and of the mind which had led others into Transcendentalism. Every sensitive man's record of his experiences could be of interest to his contemporaries not because it expressed his individuality but because it was a contribution to the understanding of human experiences.

The infinite power of God seemed a little nearer in the presence of great mountains, vast panoramas, immense rivers and ancient oaks. Most of the men who went to Europe remembered and came back, Washington Irving to his Hudson, and Thomas Cole to his Catskills. For the untravelled Easterner Bauvard painted a panorama of the Mississippi and Bingham recorded the fur traders and Indians. Kensett praised the Genesee and Lake George, Bierstadt paid tribute to Mt. Corcoran.[8] As for Niagara Falls, what poet or painter, lover or lecturer did not search for the terms in which to express this American miracle?[9] Niagara Falls was at once sublime and supernatural and real, a divine sign upon the earth visible to every eye. For the most part, however, the painters agreed with Thomas Cole who noted that " although American scenery is often so fine, we feel the want of associations such as cling to scenes in the old world. Simple nature is not quite sufficient. We want human interest . . . to render the effect of landscape complete." [10] When in the *Course of Empire* or the *Voyage of Life* he set the stage for episodes of human interest Cole commanded every appropriate " mood " of nature from snowcapped peaks bathed in a serene sunlight to thunderous skies, windwhipped trees and supernatural rainbows.

The use of the sublime as a means to greatness of art and literature is often the subject of intellectual and appreciative analysis

[7] Barzun, *Op. cit.*
[8] Corcoran Gallery, Nos. 204 and 16.
[9] C. M. Dow, *Anthology and Bibliography of Niagara Falls*, Albany, 1921.
[10] L. L. Noble, *The Course of Empire, Voyage of Life and Other Pictures of Thomas Cole, N. A.*, etc., 1853.

in the lectures of William Ware.[11] Unitarian minister, novelist, friend and biographer of Washington Allston, he taught the public to separate the sublime from the beautiful in nature. He proved the inferiority of " the natural sublime " to " the moral sublime " and warned his audiences away from " the false sublime" which deals with the merely frightful or appalling, as in *The Bloody Hand.* This was a subject taken by Allston from Mrs. Radcliffe's Italian novel, " a picture of small size which really seems unsuitable to a subject designed to awaken the emotions of the sublime."

To any American of this period unspoiled nature seems to have meant the primeval landscape, but not magnificent animals or primitive man. Perhaps nerves were still too sensitive to the dangers of frontier life to permit American versions of the Noble Savage. To be sure, James Fenimore Cooper wrote the *Last of the Mohicans* and Lydia Maria Child produced a dark-skinned hero called *Hobomok*, but the American public was certainly not ready to welcome the concept of an ideal savage. For the same reason, possibly, there are no real counterparts in American art to Delacroix's lion hunts and Barye's preying jaguars. The American public celebrated the *Last of the Buffalo* with Bierstadt,[12] or thanked Providence for the cage which separated him from the tired King of Beasts in the travelling circus.[13]

The ornithological interests of Audubon and Alexander Wilson were scientific, yet romantic for all that. No real difference existed between Science and Romanticism until much later, if ever. Turner was not the only one whose mind quickened with wonder and admiration for the railroad.[14] Tuckerman estimated Hawthorne's genius as a Romantic writer in such terms as these: " What the scientific use of lenses—the telescope and the microscope—does

[11] W. WARE, *Lectures on the Works and Genius of Washington Allston*, Boston, 1852.

[12] Corcoran Gallery, No. 17.

[13] A natural humanitarianism fostered by the Transcendental movement and focused by the passage of the Fugitive Slave Act brought Harriet Beecher Stowe to the point of writing *Uncle Tom's Cabin*. A practical sympathy for animals was oftener expressed by vegetarianism than by art.

[14] Rain, Steam and Speed, 1851.

[16]

for us in relation to the external universe the psychological writer achieves in regard to our own nature." [15]

The effect of Europe upon the American romanticist was stimulating or stultifying according to the "pattern of greatness" within each artist. How could he *not* go to Europe? It was "the home of his protoplasm." [16] There only could he hope to find in the landscape those associations with the heroes of his early reading, the associations which Cole found lamentably lacking in American scenery. If the trip to Europe was a home-going, it was also a sentimental journey out into the unknown, calculated to fill the breast of the American with nostalgia for his native shores as well as for the glorious past, and to give him simultaneously that aura of superiority which emanates still from every tourist who has passed triumphantly through the perils of foreign immoralities, bacilli and banditti.

The earlier travellers inclined towards England, the land of their fathers and their language, where they could speak with Coleridge and Southey and even with Carlyle. They soon found congenial Englishmen in Rome and Florence—Bryant heard from a friend that "four thousand English visit Florence every winter" [17]—the more congenial that both were strangers in a strange land. "Italy was classic ground, and this not so much by association with great events as with great men . . . to the American Italy gives cheaply what gold cannot buy for him at home, a Past as once legendary and authentic, and in which he has an equal claim with every other foreigner. In England he is a poor relation . . . of France his notions are purely English . . . but Rome is the mother country of every boy who has devoured Plutarch . . . Italy gives us antiquity with good roads, cheap living and above all, a sense of freedom from responsibility . . . the sense of permanence, unchangeableness and repose. . . ." [18] This analysis of the significance of Italy to the American was

[15] *Op. cit.,* p. 250.
[16] BROOKS, *Op. cit.,* p. 464, quotes T. G. Appleton.
[17] W. C. BRYANT, *Letters,* 1834.
[18] JAMES RUSSELL LOWELL, *Leaves from my Journal,* 1848.

entirely acceptable to those expatriates who sat faithfully at the feet of Raphael and the antique. Circumstances made involuntary exiles, however, of some of these students and perhaps limited their development as representative Americans. Those who came home found often an unsympathetic or an indifferent public. Washington Allston, "the American Titian," rich in friendships, pursued his painting with difficulty in Boston's colder intellectual climate. Hiram B. Powers, on the other hand, never left Florence but never forgot Vermont. Greenough, seeking confusedly through the galleries of Italy, sent home an unexpectedly impressive monument to George Washington. When finally the need for freedom brought him back to the United States, his thoughts on art and life cleared brilliantly in the form of lectures, not sculpture. Thomas Cole, whose work is to be discussed in a subsequent article, represents a fourth and more modern phase of the American artist's attitude toward Europe. Italy was a place to go for fresh material for his profession. The sunset behind St. Peter's always reminded him of his beloved Catskills, and he hurried home.[19]

Allston, who counted among his friends Coleridge, Lamb and Wordsworth, Cooper, Irving, Vanderlyn and Turner, characterized himself thus: "I am by nature, as it respects the arts, a wide liker. I cannot honestly turn up my nose even at a piece of still life, since, if well done, it gives me pleasure."[20] The implication of conflict between the accepted values of subject matter and the interests of craftsmanship is a clue to his weakness. His personal pattern of greatness was based on the high emotional intensity of Romantic drama, of the morally sublime, rather than upon an understanding of pictorial structure. For his friends he was the very model of a Romantic artist. The banditti of a Gothic novel, the supernatural ghost story, and the inexplicable grandeur of the Old Testament could rouse in him an equal passion. He had, according to his friend Washington Irving, "the

[19] NOBLE, *op. cit.*, p. 314.
[20] W. DUNLAP, *The Arts of Design in the United States*, 1834 (ed. 1918, v. II, p. 310).

sentiment of veneration so characteristic of the elevated and poetic mind. . . . His eyes would dilate; his pale countenance would flush, he would breathe quickly and almost gasp in expressing his feelings when excited by any object of grandeur and sublimity." [21]

Contemporary criticism of Allston's work invariably reveals a bias of personal friendship. He was the Romantic artist-ideal, possessing even in a casual meeting "that artist-look which seems to see pictures ever in the air, and which, if it fall on you, makes you feel as if all the world were a gallery and yourself the rather indifferent Portrait of a Gentleman hung therein." [22] His self-appointed critic, William Ware,[23] emphasizes constantly Allston's general cultivation of mind, his powers of application, his "noble and elevated principles" with regard to the filling of commissions, his truly religious mind. "Another foundation of his eminence was that he so often painted upon a large scale, the scale of life or the colossal, . . . which leads with certainty to correctness and truth of form, and gradually to a grand style of drawing, and even higher style of thinking and designing. It elevates the mind as well as improves the hand." [24] Although Ware admitted that "he was, perhaps, too various in his labors to reach the loftiest point in any one," no one failed to grant to Allston's work the quality of beauty even to the point of identity: "He dwelt in beauty, and beauty in him. He was it." "However one's notions might be modified by going to Europe, one always came back with a higher esteem for Allston," said T. G. Appleton. "Whoever has considered the speculations of Shelley on dreams, the theories of Coleridge . . . or heard Allston tell a ghost story, must have been convinced that there is a natural provision for wonder as well as for reason in select intelligences." [25] Yet returning to Boston in 1818 full of admiration for this "mighty empire" of America, Allston could never recreate the

[21] DUYCKINCK, *Cyclopedia.* Article on Washington Allston.
[22] JAMES RUSSELL LOWELL, *Cambridge Thirty Years Ago,* 1865.
[23] WILLIAM WARE, *The Works and Genius of Washington Allston,* Boston, 1852.
[24] *Ibid.,* pp. 4-14. To Horatio Greenough, on the contrary, mere size was often a matter of "the arithmetical sublime."
[25] H. T. TUCKERMAN, *Mental Portraits,* 1852.

passion which had led him to begin *Belshazzar's Feast*. His friends unanimously loved him, listened to his marvellous stories, pitied him and blamed themselves. "How narrow Boston was! . . . That unfinished Belshazzar of his was a bitter sarcasm on our self-conceit. Among *us* it was unfinishable." [26] Lowell, writing years later of this tragedy, concludes that "the daily life of the man is the greatest masterpiece of the artist."

A marble statue of Phocion in his father's garden apparently set the pattern of greatness for Horatio Greenough.[27] Washington Allston, greatly his senior, charmed the young college student and turned his thoughts from Harvard toward Rome. There Greenough followed for a time a systematic study of the antique in the Vatican, as well as drawing and painting from life at the academy. After an interval of several months at home and in Paris to recuperate from malaria, he returned to Italy, reaching Florence via the marble quarries of Carrara, to make his home there for the next twenty years. A commission from his friendly compatriot, James Fenimore Cooper, to translate into marble the chanting cherubs of a canvas by Raphael made the student feel like a professional sculptor. During these years it is probable that, like Powers, he found much pleasure in the company of fellow-Americans. In his first studio, as Tuckerman describes it, "one of the rooms was fitted up in the American style. Here beside a wood fire on winter evenings it was his delight to greet friends, . . . speculate on the news from home, criticise works of art, and tell stories." [28] Later, when he had married Miss Louisa Gore of Boston, Greenough's home became "the favorite resort of Americans." In Florence he found the legacies, the literary associations and the recreations which wholly satisfied him. But when censorship and espionage began to interfere with his freedom of speech and action, without hesitation he packed his possessions and started for home. He was eager to enter into the free social and artistic life of the United States, "inspired by

[26] JAMES RUSSELL LOWELL, *Collected Works*, v. VIII, p. 182.
[27] H. T. TUCKERMAN, *A Memorial of Horatio Greenough*, 1853, p. 13.
[28] *Op. cit.*, p. 24.

that spirit of enterprise which marks even the speculative opinions of our country. Looking around him with the eye of an artist and the heart of a patriot, he was conscious of a new scope and motive, both for his genius and sympathies." Greenough was immediately our most intelligent and courageous critic. "There was a remarkable communicative instinct in Greenough; and the results of his studies and experience were the property of his friends," writes his biographer. "A disinterested mental activity was the distinctive and invaluable trait of his character." Reading the lectures and half-prepared memoranda now, it is astonishing to recognize in Horatio Greenough our first proponent of Functionalism. Here is a man whose intellect, ripened in Italy by contact with the past, sprang into full creative activity under the impact of the energy of his native land. To the end of his life there is conflict between Greenough, the sculptor of the "ideal" and Greenough, the defender of "beauty as the promise of function." One would like to think that this could be resolved by a fresh study of the art of the man who could so early see beauty in clipper ships, racing sulkies and New England farmhouses.

Hiram B. Powers should have had marble in his very bones, born and bred in Vermont, in the region "where the hills were of solid marble and marble pigsties rose on lonely farms." [29] He too thought to fulfill his pattern of greatness by study in Italy, and chose Florence for the sake of the fine marble there. Thanks to Edward Everett and Nicholas Longworth, Powers and his Cincinnati wife arrived in Florence in 1837. The sculptor's mind was already furnished with a boyhood vision of the *Greek Slave*, but he found that American patrons and others paid cash more willingly for marble likenesses of themselves. So for years Powers patiently modelled his sitters in clay, reworked the plaster casts, and taught Italians to help him with the preliminary cutting of the marble versions. Commissions poured in. There was never enough time or strength left for more than few of the works which he felt himself equipped "by genius and by study" to

[29] BROOKS, *op. cit.*, p. 188.

create. This may explain the comment of W. W. Story, an American fellow-sculptor but an expatriate by choice, who wrote to Lowell about Powers in 1849, "He is a man of great mechanical talent and natural strength of perception, but with no poetry in his composition and I think no creative power." Certainly one must read this in the light of Story's own rather weak concepts of "poetry" and "creative power." As firsthand evidence for Power's "natural strength of perception" the portraits are supplemented by a note that he selected his models by preference from "what are called the working classes . . . because the best models are found in those walks of life where nature predominates over art." [30] In fact, far from being a neo-classicist, Powers is said to have evinced little enthusiasm for the antique sculpture of the museums, but to have had his own strong opinions of what constitutes great art. Although he made a home for his family in Florence he sought American and English rather than Italian friendships, maintaining his Vermont speech from indifference rather than from conscious pride. He would have preferred life in America to that in Florence, but there was simply never enough money with which to maintain an equally comfortable home for his wife and nine children in the United States. Other than cheaper living, there were two advantages for him in Florence: fine marble and an abundance of models. Powers resigned himself to deriving an income from the portraits, with an occasional respite for his favorite personifications.[31]

Had Powers ever returned to the United States he might have shared the experience of Horatio Greenough. "An American citizen who has gone abroad to study a refined art presents himself before his countrymen at a disadvantage. To the uninitiated, his very departure from these shores is an accusation of the fatherland. If he sail away to strike the whale on the Pacific, or load his hold with the precious teeth, and gums, and sands of Africa,

---

[30] D. E. BRANCH, *The Sentimental Years*, p. 172.
[31] For much of this material I am indebted to a grandson of Powers, Charles W. Lemmi. It will be impossible to recover the full significance of this artist's contribution to American sculpture without the publication of his letters.

it is well; but to live for years among Italians, Frenchmen, and Germans, for the sake of breathing the air of high art, ancient and modern, this is shrewdly thought by many to show a lack of genius, whose boast it is to create, and we are often asked triumphantly if nature is not to be found here on this continent." [32] There is a little of this in the attitude of Thomas Cole, as he felt his art mature in the shadow of American mountains. As soon as he could capably invent a substitute for the "associations" which he had missed earlier in his contemplation of American landscape, he frankly made a second trip to Italy (1841) only to "renovate," as he put it, his "artistic feelings." He was far more interested to introduce such Americans as Bryant and Durand to the beauty of the Catskills—but this is to trespass upon the field of the next essay.

These four men represent their contemporaries, all of whom shared the Romantic aspiration for greatness and sought a pattern not only in noble subjects and colossal size but in turning to a part of Europe where the very proximity of greatness seemed to promise achievement. That Allston was overwhelmed by the experience, that Powers endured or ignored it, that Greenough was confused for a time by it and that Cole deliberately took only what he wanted is testimony to the individualistic character of the American Romanticists. Subsequent analysis of their achievement, in the form of the works of art, as against the recorded aspirations and intentions of these artists, is a measure of American Romanticism better made in the museum than in books.

---

[32] H. GREENOUGH, *Aesthetics at Washington*; TUCKERMAN, *op. cit.*, p. 61.

THOMAS COLE AND THE ROMANTIC LANDSCAPE

by

Walter L. Nathan

SCARCELY accessible in the superintendent's apartment, the New York Public Library preserves a perfect gem of American romantic landscape painting which, for its intrinsic beauty as well as for its historic associations, deserves to be better known to the friends of American art. Through a framework of steep rocks and overhanging trees a wide view opens into a wooded valley extending in peaceful and unspoiled grandeur to the distant mountains gilded by the rays of the afternoon sun. The sound of water leaping over cascades fills the balmy air. Two middle-aged men stand on a rocky ledge at the left. One seems to enjoy the scene silently, while the other interprets its beauties to him. (*See* Pl. I.)

When we read the names engraved on the bark of the nearest tree: Bryant and Cole, and the artist's signature: A. B. Durand 1849, we realize that this painting was intended as a memorial to Thomas Cole, the painter, who had died the year before. How fitting is this fine tribute to the one whose art had first opened the eyes of his countrymen to the charm of their native land, and who had rendered in paint the romantic visions which his friend had expressed in poetic words. No one, too, could have been a worthier recipient of this tribute than the poet, William Cullen Bryant. He had been Cole's friend through many years, and had given testimony of this friendship in his funeral oration before the National Academy of Design in New York. This document will always rank high in the annals of American literature for its stirring eloquence and depth of thought, and, at the same time, it is one of our best sources for Thomas Cole's life and work.

The title Asher Brown Durand gave his painting, "Kindred Spirits," [1] throws a significant light on the close connections between painting and literature in American romanticism. For Bryant and Cole were not only personal friends, but met on a ground of common ideals and convictions. Both the poet and the painter loved nature and walked with her, like Wordsworth, in a " spirit of religious love "; they saw in her the truest revelation of God. Nature to them was always meaningful, always expressive. In each lovingly observed detail they felt the hand that had created the universe. Thus, Bryant's poems trace forms and sights with the carefully descriptive touch of a painter, while Cole's paintings vibrate with the insight and imagination of the poet. Moreover, Thomas Cole has produced poetry of unusual merit, thereby linking himself to the large group of romantic artists who sought and found expression in more than one field of creative art. Goethe, Victor Hugo, Philipp O. Runge and, most conspicuously of them all, William Blake, would not confine themselves to writing or painting, but made use of both. E. T. A. Hoffmann and, later, Richard Wagner were writers and composers; Gottfried Keller hesitated for years whether to become a painter or a poet.

This attempt to cut down the barriers between the various arts is one of the characteristics of romanticism that have led to much misunderstanding and criticism. The romantic artist will not adhere to the " laws " of poetic or pictorial form. He does not separate experiences of eye, ear, and mind into different categories. Typical is Tieck's: ". . . each of her soft, charming movements describes in lines a beautiful music," or his praise of the garden of poetry (from " Prince Zerbino," 1799) where the goddess Fantasy has united what the envious gods had separated so that " the sound here knows its color " and color, smell, song are brothers. When Coleridge dreams ". . . That with music loud and long, I would build that dome in air " (" Kubla Khan ") or Shelley speaks of " thought's melody " (" Epipsychidion "), they

[1] DANIEL HUNTINGDON, *Memorial Address for Asher B. Durand*, for the Century Club, New York, 1887, p. 33.

[25]

indicate the romantic artist's conviction that all the arts are ultimately bound together in the one-ness of the great creative power.

> And what if all of animated nature
> Be but organic Harps diversely framed,
> That tremble into thought, as o'er them sweeps
> Plastic and vast, one intellectual breeze,
> At once the Soul of each, and God of all?
>
> (S. T. COLERIDGE, *The Eolian Harp*, 1795).

The romantic artist, however, is acutely conscious that with the artistic means at his disposal, he can never hope to express his cosmic ideal, this " intellectual breeze," in the closely circumscribed sphere of a single production. His reaching over into the other arts is the result of a despair that tries the impossible. He knows that it will forever lie beyond his powers to convey the full measure and intensity of his vision; but his vision is so strong in him that he will keep trying. A work of romantic art is therefore not " finished " in its final state; we have to accept it merely as an approximation towards something greater than itself. The romantic artist scarcely ever feels satisfied with his work; he will often leave it as a fragment, or else bury his original experience under a labored, repetitious, and sometimes cumbersome effort. Romantic novels are frequently tiresome to read; romantic poetry proceeds at a pace too leisurely to fit our age of speed, and romantic painting, too, will annoy us by an insistence on detail and elaboration where we want to find rapid execution and a clear-cut design. Perhaps this explains why romantic art in general is little appreciated to-day other than in the concentrated short lyric or the quick sketch. We condemn the introduction of ideas, whether poetical, philosophical, or religious, into painting as contradictory to the nature of visual expression. In consequence, we are apt to dismiss romantic art as an aberration.

Such a point of view cannot do justice to the productions of our own romantic painters, loosely grouped together as the " Hudson River School." From the lavish praise which greeted them in their own time, they have sunk into general oblivion. But gradually

they seem to emerge again from this "undeserved disrepute." [2]
We begin once more to see the passages of compelling beauty, the
flashing revelations of a breath-taking immediacy of vision that
romantic art has in store for us if we grant it time to grow upon
us. While not overlooking the self-confessed limitations so appar-
ent in these works, we are taking a renewed interest in what they
have to tell us. In the wake of carefully planned and organized
exhibitions such as the Whitney Museum's " Century of American
Landscape " of 1938, voices were heard that asked for a revised
estimation of Allston, Cole, Inness, and even Whistler.[3] The
severely critical attitude of a decade ago appears already dated.[4]
It is to be hoped and expected that this reawakened interest will
bring to light many paintings mentioned in the older sources
which have not yet been located; until that time, our understanding
of American romantic art must needs remain incomplete.

What has just been said of the Hudson River School applies
with equal force to its most eminent member, Thomas Cole. More
than a third of the eighty-two pictures assembled for the memorial
exhibition held shortly after the artist's death in 1848, without
including all his then known works, are still unaccounted for.
Fortunately, we are well informed about the painter himself,
thanks largely to his early and enthusiastic friend and biographer,
the Rev. Louis L. Noble.[5] Bryant's funeral oration, and the chapters on Cole in Dunlap[6] and Tuckerman[7] furnish additional
material.

As reflections of very personal experiences the works of a ro-

[2] "Paintings of the Hudson River School," *Supplement to the Bulletin of the
Metropolitan Museum of Art*, New York, Oct. 1917, p. 3.

[3] HELEN A. READ in *American Magazine of Art*, March 1938, p. 168. Cf. also
EDWARD A. JEWELL in the *New York Times*, Jan. 23, 1938.

[4] Cf. SUZANNE LaFOLLETTE, *Art in America*, New York, 1929, pp. 128 seq.,
and RILLA E. JACKMAN, *American Arts*, Chicago, 1928, p. 64.

[5] (The Rev.) LOUIS L. NOBLE, *The Course of Empire, Voyage of Life, and
other pictures of Thomas Cole, N. A.*, with selections from his letters and miscellaneous writings . . . , New York, 1853. (Hereafter referred to as NOBLE.)

[6] WILLIAM DUNLAP, *History of the Rise and Progress of the Arts of Design in
the United States*, New York, 1834, vol. ii, pp. 350 seq. (Hereafter referred to
as DUNLAP.

[7] HENRY T. TUCKERMAN, *Book of the Artists*, New York, 1867, pp. 223 seq.

mantic artist are closely linked to the inner and outer rhythms of his life, and to the factors of environment which he assimilates or rejects. Thomas Cole's love of nature; his interest in great history, his pessimism, and finally his trust in the benevolent guidance of a superior wisdom, are alike traceable to the various stages of his life.

From his early years on, Thomas Cole learned to look upon nature as a refuge from the vicissitudes of poverty, and a solace for the lonely heart of a poet. His family lived in poor circumstances in Bolton-le-Moors, home of cotton-spinning industries in Lancashire, England. There the painter was born on February 1, 1801, as the youngest but one of eight children. The boy was soon sent to work on engravings for calico in a print works, and came to know the hardships of child labor. From tedious hours of toil, he would seek relaxation in long walks with one of his sisters, in playing the flute, listening to the ancient ballads of the hills, and writing poetry. It is easy to imagine that the inspiring verses of the poets of recent fame, Wordsworth, Coleridge, Shelley, Sir Walter Scott, or Lord Byron, must have found in him an eager disciple. We can also assume that already at this time his mind was impressed by the dramatic visions of Milton's poems; their rhetoric and imagery formed one of the elements of Cole's later style, as they had also guided William Blake's receptive soul into the solitudes of prophetic thought and form.

The hope of finding a promised land across the Atlantic caused Cole's family to immigrate to the United States where, in 1819, they made their first home in Philadelphia, soon after proceeding to Steubenville, Ohio. Some of their relatives had already settled near Baltimore, and the family soon became americanized. But the eagerly expected financial success did not come. In what was then the frontier region, the craft of the father was doomed to failure as a luxury. (He printed wallpaper.) Poverty remained their constant companion. For some time after the departure of his family, Thomas Cole had stayed in Philadelphia, and we hear of a voyage to St. Eustatia—enlivened by an encounter with a pirate—where he sketched a view of the island. Later, he set out on foot, with a friend, to join his family. The narrative of this trip reads like a translation of one of Eichendorff's romantic novels; all the carefree gaiety, the music, and the boundless optimism of that German masterpiece, the "Taugenichts" ("Good-for-Nothing") seem to have sprung to life.

Cole was as lonely in Steubenville as he had been in England. He was of a reserved and shy nature, and, we can say like all romantics, of a somewhat feminine disposition. For the helplessness of his situation, he sought relief in rambles along the Ohio, in melancholy hours in the woods, in poetry and music. These years laid the foundations for the deeply poetic attitude towards nature which he retained through life. Noble is certainly right when he suggests that much less important at that time was what he *did* than what *was doing in him*.[8]

Cole had already shown interest in drawing and copying from whatever illustrations he could find when the visit of an itinerant painter finally decided him on his career as an artist. Stein gave him an English book where the boy found the great masters treated as heroes and pillars of human civilization. From that moment on Cole had found his vocation. He improved on his sketching and painting and, after some landscapes, tried his hand at portraiture, because that was the only branch of art likely to offer some prospects of success in the hinterlands of America. The country, during the first decades of the nineteenth century, was much too busy extending frontiers and conquering the newly won soil to hold out much encouragement to artists. Outside the leading cities of the East and the plantations of the South, artistic life was practically non-existent, though the eternal urge for self-expression has wrung from many an unsophisticated farmer or craftsman pictures which charm us in their "primitive" simplicity. What itinerant "limners" there were barely eked out a living by producing those "likenesses" that served in the place of our family photographs. They were frequently obliged to accept the oddest painting jobs in order to keep body and soul together.

When Thomas Cole went to try his luck and establish himself

[8] NOBLE, p. 26.

as a bread-winner independent from his family, he met nothing but disappointment, suffered great hardships, and ran into a debt that haunted him for years. In Pittsburgh, where the luckless family made their next home, he studied nature first-hand, sketching details of trees, plants, and rocks, and advancing to the careful execution of whole landscapes. Little as we know of these early efforts, they proved of greatest importance for his art.

But the lowest point in his fortunes was reached when after a dreary journey he settled in Philadelphia in a renewed attempt to break loose from the care of his family. The account of his utter poverty there, aggravated by sickness and solitude, is immensely moving. It would have broken the spirit and courage of anyone less enthusiastic, ambitious, and visionary. But the lonely young dreamer did not give up. His nature remained amiable and unembittered as we know from various accounts of people who met him then. Nonetheless, the dark outlook on life and the feeling of despondency formed within him in these disastrous years tinged all his later work, finding expression not only in the gloomy mood of the "Course of Empire" and "Voyage of Life," but likewise in his romantic preoccupation with death which runs through his journal and produced the contrast between the tragic "Return" and the gay "Departure." Perhaps these sufferings help to explain why he loved the dark sides of nature, thunderstorms and deluges, and why his evening landscapes with all their loveliness almost invariably make us sad.

Cole survived the ordeal of two winters in Philadelphia. He got a few commissions for commercial work, once published a tale, "Emma Moreton," in the Philadelphia *Saturday Evening Post*, and occasionally drew at the Academy. However, he never got proper instruction in anatomy, and this made itself felt in the weakness of his figure-drawing. Altogether he has to be considered as a self-taught artist.

When he followed his family to New York, he did not acknowledge defeat, but continued to paint, a narrow garret of his father's house on Greenwich Street serving as studio. His unbroken faith was finally rewarded. Some little landscapes which he exhibited in a shop sold for forty dollars and, what was more important, brought him into contact with one of the buyers, who took enough interest in the young artist to make it possible for him to visit the upper Hudson valley and the Catskills. It was the turning point in Cole's life. The landscape paintings which he brought home soon caught the attention of two leading New York artists, John Trumbull and Asher B. Durand, and the critic, William Dunlap. They bought his pictures and made his acquaintance, acclaiming him as a new genius. " This youth has done what I have all my life attempted in vain," Trumbull is quoted as saying.[9] Dunlap brought Cole's name before the public, and soon after he received enough commissions to paint landscapes so that he could increase his prices, " and his faculty of handling, as well as his truth and power of coloring." He spent the following summers in Catskill, N. Y., in the house where he later was to make his home, and went to the City only for the winter. These years saw the spectacular unfolding of his talent until his renown was such that Dunlap could call him, in 1834, " one of the first painters in landscape, as I believe, that the world possesses, and one of its most amiable of men." [10]

Was it pure coincidence that brought Cole to the historic valley of the Hudson at the critical stage of his career? This part of the country had just won its greatest popularity. Romantic history had been enacted here not so long ago, and romantic fancy was busy weaving a shimmering net of poetry and fiction around it. In the year 1821, James Fenimore Cooper had published his first novel, " The Spy." In 1823, " The Pioneers," and in 1826, " The Last of the Mohicans " had followed. In the same year 1821, William Cullen Bryant, Cole's senior by eleven years, gave the nation his first volume of verse, including the famous " Thanatopsis." One year before, Washington Irving's " Sketch-Book " with the tales of Rip van Winkle and Sleepy Hollow had appeared and been received with applause. These books gained full recognition for the romantic movement in American literature. Inspired by the pride with which Americans began to look upon their country and

[9] DUNLAP, p. 360.   [10] Ibid., p. 351.

its now firmly established freedom, they in turn spread a wave of enthusiasm for things American through the United States. As America had no mediaeval castles or cathedrals to evoke romantic longings for the past, her writers—and, shortly after, her painters—responded to the appeal of her picturesque nature and colorful history. In fact, the "picturesque" was rediscovered. Robert Rogers of the "Rangers" had been one of the first to note the "romantic and noble scenery" of the mountains and lakes of Northern New York and New England.[11] The great change of taste in favor of the "picturesque" was, however, a result of the romantic movement. England had taken the lead with a new conception of beauty in nature. Pope, Addison, Horace Walpole had ridiculed the French idea of embellished nature; the formal garden gave way to the "picturesque" English type of landscape architecture which, together with the revival of the Gothic style, spread like wildfire through Europe and the United States. Country houses sprang up all along the Hudson imitating the Tudor mansions of Old England, and surrounded by extensive grounds where the hand of the gardener had arranged charming groups of trees so as to give an always varied impression of (what appeared to be) free nature at her best. Gardens were made to flow into the neighboring landscape without a perceptible break, and presented the pleasing effects of Claude Lorrain's or Salvator Rosa's popular paintings. A. J. Downing, the landscape gardener, even suggested planting trees of different foliage so that they imitated, by the gradation of their hues, the "aerial perspective" found in landscape painting and created as it were, an "artificial distance."[12]

There can be no doubt that Cole was deeply impressed by this rediscovery of the romantic landscape. He brought with him from the frontier a sense for the beauty of unspoiled nature, and his own poetic leanings welcomed the associations which Irving,

[11] As quoted by EDWARD E. HALE in "The Early Art of Thomas Cole," in *Art in America*, vol. 4, New York, 1916, p. 24.

[12] A. J. DOWNING, *A Treatise on the Theory and Practice of Landscape Gardening, adapted to North America* . . . , New York, 1856, p. 136 *seq.*

Cooper, and Bryant had found in the Hudson River scenery or brought to it through their works. Among his early paintings is a " Scene from The Last of the Mohicans" in the Wadsworth Atheneum in Hartford. It illustrates the dramatic scene near the end of the book when Cora proudly defies the schemes of Le Subtil, Uncas arriving too late on the spot to save her life. Cole laid the scene in a romantic wilderness. Huge crags overlook the rocky platform where the warriors have formed a wide circle round the main actors of the drama. To the left, the mirror of a lake is visible behind the mountains. A dark pond partly fills the right foreground. The artist was chiefly interested in the grandeur of the mountain scenery against which the figures almost disappear, a peculiarity often found in his landscapes. The incident itself is well expressive of the character of the setting, and was certainly not added as an afterthought, as the arrangement of horizontal and vertical planes is clearly intended to set the figures into relief. The literary and the pictorial thus go together in Cole's work from its very beginnings, and the picture is a valuable document for the strong influence on him of contemporary romantic literature.

Thomas Cole soon felt deep in love with the picturesque beauty of the mountains near the Hudson. He was an untiring walker and discovered, to his ever increasing delight, the unending variety of hills and dales, woods and streams which were still close enough to the frontier to have remained in a state of almost unbroken wilderness. The country became so dear to him because there was always a new horizon behind the last. One of his later remarks is significant. "Why," he asks, "do not the younger landscape painters walk—walk alone, and endlessly? . . . How I have walked, day after day, and all alone, to see if there was not something among the old things which was new!" [13] Here speaks the same romantic Wanderlust and longing for the far-away which the German romantics embodied in the symbol of the elusive blue flower. After a day's rambles, Cole would write down some description of the scenes and incidents witnessed, or express in verse

[13] NOBLE, p. 81.

a thought or sentiment. It became an axiom with him that "to walk with nature as a poet" was the necessary condition of a perfect artist.[14] The friendship with William Cullen Bryant further strengthened this conviction. Cole developed into a master of prose and poetry himself, and were his writings collected and edited, he would occupy his rightful place in American literature. His descriptions of nature are always vivid and imaginative, and even antedate, in "The Bewilderment," the weird mixture of fact and fancy of Edgar Allan Poe's romanticism.

"The Bewilderment" gives a fascinating glimpse of a hurricane which surprised the artist in the mountains. He relates his plunge into a dark pond, and how he floated down a subterranean stream on a broken tree, until he landed on firm ground again and found his way to a solitary farm-house. The "Cascade in the Catskills," a painting of 1826 in the Wadsworth Atheneum, has a similar air of suspense, of solitude, and the mysterious silence of the woods. The fall of the waters from an unseen source into an unseen abyss, the ghastly forms of broken trees, and the darkness of the sky are fitting expressions of the spirit of wilderness. Technically the picture is but the work of a beginner, yet it proclaims the poetic inspiration of a true Cole.

A different, but equally poetic mood is touched in a beautiful little panel in the same collection—Mr. Wadsworth was one of Cole's earliest patrons and collectors—"North-West Bay, Lake Winnepesaukee, N. H." of 1825. With its solitary lake in endless woods it is a truly American scene. We can understand how his friends and the discriminating public felt delighted at finding the painter represent native landscape at its most picturesque. There was no landscape painting prior to Cole that could claim this distinction. His immediate predecessors, Birch and Doughty, had seen their aim in landscapes of a more topographical character. Ralph Earl's graceful "Looking East from Leicester Hills" of 1800 in the Worcester Art Museum owes its charm to the faithfully portrayed landscape rather than to merits of artistic treat-

[14] *Ibid.*, p. 62.

ment.[15] And Washington Allston, friend of the poet Coleridge, had imbued his "Deluge" and "Elijah fed by the Ravens" with romantic spirit, but had never attempted a specifically American landscape. (*See* Pl. II.)

Cole's landscapes, in particular those of his early years, have usually been labelled "realistic." But Cole never was intentionally a realist. We need only compare his landscapes with Doughty's, Kensett's, or even Durand's to know that realism is not their characteristic sign. Cole never treated his landscapes as delineations of particular scenes in a topographic sense. They are "composed" landscapes, free transcriptions into the language of a romantic poet. Line, form, and color work together to create a picture which does not exhaust its significance in their pleasing arrangement, but evokes a distinct mood. In the "North-West Bay, Lake Winnepesaukee," for instance, the branches of the four slender trees at the left, curving gracefully upward before the sloping lines of the woods, express the same longing and devotion that live in every other part of the picture. The quiet expanse of water, the rhythmical line of the mountain ridge, the delicate silhouette and reflection of the bending tree on the island, and the gently receding right shore leading the eye into the distance, all fit into this poetic mood of stillness, solitude, and love. Cole has found expression for the hidden spirit of nature. The single hunter, or in other cases, herdsman or canoeist, often with his back to the beholder, only serves to emphasize this spirit. These are scenes such as Irving, Cooper, or Bryant had envisaged them.

Where a specific commission made closer adherence to topographic truth necessary, as in the "Mt. Washington" in Hartford, Cole found means to bring out the poetic element by sharp contrasts of lines and light and dark masses. The "Mt. Washington" has great depth, but the foreground and middle distance show a certain dryness, and the total effect is not concentrated enough to be convincing.

From the poetic to the spiritual was only one step. Cole some-

[15] Cp. LLOYD GOODRICH in "A Century of American Landscape Painting, 1800-1900," *Whitney Museum of American Art*, New York, 1938, p. 6.

times would ascend a mountain not to make sketches or enjoy the view, but " for thought." Face to face with nature, he would burst into song. Far in the distance rose a sacred hill; if he could sleep there for an hour and awake inspired with poetic fervor! Then would he tell of the pleasures that spring like flowers in the bosom of the wilderness, and call his fellow-men

> . . . to kneel in Nature's everlasting dome,
> Where not the voice of feeble man does teach,
> But His, who in the rolling thunder speaks,
> Or in the silence of tenebrious night
> Breathes in his power upon the startled ear.[16]

Experiences of this kind had to find an outlet in his art. They point towards symbolism as a logical consequence. It appears in outwardly " realistic" landscapes as an undercurrent that grows stronger with the years, and is the motivating force behind Cole's religious and historical paintings. Symbolism unites his whole work and stamps it with the personal style which distinguishes Cole's pictures from those of his contemporaries. While landscapes of the " Hudson River School " often look very much alike, one who has entered the spirit of Cole's nature poetry will identify his hand instinctively wherever he paints with real inner concern.

Two of his earliest ventures into the "allegorical" are the " Expulsion from Eden " and the " John the Baptist in the Wilderness." The "allegorical" was particularly sought by the romantics. " All beauty is Allegory. The most sublime, being inexpressible, can only be said in an allegorical way," Friedrich von Schlegel had said in his " Discourse about Poetry." [17] " The Expulsion " of 1828 now hangs in the superintendent's apartment of the New York Public Library near Durand's "Kindred Spirits." Unfortunately it has darkened to such an extent that local color is almost gone. Even close inspection does not reveal all the details. But the main features of the composition still stand out

---

[16] From " The Wild," NOBLE, p. 64.
[17] As quoted by GERSTENBERG-RAVE in *Die Wandgemälde der deutschen Romantiker im Casino Massimo zu Rom*, Berlin, 1934, p. 170.

clearly. A pointed rock gate in the center divides the picture in two sharply contrasted sides. On the right, a sunny, fairy-tale like view of the flowery grounds of Paradise; on the left, dark horror and desolation. A volcano in fiery outburst mounts over a wild pile of forbidding rocks. Streams rush down in cascades into a black abyss in the foreground, and a terrific thunderstorm blots out the smiling sky of Paradise. Arrows of unearthly light shoot from Eden's gate and point out the pitiful figures of the first pair crossing a stone bridge. They wander away into a windswept barrenness. A huge wolf stands over the carcass of a freshly killed stag, and the twisted trees are contorted into the grotesque shapes of hideous masks.

Though in a very poor state of preservation, the picture still impresses through its inspired conception and bold execution. But it lacks persuasive power. The dramatic left half outweighs the other too much, especially as the garden of Eden is treated in too minute detail to allow of a clear impression. The painter obviously felt more at home with scenes of wilderness. But his imagination has run away with him. We pity the poor sinners in the horrors of wildest nature, and cannot believe that such was their just punishment. Details such as the volcano, which reminds us of the famous " Cotopaxi " by Frederic E. Church, Cole's pupil, in the New York Public Library, or the fantastic trees in front reminiscent of Baldung, Rosa, or Magnasco, can still be admired.

Being less crowded, the " John the Baptist in the Wilderness " of about the same year—in the Wadsworth Atheneum—is more effective. All the ingredients of romantic landscape are here: the towering cliffs, the sunlit, sharp-ridged mountains, the cascades, the upward sweeping curve described by areas of brightest light. Purely imaginative details added to motives from the Catskill mountains combine to an astonishing landscape of very " nordic " character, where only the palm-tree looks strangely out of place. The small figures are again nothing but accents on important spots of this expressive vision, placed where they seem to belong. (See Pl. III.)

Cole was to learn that the public preferred his native landscapes and did not willingly follow him into the spiritual. But the voice in him was stronger than considerations of worldly success, and a straight line leads from these first attempts to the " Course of Empire," " Voyage of Life," and " The Cross and the World." Before they were started, Cole passed through the great experience of his first visit to Europe.

It had become a well established tradition among American painters to visit Europe. West, Copley, Vanderlyn, Allston, and Trumbull had set the example. Cole felt that a pilgrimage to Italy was a painter's " duty." [18] His itinerary led him first to his native country, England. It was a disappointment. He could no longer feel at home there. The climate, the absence of unspoiled scenery, and the rather meager success of his exhibitions threw him into a depression which a brief stay in Paris did not help to alleviate. The atmosphere of perfect freedom in Italy, the congenial people he met, and the great impressions of nature, history, and art, finally broke the spell. He worked and studied in Florence, Rome, and the Campagna. News of his parents' sickness called him home in 1832 after spending three years in Europe.

With somewhat mixed feelings, Cole's friends has bid him godspeed for his voyage. They had greeted enthusiastically his American landscapes and were afraid lest Europe's scenery and great masters might overwhelm the young artist and estrange him from the very different nature of his home country. In a sonnet " To Cole, the painter, departing for Europe," Bryant implored him to " keep that earlier, wilder image bright." But while he was still young in years and unknown outside of the States, Cole no longer considered himself a beginner. The good and bitter experiences of his life had already determined his outlook, and the romantic nature of the North-East was so well suited to his temperament that he stood in little danger of being diverted from his true course. On the contrary, his convictions and predilections made him a biased critic at least of contemporary European art, taking encouragement and giving praise only where he felt an inner relationship. His notes on European art and nature are

[18] NOBLE, p. 104.

therefore highly revealing for the influences which must have worked on him in some way or other.

In London, he met Sir Thomas Lawrence, Constable, and Turner. The art and technique of Constable was too far removed from his own to elicit much of comment, neither did he seem to care for Old Crome and his school. Of Turner's work he preferred the earlier, Lorrainesque period and particularly admired the " Dido Building Carthage" of 1815 in the National Gallery. In the productions of Turner's more recent periods he missed stability of form and the spirituality that had become of prime importance to him. Always somewhat weak as a colorist, he suspected quite naturally in Turner's color-fantasies a form of art that served only as " food for the gross eye, which is as well satisfied with the flash and splendour of jewelry." [19] The one English landscape painter who was really to his taste was Richard Wilson, early romantic of the eighteenth century, whose solid forms, luminous skies, and clear distances appealed to him. The only copy that Cole made from a painting during his entire stay in Europe was from a Wilson. One wonders that he did not notice the art of Patrick Nasmyth (1787-1831) who in some romantically inspired landscapes comes fairly close to his own style without, however, sharing Cole's deeper insight.

While in London, Cole painted one of his grandest visions of romantic nature, the " Tornado" of the Corcoran Gallery in Washington, D. C. Perhaps it has a trace of Salvator Rosa's wild picturesqueness, then highly popular, but the main impression is one of strength, originality, and actual experience. In fact, a prose description, in Cole's journal, of a storm in the Catskills reads almost like an interpretation of the painting. Magic light from a rift in the dark clouds hovers over a turbulent place of turmoil and disruption. Howling, hissing, roaring sounds of the windstorm lashing the treetops seem to burst from the canvas. The cracking noise of splitting wood, the splash of rain, and the bellowing of thunder unite to a fortissimo painted in almost impressionistic dashes and with a surpassing power of suggestion.

[19] *Ibid.*, p. 116.

The " Blocksberg " scene from Goethe's Faust, or the " Wolf-schlucht " from Weber's opera " Der Freischütz " translated into American! Yet we do not get a feeling of theatricality. The helpless wanderer behind the tree might be Cole himself who during a similar storm and cloudburst could note that his situation was becoming every moment less comfortable, but more " romantic." [20]

Cole loved such moments of magnificent uproar when earth and heaven are instruments in one great cosmic orchestra performing a grandiose symphony. The " Expulsion from Eden " showed one of these thunderstorms, the " Oxbow," the first and fourth pictures of the " Course of Empire," and the third of the " Voyage of Life " repeated the same motive in variations. A very fine " Land-scape " in the Rhode Island School of Design, datable shortly after his return from Italy as similarities to the first picture of the " Course of Empire " indicate, represents perhaps the finest version. Unlike the " Tornado " it does not show the storm at its height. The weather is drawing off, obliterating behind its dense curtain of rain the whole right distance. On the left, in one of Cole's favorite sharp contrasts, the summit of a lofty hill that is bathed in glorious sunshine rises majestically behind a shadowy ridge in the middle ground. The mountain lake in the center reflects rocks, trees, and the sky. This landscape shows the painter in full possession of his means of expression. The composition is easy to understand in its essentials, with diagonal lines leading into the distance, contrasts of light and shadow in sharp relief, the chiaroscuro so dear to him, the splendid light blues and greys of the transparently clear sky, and the romantic gnarled trees and few sketchily painted plants near the lower border. These trees are no " mannerisms " [21] though they became standing parts of his repertoire. For Cole they were always expressive, and not only because their sinuous lines repeat and enhance the main lines of the composition. In a description of a similar lake scene we read: " The dead trees are a striking feature in the scenery of the lake, and exceedingly picturesque. Their pale forms rise from the

<hr>

[20] *Ibid.*, p. 69. [21] HALE, *op. cit.*, p. 39.

margin of the deep, stretching out their contorted branches, and looking like so many genii set to protect the sacred waters. . . . What a place for music by moonlight! It would be romance itself!" [22]

We may object to such an attitude towards nature as not " naïve," but we cannot deny its being perfectly genuine. If we adopt Schiller's classic definition of the naïve and sentimental poet, Cole—like all other romantic artists—very decidedly belongs to the " sentimental " side. The " sentimental " artist is less concerned with the actual forms of nature than with the feelings and emotions they call up in him. Long hours of solitary thinking, and his poetic inclinations, caused Thomas Cole to react on nature in such a " sentimental," that is, self-conscious way. He was denied the purely visual joy of a Monet or Renoir; his experience of nature was always emotional or symbolic. So when he felt an " indescribable melancholy " in the wildernesses or saw, in a lull during a thunderstorm, " expectation hung on every crag." [23]

No wonder then that the painter registered only disgust before the specimens of contemporary French art. Neither the coldly academic style of the David-Ingres school, not the " murderous and bloody scenes " [24] of the romantic painters, especially Delacroix, could find sympathy with him. The German romantics in Rome were more to his heart. Significantly he applauded them for painting " with more soul." [25]

Cole offers indeed a striking parallel to the tendencies of the German romantic school. Philipp Otto Runge (1777-1810) and Caspar David Friedrich (1774-1840) were deeply emotional painters who like Cole refused to content themselves with the perceptible aspect of nature. Cole would have agreed wholeheartedly with Friedrich's doctrine: " The painter should not only paint what he sees *before* him but also what he sees *in* him. If he does not see anything in him, let him cease painting what he sees before him." [26] Friedrich was a solitary dreamer who put

[22] NOBLE, p. 203.   [24] DUNLAP, p. 363.
[23] *Ibid.*, p. 68.   [25] *Ibid.*, p. 365.
[26] KURT K. EBERLEIN, *Deutsché Maler der Romantik*, Jena, 1920, p. 57.

down on canvas, in his bare Dresden studio, the great visions that nature inspired in him. Often before Cole's finest landscapes we feel reminded of Friedrich's. The "Roman Aqueduct" in the Metropolitan Museum in New York, painted 1832 in Florence, approaches perhaps most closely the German's style. It is remarkable for the expressive sky and the delicately painted vapors drifting up somewhat like those in the " John the Baptist in the Wilderness," only with more subtlety. The general impression is not of an Italian scene but of a romantic, almost nordic landscape. Dorner has noticed the affinity between Cole and Friedrich,[27] yet it seems little probable that Cole ever saw one of the latter's beautiful compositions. A similar outlook on life has led to similar solutions in art. Neither could Cole get into contact with the work of Runge, unless through engravings. He would have found in Runge, whose untimely death was a severe loss to German art, a soul tuned to the same key as his own: " What now are the exigencies of art? First, our intuition of God, second, the perception of ourselves in harmony with the universe, third, religion *and* art, that is to express our highest feelings through words, music, or pictures." [28] Both Runge and Friedrich were " symbolic" artists; they were convinced of the unity in all the manifold forms of nature.

Still another parallel between Runge and Cole deserves mention. For many years Runge experimented with colors to find out about their symbolism. In his never completed " Vier Tageszeiten" ("Four parts of the Day") he planned to give an immense " abstract, picturesque, fantastic, musical poem with chorus, a composition for all the three arts together, for which architecture had to erect a unique building." Sketches for this utterly romantic plan of a " total " work of art show colors built up like the melodies of a symphony and assigned to (painted) instruments so that "tones of color and music embrace each other." [29] Thomas Cole, too, thought of the music of colors. " I believe that colors are capable of affecting the mind, by combina-

[27] *Bulletin, Rhode Island School of Design*, vol. XXVI, April, 1938, p. 8.
[28] EBERLEIN, *op. cit.*, p. 30.   [29] *Ibid.*, p. 36.

tion, degree, and arrangement, like sound. . . . It is evident that there is an analogy between color and sound. . . . An instrument might be constructed by which color could be played, and which would give to those, who had cultivated their taste in the art, a pleasure like that given by music." [30] The kind of color-piano envisaged here was actually built in 1877 by Bainbridge, Bishop of Essex County, New York. Other scientists are still experimenting in the same field. But the romantics were less interested in the physical aspects of color and sound than in their symbolic, that is to say, spiritual relationship.

Germany's greatest romantic landscape painters never went to Italy. But the flourishing colony of German artists in Rome could boast of many talents who deserved Cole's praise as painters of the soul. He did not mention names, but most likely had in mind the two leading figures, Johann Christian Reinhart (1761-1847) and Joseph A. Koch (1768-1839). In their universally admired works, the idyllic and the grandiose enter into an alliance equally typical of Cole's own style. Reinhart's best canvasses "bear witness of a grandeur and repose of the landscape element which can only come from a sublime spirit, and which is a matter of conviction." [31] Cole's "Arcadian Landscape," second in the "Course of Empire" series, shows a strong resemblance to some of Reinhart's etchings, such as the "Great Heroic Landscape" of 1800, in the clearly defined planes, the introduction of architecture in the middle distance near the intersection of vital diagonals, and even the odd detail of the two men on horseback half hidden behind some rising ground. In Reinhart's painted and graphic work, Cole found the "bright, happy air under a sky full of the purest clarity of light," and a type of scenery not outspoken Italian, yet definitely southern which he liked to depict himself. [32]

Dorner compares the two versions (in Leipzig and Munich) of Koch's "Schmadriba-Bach" with Cole's late landscape with waterfall in the Rhode Island School of Design and thinks of

[30] NOBLE, p. 191 *seq.*
[31] PAUL F. SCHMIDT, *Deutsche Landschaftsmalerei von 1750 bis 1830*, Munich, 1922, p. 20.
[32] *Ibid.*, p. 26.

a possible influence. This landscape, though, was not painted until eight years after Koch's death, and its softness and lacking clarity of spatial relations is alien to Koch's concentrated and strongly monumental style. Koch is closer to Cole in his more lyrically romantic landscapes such as the " Ideal Landscape with St. George " in Munich which introduces the motive of mediaeval romance as does Cole's " Departure " and " Return," or the landscape with castles in Berlin.

How far the German romantic landscapists actually influenced Cole will remain conjectural. He entered the artistic atmosphere of the Italian capital and took in what appealed to him and confirmed him in his own direction. One great master overshadowed all others in his esteem, the same whose conception of the " landscape of the soul " was the ultimate source for Reinhart and Koch: Claude Lorrain. Cole never ceased to admire his works. He ranked him next to Raphael and Michelangelo as one of the greatest masters of art, insisting that landscape painting was as important and varied as any other branch of art. (It is noteworthy that Dunlap still refused to accept this view.) Claude, to Cole, was even more than Poussin or Ruysdael, while Salvator Rosa in fact disappointed him as being " limited."

Claude has always been a great favorite with landscape painters of lyrical temperament. Goethe once gave a fine interpretation of his art when he said: " There is no trace of realism in his pictures, but the highest truth. Claude Lorrain knew the real world by heart, up to the last detail, and he used it as the means to express the world of his fine soul. . . . " [33] His landscapes have the free breath of classicism and the magic of light that may be called his northern inheritance. No landscape painter before him brought such floods of light to his canvasses. They link the parts of his compositions to one another, give life and melody to every form. There is no excitement, no drama in his wide views, only the quietude and beauty of peaceful harmony.

Claude carried on what Nicolas Poussin had developed in the

[33] NIKOLAUS PEVSNER and OTTO GRAUTOFF, *Barockmalerei in den romanischen Ländern* (Handbuch der Kunstwissenschaft), Wildpark-Potsdam, 1928, p. 282.

last twenty years of his life, when from classic figure scenes he had turned to the heroic landscape. Poussin's dramatic style, as exemplified by the "Winter" in the Louvre, seems to have inspired some of Cole's more agitated landscapes, such as the landscape with thunderstorm in the Rhode Island School of Design.

The great impressions Thomas Cole got from the works of the masters in Rome, to which we have to add those of the Colosseum at night, classical ruins in Rome, Tivoli, and Paestum, Alpine and Mediterranean scenery, mediaeval castles along the Rhône, and the cosmopolitan life on the continent, could not fail to make themselves felt in his later work. No more could he lose out of sight the new horizons that had opened before him. His fertile imagination had received the stimulus it needed, and the years after this first visit to Europe see him at his height.

He had not lost the "earlier, wilder image." Never before could he have painted so majestic a mountain scenery as the "Catskill Mountains" of 1833 in the Cleveland Museum of Art. A single glance at the "Mt. Washington" in Hartford of about 1828 tells the difference. The timidity and minute elaboration have disappeared. Instead, bold masses in simplified outlines sweep up unbroken towards one center of interest. The grandeur of the scene has found congenial expression. Nothing "provincial" clings to this canvas. The "Oxbow" of 1836 in the Metropolitan Museum is not equally concentrated; it shows how Cole endeavored to bring this element of grandeur into a scene of more panoramic character. To heighten the picturesque effect he conjures up another of his storms, the edge of the clouds forming a wide curve essential for the composition. It is a big canvas and effective in spite of a certain lack of coherence.

From this period date also some of Cole's finest evening landscapes. The "Summer Sunset" in the New York Historical Society shows a river winding quietly through the middle distance; the foreground is broken, a dimly lit mountain range closes the far distance. The sun is setting, lovely evening colors spread over earth and sky. Peace, stillness, shadows creeping up, and the wide, wide sky. One has to study it from close by; then slowly more

[45]

and more little details emerge; a cottage roof, a fence, a man with axe returning from work, some white sheep, cows silhouetted against the river, a sail on the water. Such pictures appeal more to the heart than to the eye; they touch us like one of Bryant's sonorous nature poems. Similar moods govern two other landscapes in the same collection, "On the Catskill" of 1833, and "Autumn Scene, Conway Peak, White Mountains, N. H." of 1834. These unpretentious little pictures have real charm. They are unmistakably American in character without aiming at the topographical, and less so these works of his maturity than his earlier productions. The tone is subdued to express better the hushed silence of evening. Forms are studied carefully from nature—Thomas Cole has left numerous sketches—but changed and modified in the finished composition. The "Hudson River Scene" (more likely a scene on the Catskill Creek) in the Brooklyn Museum and the Metropolitan Museum's "In the Catskills" of 1837 show an almost identical spot, but by subtle changes in details and proportions Cole enhanced the lyrical and romantic effect of the latter.

Like Claude Lorrain and the romantic painters of his succession, Cole did not consider such changes deviations from truth. When he insists on truth as the foundation for art he means the higher truth of nature's spirit. He believed the artist to be entitled to combine the most lovely and perfect parts of nature into a whole that should surpass in beauty and effect any picture painted from a single view.[34]

These tendencies and experiences prepared Cole for the great series of five pictures in the New York Historical Society, "The Course of Empire," which represent the climax of his early development. In Florence he had already started a composition of what he called "a romantic country, or (sic!) perfect state of nature, with appropriate savage figures."[35] We have here the germ of the later series and other "ideal" landscapes painted after his return from Italy. James Fenimore Cooper considered the "Course of Empire" to be the work "of the highest genius

[34] NOBLE, p. 336.   [35] Ibid., p. 144.

this country has ever produced," and esteemed it "one of the noblest works of art that has ever been wrought." [36] Since Cooper, no critic has registered equal enthusiasm. And yet one cannot help feeling impressed by these canvasses. The first reaction is one of surprise at the bright color scheme especially of the second and third piece; then, the astonishing skies compel admiration. Sober criticism denies the artistic possibility of the whole idea, points out the garish effect of the colors in the third picture, and contends that the artist's knowledge of the human figure was inadequate to the task.

All this is true, and we know that Cole himself was far from satisfied when he put the finishing touches to the last canvas. But we must not judge romantic art from the standpoint of any other form of art, for the simple reason that its aims lie not in the pictorial only. Cole spoke of the "philosophy" of the series, and Cooper calls it a great epic poem. We could as well compare it to a symphony. The five pictures evoke different emotions like the successive movements: allegro—andante, allegretto—tempo di marcia—furioso—largo. The identical scenery given in each instance in different light and from a different angle forms the "leitmotiv" with its variations in various keys. A spell emanates from the pictures that will touch responsive chords in us, and the longer we study them the more we grow conscious of the grandeur of conception and beauty of detail. While so many other romantic artists failed to carry out similarly ambitious plans, Cole had the courage and energy to bring his to completion.

The curtain opens almost visibly in the first scene, "The Savage State or Commencement of Empire." A sheltered bay opens to the left. In the foreground, green and brownish broken ground rises and falls in waves towards a stream that sheds its waters into the bay. Beyond, a green wilderness mounts in several stages to a steep hill with a huge boulder on top. One of Cole's violent thunderstorms is drawing away to the right; mists rise from the stricken woods. Under the glorious rays of the early morning sun, groups of men with bow and arrow are pursuing the deer,

[36] *Ibid.*, p. 226.

while a big fire has been kindled in the circle of rude tents on the opposite bank of the stream.

It is a beautiful picture in its fresh colors, its wide views, and formal logic. Staccato lines, dashing alleys of light, broken forms, and rapid changes of dark and light spots suggest vigorous life and movement. The wide sweep of the main curve brings together the diagonals of the composition; one motion pervades everything, and allows of no reposed and self-centered forms. A bugle-call of awakening sounds. The human figures, all but one of the type met in the " John the Baptist in the Wilderness," again serve as accents on vital spots. Taken by itself, the picture is too restless to be pleasing; the painter clearly intended it as an overture to the whole work.

The second picture, " Arcadian or Pastoral State," offers a striking contrast. The peaceful serenity of a melodious dream has taken the place of vehement action. The clouds are dispelled, the waters quiet. The broken and rugged country has changed to softly modulated pastures, and a stately mountain lifts head and shoulders above a thin veil of mists into the tender blue and grey of the sky. Every form shares the tranquillity and repose. The light envelops the scene evenly instead of rushing into it abruptly. The trees are round and of soft curves. Even the pointed tents are gone; a massive temple, much like Stonehenge, crowns the promontory as if it had always been there. The few figures (the woman at the right badly out of proportion) almost melt into the landscape in attitudes of peaceful enjoyment.

The romantic soul will always dream of an Arcadia. Shelley, Coleridge, Wordsworth, Schiller, had sung of it in the painter's own time. Claude Lorrain's arcadian tradition was still very much alive, as we have seen; and Blake, Calvert, Runge had joined in their own way the choirs of blissful harmony. The dancing shepherds on the right side of Cole's picture even remind us of Corot's idylls.

Cole treated the same idea in several other works, among them the " Dream of Arcadia " in Toledo, a sketch in the New York Historical Society, another sketch for a " Landscape with Greek

Temple " in Hartford, and the lost " Allegro." A projected picture to illustrate Coleridge's poem " Love " would have combined the arcadian motive with feudal romance.

The center piece of the " Course of Empire," larger than the others, is called " The Consummation of Empire." It is the least enjoyable of all. A conqueror returns in triumph to his metropolis. He is riding on a curiously shaped chariot drawn by elephants. Immense temples, colonnades, and porticoes fill both banks of the river which the emperor is just crossing. In the immediate foreground, the queen sits at the foot of towering columns and watches the throng of dignitaries, soldiers, maids of honor, and people of all ranks of life following the emperor, or waiting for his arrival. Innumerable figures of spectators crowd every inch of space. Fantastic galleys move on the bright water, and the noon-day sun shines from the clearest zenith on all this profusion.

It was too much glitter and gaud even for the painter. He had showered over the canvas colors of greatest brilliancy in rainbow contrasts, with gold, purple, red, and green dominating. The total effect of this clash of local colors with the white of the buildings and the blue of the sky is like that of a brass band playing fortissimo. The only bit of nature left without traces of man is the solitary mountain ridge barely visible in the left center. Everywhere else man has pushed nature aside. Did the artist try to express his misgivings of the vainglorious pomp of the big cities? We know that he could never feel happy there.

A black and white reproduction of this painting makes almost a better impression than the original because it hides the glitter and brings out to advantage the ingenious solution of intricate problems of perspective and architectural detail. Cole took an active interest in architecture, and is credited by his biographer with the plans for the State House of Ohio. An imaginary landscape called " The Architect's Dream " is described as a fantastic assemblage of buildings in all possible styles. It was painted on commission, but not accepted. Architectural fantasies are not uncommon with the romantic painters; Cole's contemporary, the German Karl F. Schinkel, is well known for them.

The " Consummation of Empire " as a whole is a huge opera-like spectacle. Memories of Italy are exaggerated with the riotous fancy that we find in William Beckford's ultra-romantic " Vathek " when he gives the glowing account of the five palaces of Alcoremi.

In the next scene, " Destruction," the expected blow is falling on the proud capital. An earthquake has shattered bridge, light-houses, and colonnades. Fire spreads through the stately halls, a terrible cloudburst threatens to engulf friend and foe in one torrential downpour, and the despairing defenders are besieged on all sides by a merciless host of bloodthirsty invaders. Horror is heaped upon horror. On the right side, a symbol of vain defiance, towers the gigantic statue of an onrushing gladiator, its head and sword-hand broken off, its shield cracked. (*See* Pl. IV.)

It is a stupendous conception, oppressive like a nightmare in its fury and helplessness, and almost surrealistic in the implications of the headless statue. Greys and flaming reds dominate, with specks of color in the figures. The story is unfolded in a sort of motion-picture technique; our eyes are shifted from mass scenes to details treated almost like " close-ups." But the painter did not possess the mastery of the human figure that makes Rubens' equally dramatic vision of the " Last Judgment " in Munich so impressive. His attitudes are frozen and create an effect similar to sudden stops in the performance of a motion picture. A strange immobility contrasts sharply with the violent action. Cole realized the danger and tried to overcome it by means of great com-positional lines which keep the eye in perpetual motion around the picture field. They motivate the distribution of details and their form even to the pathos of gestures approaching, in some instances, the grotesque. The very minute treatment of these de-tails, however, counteracts the coherent movement of the com-position by arresting our attention. The gladiator is a charac-teristic example; though painted to suggest the most aggressive motion, he remains for ever rigidly fixed in his posture. As a result a feeling of balance or suspense exists as if the fate of the city were not yet finally settled, though one look at the sky is sufficient to convince us of impending doom. There, the sense of rapid movement is actually realized.

"Desolation," the last picture of the series, once was considered its best. Daniel Huntingdon claimed for it absolute perfection in texture and color,[37] and as recent a critic as Sadakichi Hartmann believed that it had few superiors " in solemn majesty and depth of thought." [38] Calm, empty waters, a nearly empty sky with a pale moon, and clouds approaching from the left as if to pull down the final curtain. Jumbled masses of masonry, ruined arches and porticoes, gradually fade back into nature. One stately column only stands erect, greyish-white and half overgrown with the dark vegetation that is claiming the site of man's short-lived triumph. A few birds hover over the river, and the low murmur of water ceaselessly running through broken architraves is the only sound in all that stillness. Silvery tones combine with blues, greys, browns, and dark greens to a picture of sadness and melancholy. How the romantics loved to sit among ancient ruins and dream of the passing of splendor and beauty! The past, being distant, had for them always the shimmer of something mysteriously greater and better than the present. It may be noted that " Past" and "Present" were titles of two companion pictures mentioned among Thomas Cole's works. Bryant calls them " rich, solemn, full of matter for study and reflection, in producing which Cole had no rival." [39] A similar note was intended in a landscape with a " ruined and solitary tower on a craggy promontory, laved by the unruffled ocean " where a lonely shepherd boy was lost in " dreams of distant lands." [40] It never occurred to the painter to question whether art could express thoughts. He believed the picture would be a truly poetic one; there would be a stillness, a loneliness about it that might reach the imagination. We are inclined to smile at the idea of painting the romantic dreams of a

[37] Quoted by G. W. Sheldon, *American Painters*, New York, 1879, p. 100.
[38] SADAKICHI HARTMANN, *A History of American Art*, New York, 1907, vol. 1, p. 47.
[39] WILLIAM CULLEN BRYANT, *A Funeral Oration occasioned by the death of Thomas Cole* . . . , New York, 1848, p. 25.
[40] NOBLE, p. 264.

shepherd. But are the attempts, in the art of the Surrealists, to reveal hidden secrets of the subconscious, not fundamentally the same? Surrealism with its insistence on " meaning " as opposed to mere visual statements may help towards a renewed appreciation of romantic art. Sherman [41] very correctly said of the works of Allston, Cole, and Church: " Whether one does or does not care for them in no wise affects their artistic merit as examples of a mode of graphic expression which has its own importance."

The standards by which we have to judge romantic art are clarity, persuasive power, sincerity, depth and human significance of idea as well as perfection and convincing truth of formal organization. Cole's " Course of Empire," because of inadequacies in form, cannot be ranked with the great masterpieces of art, but the timeless significance of its idea makes it the outstanding example of American romantic art. Morning—noon—full noon—evening—night; man's coming and going, his rise and fall: our war-torn world is perhaps ready again to understand the sadness and tragedy of this idea.

Two years after the completion of the great series, Cole produced the epitome of mediaevalism in American painting in the two companion pictures " The Departure " and " The Return " of 1837, now in the Corcoran Gallery. They are the outgrowth and, at the same time, the climax of the " Gothic revival " of the early half of the nineteenth century. The artist did not acknowledge specific literary sources for his story; love for the feudal institutions of the Middle Ages was so widespread among the romantic writers of all countries that he could find material enough in Sir Walter Scott's poems and novels, Uhland's and Chamisso's ballads, popular through Bryant's translations, and the many " Gothic " tales of the time. In addition, he could draw on his memories of sights seen in Europe. The picturesque castles along the Rhône had stirred his imagination. " Through the crumbling gate-ways fancy easily calls forth the steel-clad warriors and sounds the trumpet, or sees the dark-eyed ladies looking through

[41] FREDERIC F. SHERMAN, *Early American Painting*, New York, 1932, p. 211.

the narrow windows of the mouldering towers for the return of their beloved knights from the wars." [42] This was written six years before; now he felt called to paint it. The story content of the two pictures cannot be told better than in William Cullen Bryant's words. "In the first, a spring morning, breezy and sparkling, the mists starting and soaring from the hills, the chieftain in gallant array at the head of his retainers, issuing from the castle—in the second, an autumnal evening, calm, solemn, a church illuminated by the beams of the setting sun, and the corpse of the chief borne in silence towards the consecrated place." The poet added: "There could not be a finer choice of circumstance nor a more exquisite treatment of them." [43] (See Pl. V.)

The two large paintings belong indeed to Cole's most characteristic works. The coloring is highly effective, the skies are painted brilliantly, and the composition is not only pleasing and clearly defined in each individual canvas, but carefully correlated to that of the other. Horizontals, verticals, and diagonals correspond, masses are evenly balanced, and enough subtle contrasts are introduced to avoid monotony. The romantic story has lost its meaning for us, but the two landscapes will retain their appeal as the most beautiful documents of "Gothic" romanticism in America.

Cole had firmly established himself among the leading artists of his day. He had married, he enjoyed the friendship of Bryant, Durand, and other men prominent in arts and letters, and he continued to love the country near his home with deep affection. Yet he could not shake off the memory of his unhappy youth; nor could he fail to see the inner and outer limitations of his own endeavors. He must have felt how much a good artistic education would have helped him. Also, as the son of an idealistic age he carried deep within himself the conviction of the artist's mission. Sometimes he would despair ever to produce " pictures that shall delight, and improve (sic!) posterity." [44] Premonitions of death beset him. The strain of years of intense work began to be

[42] NOBLE, p. 127.   [43] BRYANT, *op. cit.*, p. 25.   [44] NOBLE, p. 263.

felt. He was afraid he might find himself in Giant Despair's castle. Out of these moods grew the idea for the "Voyage of Life," a series of four canvasses. They were immensely popular once. The Editor of *Harper's Magazine* could declare in 1856 that with the exception of one or two pictures of West's, ". . . there are no works so famous as the series of the Voyage of Life. . . ."[45] The New York Art Union, which carried out an extensive program of distributing works of art by way of lottery, acquired them after the artist's death and presented each member with an engraving after them. Their original cost was figured at $6,000.00, and as late as 1885, Mrs. Sarah Knowles Bolton testified that they were hung in thousands of homes.[46] To-day, they are almost forgotten. They hang in a dimly lit back stairway of St. Luke's Hospital, New York.

Cole has given a lengthy explanation of the four pictures from which we may gather his meaning. "Childhood" and "Youth" are seen in the rosy light of hope and enthusiasm, while "Manhood" and "Old Age" are steeped into the darkness of vain struggle and defeat. Blissfully unaware of the dangers to come, the radiant child sails forth in a fanciful boat (much like the one in the new screen version of Maeterlinck's *Blue Bird*) on the stream that issues from a dark cavern in a rocky mountain. His guardian angel stands at the helm. Youth has left the angel behind; relying only upon himself he steers on, a fragrant landscape around, glorious visions of a silver castle in the sky before him. Suddenly all is changed. "It is only when experience has taught us the realities of the world, that we lift from our eyes the golden veil of early life; that we feel deep and abiding sorrow," the artist explained. His tendency is a fatalistic one; man is helplessly drifting along on the dark rapids with nothing but prayer to assist him against "the demon forms of Suicide, Intemperance, and Murder, which are the temptations that beset men. . . ."[47]

---

[45] *Harper's New Monthly Magazine,* vol. XIV, Dec. 1856, p. 130.
[46] SARAH K. BOLTON, *Lives of Poor Boys who Became Famous,* New York, 1885, p. 270.
[47] *Bulletin of the Art Union,* New York, No. 7, July 25, 1848.

We are reminded of Bunyan's Christian pilgrim without Hope, his companion. Finally, the stream of life reaches the ocean. But man does not throw himself joyfully into the arms of the eternal father; the pitiful figure of a feeble old man is gliding sadly towards the dark shadows overhanging the vast solitude. Then and there the clouds open; a broad avenue of celestial light, and angels beckoning him to come, promise a fairer land of rest and peace. This vision of light, almost Rembrandtesque in its chiaroscuro, is touchingly poetic, if only the guardian angel would not proclaim the message so overtly.

A mood of "Weltschmerz" pervades the series, perhaps suggested by Shelley's "Alastor" where similar scenes are described; Cole, however, did not mention this poem as his source. The moral of the "Voyage of Life" was severely criticized as early as 1856 in the "Crayon," and it must not be considered as Cole's last word. Fortunately, he overcame its stark pessimism in his later works.

The painter felt the need for new and refreshing impressions. He began to miss in American scenery the associations that cling to scenes in the old world. "Simple nature is not quite sufficient. We want human interest, incident and action, to render the effect of landscape complete." [48] A second voyage to Europe, he hoped, would restore his self-confidence, and renew his powers. He went in the summer of 1841, first again to London, also visiting this time the Shakespeare country; then to Paris, where he was deeply impressed by the old masters in the Louvre, especially Nicolas Poussin and the masters before Raphael; on through part of Switzerland and the valley of the Rhône to Italy. From a drawing made on the spot he painted in Rome the big landscape of the "Valley of the Vaucluse" in the Metropolitan Museum. At first sight it seems like the work of a different Cole, so free and broad is the handling. Petrarch's castle stands out boldly on an imposing rock. Clouds partly hide the massive cliff in the background against which a smaller, pyramidical rock is sharply silhouetted. The tones range from greys to yellows and browns, with greens in

[48] NOBLE, p. 294.

[55]

the mountain stream and the pastures on the slopes of the castle hill. (*See* Pl. VI.)

Though the technique is different, the romantic spirit is as conspicuous as in the " John the Baptist in the Wilderness " and other early pictures. It is visible in the surging lines of the composition, in the contrasts of light and shadow, the rugged wildness of the natural setting, and the poetic effect of the whole.

Cole's later work in Italy does not live up to the freshness and quality of the " Vaucluse." The " Italian Landscape Composition " and the " Vale and Temple of Segestae " in the New York Historical Society, or the " Mt. Aetna Seen from Taormina " in the Wadsworth Atheneum, painted from sketches after his return, are labored and unappealing in tone. Local color is too subdued to create the impression of southern landscape. Romantic detail such as ruins, broken columns, shepherds and shepherdesses, cannot hide the emptiness and lack of organization in the middle distances. Still, a feeling for the grandeur of the scenery is undeniable, particularly in the fine outline of Mt. Aetna. Cole did not tire of painting views of this magnificent mountain, the ascent of which, during his tour through Sicily, he described in a vivid account.

From his return to America, he wrote to his friend Greene, the American consul in Rome: " Must I tell you that neither the Alps nor the Apennines, no, nor even Aetna himself, have dimmed, in my eyes, the beauty of our own Catskills? It seems to me that I look on American scenery if it were possible, with increased pleasure. It has its own peculiar charm—a something not found elsewhere." [49] Two of Cole's finest works bear witness of his unchanged love for American nature: the " Mountain Ford " of 1846 in the Metropolitan Museum, and the " Catskill Creek " of 1845 in the Public Library, New York. They have all the characteristics of Thomas Cole's art at its best: harmony of form and spirit, structural logic of composition, interesting detail contrasted with broad masses, and a romantic poetry so self-evident that it needs no commentary. We think of the lovely evening sky of the

[49] *Ibid.,* p. 333.

"Catskill Creek" when we read his poem "Twilight" of the same year:

> The woods are dark; but yet the lingering light
> Spreads its last beauty o'er the western sky.
> How lovely are the portals of the night,
> When stars come out to watch the day-light die.
>
> The woods are dark; but yet yon little bird
> Is warbling by her newly furnished nest.
> No sound beside in all the vale is heard:
> But she for rapture cannot, cannot rest.

Thomas Cole's heart, too, was overflowing with rapture. The gloomy dejection of the last two pictures of the " Voyage of Life " had lost its hold on him. He wished he could paint it all over again, not copy it as he had done in Rome, where Thorwaldsen, the great Danish sculptor, had admired it in his studio. What had dispelled the clouds from his mind was a truer insight of the Christian conception of life. (*See* Pl. VII.)

Cole had never received regular religious training in childhood, but his whole nature was religious, and his art from the first shows a reverent, almost devotional approach towards nature. Now his ideas became clarified. " Art, in its true sense, is . . . man's lowly imitation of the creative power of the Almighty," he said in 1842.[50] He became a member of the church, a Bible lay open in his studio, and Noble tells us that he prayed before painting. His lofty idea of the artist's mission won greater depth. The artist, to be great, must work always, he maintained. Like a magician, he must draw a circle round himself and exclude all intrusive spirits. " And above all, if he would attain that serene atmosphere of the mind in which float the highest conceptions of the soul, in which the sublimest works have been produced, he must be possessed of a holy and reasonable faith." [51]

This positive religious attitude is a typical characteristic of romanticism. Wordsworth, Blake, Bryant, the German romantic poets expressed it in their works; the group of romantic youths forming the " Brotherhood of St. Luke's " or, as they called them-

[50] *Ibid.*, p. 336.　　　　　[51] *Ibid.*, p. 380.

selves, the " Nazarenes," devoted their lives to religious art; Runge and Friedrich saw the essence of art in the spiritual. In his essay on the German paintings exhibited at Rome in the year 1819, Friedrich von Schlegel outlined the esthetics of " Christian " art. Granted a technical skill based on natural talent and serious study, the artist must embrace the " beautiful truths " of the Christian faith with an earnest conviction of their reality. To reach perfection, he further needs the inspiration that emanates from heaven like a celestial light. " His very soul must, so to speak, become itself illuminated, a glowing center of holy radiance, in whose bright beams every material object should be reflected, and even his inmost conceptions and daily thoughts be interpenetrated by its brightness, and remodelled by its influence. This in-dwelling light of the soul should be recognized in every creation of his pencil, expressive as a spoken word; and in this lies the peculiar vitality of Christian beauty, and the cause of the remarkable difference between classical and Christian art. . . . Even in the choice of subjects for painting, this ray of inborn inspiration, this divine enthusiasm, must guide and govern the painter's decision. A more than earthly aspect subduing the soul; a state of heavenly illumination and exaltation; an upspringing from the dark night of mortality, like the morning dawn breaking through heavy clouds; a spell of love and fascination in the midst of suffering nature, or a flash of intense beauty, created from the very anguish of the soul's despair;—such are the peculiar and not merely pleasing themes which afford subjects to the Christian painter, and such is the spirit in which they ought to be rendered." [52]

In his late works of the 1840's, Thomas Cole fought for a pictorial expression of such ideas. Most of them unfortunately are lost, others remained unfinished, a third group was contemplated but never executed. To these belong the three pictures of a series, " Life, Death, and Immortality." Life: a magnificent daylight landscape; Death: a wild and dreary night scene with a funeral procession; Immortality: angels conducting a spirit to-

<hr>

[52] FRIEDRICH VON SCHLEGEL, *The Aesthetic and Miscellaneous Works*, translated by E. J. Millington, London, 1860, p. 306 *seq.*

wards the gates of heaven; a flood of light bursting in from on high. The progress of the artist away from the pessimism of the " Voyage of Life " is evident. We hear of a " Cross in the Wilderness," of an " Elijah at the mouth of the cave in the mount of God," and of a final series commenced at the end of the year 1845, " The Cross and the World." It was to be a correction of the naturalism of the " Course of Empire," more expressive of his Christian faith than the " Voyage of Life." The main idea was a rather involved one of two pilgrims finally arriving at the Holy City. One after fearful trials with the divine light as his only guide, the other saved by grace from the plenitude of sin. Such subtleties are included as a sunny landscape where nature flatters the sinner, " and in their unreal splendor and profusion, the very flowers lie." [53] Romantic art here tried the virtually impossible.

In the Brooklyn Museum's " Vision " we have the final picture of the series, the " Triumph of the Pilgrim of the Cross." It was painted in a devotional solitude, not even the artist's wife being allowed to see it until it was finished. (*See* Pl. VIII.)

The picture is purest symbolism. Darkness fills the foreground. Cloud-like shapes ascend on the right and left, dark first, brighter near the radiating cross in the center sky from which beams of light pour forth in all directions. Their reflections in the air create a path towards the pilgrim standing on the summit of a mountain in front, his arms opened in a gesture of joy and hope. Angels approach him to lead him upward. It is a vision such as a pious soul might experience in the last moments on earth, when, the shadows recede, and the inner eye beholds the first glory of eternal light. Wagner's Parzifal-music is keyed to the same ecstatic tone, Goethe's *Faust II* and Shelley's *Adonäis* end on equal notes of rapture. We might wish there would not be the feeble pilgrim nor the tiny angels to interrupt the austere silence; they threaten to make a stage scene out of what is otherwise a message directed to our own heart. This message is that of Fra Angelico's " Last Judgment " in Florence, of Dürer's " All Saints " in Vienna reduced to a puritanically abstract form. What they

[53] NOBLE, p. 393.

impersonated in choirs of human and celestial beings, is here expressed in the language of light.

There are dangers in this symbolism. An artist less sincere than Cole might easily make empty pretense stand for high thought. In art, too, it is only one step from the sublime to the ridiculous. Romantic art always stands on the borderline. An age of reason will condemn it as absurd: the old Rembrandt, Blake, Friedrich, Ryder, Davies have in their times met the same lack of understanding. With their return to favor, the art of Thomas Cole may also hope to emerge from near-oblivion to just appreciation.

On the first of January, 1848, Thomas Cole wrote in his journal: " I thank God for the blessings of the past year. They have been manifold. Another year, a stranger whose face is yet unknown to us, is announced. Mysterious strangers they are, these years. Pilgrims of time that wander through eternity to do homage, and sing praises at the foot of God's throne. . . . " [54] A few weeks later, the artist himself was called to his Maker. He died suddenly, of an inflammation of the lungs, on February 13, 1848. His death was widely lamented. The day of his funeral was a solemn day and a sad one in Catskill; the shops were closed and business was suspended in obedience to a common feeling of sorrow.[55] Not often was such an honor awarded to an American artist.

The Metropolitan Museum in New York owns a fine marble bust of the artist by Henry Kirke Brown (1814-1886), and there are portraits by Durand and Huntingdon.[56] They show a spirited, sensitive face in a long and delicately modelled head with deep-set eyes and a prominent forehead. A certain softness around mouth and chin is unmistakable. It is a face that goes well with the warm tributes unanimously paid by his contemporaries to a tender-hearted, generous, idealistic, and deeply religious personality.

It was perhaps Cole's tragedy that he was so exclusively a romantic. That made him extremely popular during the days of

[54] *Ibid.,* p. 378. [55] BRYANT, *op. cit.,* p. 36.
[56] Durand's was reproduced in *Harper's Magazine,* vol. 80, Jan., 1890. Huntingdon's is in the New York Historical Society.

romanticism; his name became almost a household word, his paintings were found in many private collections. On the other hand, with the passing of romanticism his work soon grew obsolete. The industrial and social developments of the second half of the nineteenth century asked for a different temperament. The other painters of the so-called Hudson River School lowered the tone of romantic fervor to one of clear and factual statement. Durand, Kensett, Church, and Gifford still feel the poetic element in nature, but they try to express it through faithful adherence to her objective forms. Durand, who had started as an engraver, was mainly a portrait painter and turned to landscape only later in life, probably stimulated by Thomas Cole's work. He, too, belonged to the Bryant circle, and saw nature with the loving eyes of the poet. Some of his wood interiors are very impressive in the treatment of individual trees, rocks, ferns, and mosses, and the green haze of the distance; they lead us into the heart of nature untrodden by man. His whole outlook, however, was more governed by insistence on actual truth than Cole's had been. Even in Claude Lorrain's landscapes he criticized liberties; to him, nature was always more beautiful than art—in essence the standpoint of realism.[57] As a consequence, his style presents a sort of romantic realism much like that of the contemporary Barbizon School in France. "Kindred Spirits" represents his strength and his weakness: a poetic feeling, a fine sense for the beauty and individuality of American scenery, and a pleasing and logical composition, against which stand a lack of coordination, and overelaboration of detail. Compared with some of Cole's landscapes it looks almost dry and matter-of-fact. His canvasses are more characteristically American than most of Cole's, and he never followed the latter into pure symbolism. While thus more firmly established on solid ground, he did not attain the sublimity of Cole's best works.

John F. Kensett and Sanford R. Gifford likewise surpass Cole in the faithful portrayal of natural scenes without equalling his poetic vision. They show lyrical grace combined with careful

[57] SHELDON, op. cit., p. 132.

observation especially of atmospheric effects. Their works are pleasing and enjoyable but do not stir us to enthusiasm.

The greatest merit of these painters and their friends and followers—Worthington Whittredge, William and James Hart, Jervis McEntee, Thomas Moran, John W. Casilear, and others—is their success in awakening a widespread interest in art among the American public. They treated familiar scenes of America, England, and Italy; Frederic E. Church, Cole's only direct pupil, preferred those of exotic grandeur. The romantic longing for the distant led him, like Delacroix, into foreign countries. The mountains and volcanoes of South America, or the icebergs and aurora borealis of the Arctic north were sights that Church knew how to render impressively. From his master he had learned to build up great compositions—compare, for instance, the "Aegean Sea" in the Metropolitan Museum—, to which he added an almost photographic realism of detail. This realism found the full approval of a generation ready to pay the highest sum ever paid for an American picture up to that time, $12,500.00, for his "Niagara," now in the Corcoran Gallery in Washington. Once a newly discovered arctic peak was called after him.[58] In the panoramic views of Albert Bierstadt, topographic realism reached an extreme. Some last trace of Cole's romantic feeling for the grandiose is still discernible, but merely serves as a convenient form in which to present objectively painted scenery instead of leading to visions expressive of personal experience.

Yet the romantic conception of landscape did not die. It lived on in the work of Jasper F. Cropsey, and pervaded the dreamy landscapes of George Inness with mysterious enchantment. "It was only a short step to the lyric interpretation of landscape which has been the mode from Inness on down to the present day";[59] Albert P. Ryder's "landscape of the unconscious mind,"[60] Arthur B. Davies' fantasies, and the moody watercolors and oils of Charles Burchfield marks this continuance of the romantic spirit in forms of modern art.

[58] Cf. the autograph letters to Dr. Isaac I. Hayes, in the Library of Congress.
[59] ALAN BURROUGHS, *Limners and Likenesses*, Harvard Univ. Press, 1936, p. 147.
[60] LLOYD GOODRICH, *op. cit.*, p. 18.

THE ROMANTIC LADY

by

Ralph P. Boas

The ideal woman of early nineteenth century literature is a descendant of Richardson's Clarissa. In the pure line of descent she is delicate; full of "sensibility"; dazzlingly fair of complexion; "enthusiastic"; and later, "romantic"; not too strong physically, but mentally, except in one particular, resolute; a girl of wealth, or at least connected with a family which had once been wealthy; and, up to a certain point, well educated. She has one weakness which is always causing her "distress": she has a sex-appeal so magnetic that no descendant of Lovelace can pass her by without immediately plotting for her possession. Her high ideals of "honor" will not permit her to yield, however much she loves her predestinate seducer; and so the Lovelace of the particular book must, if he is to conquer her virtue, resort to stratagem. If she remains in the pure line of descent she is vanquished. Once seduced she either dies like her great ancestress or lives a life of spurious gaiety descending from one "distress" to another until eventually she perishes miserably.

The pure line of descent was, however, modified both in America and in England. Changing ideas of morality, social ethics, education, and etiquette ended the power of the amatory villain, and though he remained, he ceased to be inevitably successful. As the pure, graceful, religious, blonde girl became more and more the ideal to be won as a wife, it became less and less fitting that she should be ruined for wifehood. As time went on, seduction yielded to unsuccessful assault, and the incident which once produced a moral lesson now produced a romantic glow. A beautiful girl escaping from the clutches of a predatory man not only provided more thrills but gave an opportunity for heroic action. The tempting sex-appeal of the inviolate maiden yielded such titillating interest that her once gentlemanly pursuer developed into the anti-social villain predestined to failure.

With a new emphasis upon the inviolability of a noble chastity came a new ideal of womanhood. If woman was to be chaste she must be cold. If Caesar's wife must be above suspicion she must, for all her beauty, be pure in mind as well as in body, no longer " the hapless victim of imprudence and evil counsellors." [1] The ideal woman became the standard heroine of the romantic era (1812-1860), the heroine of novels, poems, and plays.

It is a mistake to think of the idealized heroine as the weeping, fainting, delicate female. " The desired feminine type of the time " was not " delicate, consumptive, given to fainting, and languidly lying upon invalid couches; saying incredibly refined and sentimental things, and listening to denatured artificial rhapsodies " nor did she waste " away in her wailing lovers' arms, leaving them stricken with sorrow or touched by madness to haunt the lovely grave, forever inconsolable." [2]

The evidence shows that the idealized female was quite another person. She was Lowell's " Irene ":

> Hers is a spirit deep, and crystal-clear;
> Calmly beneath her earnest face it lies,
> Free without boldness, meek without a fear,
> Quicker to look than speak its sympathies . . .
>
> She hath a natural wise sincerity,
> A simple truthfulness, and these have lent her
> A dignity as moveless as the centre . . .
>
> For she unto herself hath builded high
> A home serene, wherein to lay her head,
> Earth's noblest thing, a Woman perfected.[3]

---

[1] Mrs. Susanna Rowson, *Charlotte: A Tale of Truth*, 5th ed., Harrisburg, Pa., 1802, p. 90.

[2] Hervey Allen, *Israfel: The Life and Times of Edgar Allan Poe*, 2 vols., New York, 1927, vol. I, p. 389. This statement is made by Mr. Allen partly on the basis of the sentimentality of the 1880's, partly because Poe's wife was a consumptive invalid, and partly because of the strange women of Poe's tales. As a generalization, his statement is contrary to the facts.

[3] *The Poetical Works of James Russell Lowell*. Introduction by W. M. Rossetti. London, n. d., p. 3.

She was the girl of Longfellow's "Maidenhood":

> Standing with reluctant feet
> Where the brook and river meet.[4]

She was Priscilla of *The Courtship of Miles Standish*, like all

> Puritan maidens
> Modest, and simple and sweet.[5]

She was Anneke of Cooper's *Satanstoe:*

> If beauty, and modesty, and grace and gentleness and spirit, and sense, and delicacy, and virtue, and piety, can make any woman of seventeen a sweet creature . . . then Anneke is sweet.[6]

She was Bessie of Mrs. Sedgwick's *The Linwoods* (1836):

> . . . she resembled the exquisite instrument that responds music to the gentle touches of the elements, but is broken by the first wide gust that sweeps over it.[7]

And in Mrs. Sedgwick's *Redwood* (1824):

> "This Ellen Bruce," thought he, . . . "has such a look of spirituality, so bright, and so tranquil too, that if there is a heaven she is surely destined to it." [8]

The idealized American girl begins at least as early as the heroine in Charles Brockden Brown's *Wieland* (1798) continuing her life of piety, "sensibility, enthusiasm, pliability, charity, and devotion" throughout the romantic period down to the "white-souled" Hilda in Nathaniel Hawthorne's *The Marble Faun* (1860) where she is "a slender, brown-haired, New England girl, whose perceptions of form and expression were wonderfully clear and delicate." [9]

As the idealized girl of the first half of the nineteenth century

---

[4] *The Complete Poetical Works of Henry Wadsworth Longfellow*, Cambridge ed., Boston, n. d., p. 18.
[5] P. 169.
[6] JAMES FENIMORE COOPER, *Works*, 10 vols., Satanstoe, vol. 8, New York, 1891, p. 315.
[7] New York, 1836, 2 vols., vol. 1, p. 36.
[8] New York 1850, p. 200. [9] Boston, n. d., p. 21.

developed she became no longer the maiden to be sought as a bride " laughing, lovely, star-eyed " [10] but the wife and mother. She kept her house, she brought forth her large family, she fulfilled the promise of the mind that her lover had recognized even in her glowing youth.

> She was also a girl of thought and intellect—something too, of a dreamer. . . . [11]

In short, she became " the sainted mother." To speak of such a woman in connection with words like " love " and " passion " seemed sacrilege. " Passion " belonged to another type of woman. As the ideal became the normal, it lost the quality of romance which it had had when it was new and strange, and another type appeared, the romantic lady.

She was born at least as early as Charlotte Temple as another character in Mrs. Rowson's famous book:

> Julia Franklin was the very reverse of Charlotte Temple: she was tall, elegantly shaped, and possessed much of the air and manner of a woman of fashion; her complexion was a clear brown, enlivened with the glow of health; her eyes, full, black, and sparkling, darted their intelligent glances through long silken lashes. . . . [12]

Julia Franklin thus anticipates the standard characteristics of the romantic lady; she is a brunette, she is strong and capable, she is beautiful, she is resolute and self-willed, and she has an aggressive sexuality.

The romantic lady is, then, the direct opposite of the innocent girl who had become the ideal. For inspiring passion a lady needed no excuse; the misfortune might happen to anyone and was, indeed, inevitable when a lady met the predatory male. Her guardian must be her innate chastity supplemented by the chivalrous gentleman supposedly always available in a crisis. The wrong was in feeling passion herself, in meeting a man on frankly even terms. In responding to passion the lady became romantic, but at

---

[10] WILLIAM GILMORE SIMMS, *The Yemassee*, Richmond, n. d. (1st ed., 1835), p. 48.

[11] P. 159.   [12] *Charlotte; A Tale of Truth*, p. 114.

[66]

the same time she lost the respect of good people, both male and female. Hence the romantic lady who loved with a greater freedom than the American code permitted needed the excuse of distant times when American civilization was yet unknown, of foreign lands which had not yet achieved the new democratic freedom, or of a racial heritage which made of her, in part at least, a woman doomed to tragedy.

Charles Brockden Brown like Mrs. Rowson provides prototypes of the romantic ladies. *Ormond* (1799) has a heroine deserted and forlorn. Helena Cleves illustrates the Ariadne motif, not popular in novels and plays, but used by female poets and popularized by Vanderlyn's famous painting. The real romantic lady in *Ormond* is Martinette de Veauvais who explains herself:

My mother was a Greek of Cyprus, my father was a Sclavonian of Ragusa, and I was born in a garden at Aleppo. [13]

The pattern continues with Ailsa Fielding in *Arthur Mervyn*, who possessed the fatal magnetism which always masked the romantic lady:

Never saw I one to whom the term *lovely* more truly belonged. And yet in stature she is too low; in complexion dark and almost sallow; and her eyes, though black and of piercing lustre, have a cast which I cannot well explain . . . all personal defects are outweighed by her heart and her intellect. There is the secret of her power to entrance the soul of the listener and beholder. . . . [14]

Brown's women are, however, only anticipations of the later romantic ladies. He is preoccupied with a type which never became popular in America, the intellectual soul-mate, such as Constantia in *Ormond* whose name Shelley took for a poem to Claire Clairmont [15] and who had one exemplar in real life, Margaret Fuller.

The real romantic love-lady as she appears in poems, novels, and plays is usually seen through the eyes of a passionate male.

[13] CHARLES BROCKDEN BROWN, *Ormond,* ed. E. Marchand, New York, 1937 (1799), p. 159.
[14] BROWN, *Arthur Mervyn*, Phila., n. d. (1799, 1800), p. 197.
[15] To Constantia, Singing."

He is, naturally, often the man who most devotedly sings the praises of the cold, controlled, religious girl whom he will marry and who will bear his children. Lowell, who wrote " Irené," wrote also of a romantic woman. " A Legend of Brittany " [16] is a dream of a woman of his romantic imagination quite different from the idealized woman of whom he wrote

> I love her with a love as still
> As a broad river's peaceful might.[17]

The romantic lady is Margaret who was " fair as a summer dream." Her heart

> . . . grew brimming with the lore
> Of love's enticing secrets. . . .

Innocent as she was, her " ripe beauty " ensnared a celibate Templar, " a dark proud man " [18] who falls in love with " sharp thrills of tingling flame." When Margaret saw him in the forest " She thought of Tristrem and of Lancilot " and gave her heart to him

> Freely as she would have thrown
> A rose to him.

Unfortunately the Templar tired of his easy prey especially since Margaret was to have the inevitable " babe " and so

> Enough that Margaret by his mad steel fell.

Margaret represents the romance of passionate love filling the mind of a young poet. As an emotion it was, from the point of view of American ethics, abnormal, but both Margaret and the poet can expiate their abnormal feelings by the lady's death and by the implied argument that all this happened long ago in a forest on the edge of fairyland.

In Longfellow's " The Spanish Student " Preciosa, the Gypsy

[16] *Poetical Works of James Russell Lowell*, Boston, n. d., vol. VII, p. 78.

[17] " My Love," *Poetical Works*, p. 17.

[18] The Byronic influence is obvious, as the influence of Keats is strong in the lush details of passion and in such passages as

> Faint heatings in the calyx, ere the rose
> Its warm voluptuous breast doth all unclose.

Girl, can be romantic and yet decent reading for the American public because she is a Spaniard and Spain is a naturally romantic country. She is a Gypsy and Gypsies belong to a race congenitally given to romantic behavior. One expects a Spanish Gypsy not only to inspire love but to be violently in love herself. But she is in love with Victorian, a Spanish gentleman who is too proud to marry a Gypsy and too virtuous to seduce her. The normal outcome of such a situation is tragedy, either death or self banishment. Longfellow is kind, however, and resolves the situation by having Preciosa discovered to be a nobleman's stolen daughter. So she can marry her Victorian with no objection from the reader. After all she is marrying a Spaniard.

A safe source for romantic exploitation was obviously Italy with its Renaissance tradition of poisons, vendettas, banditti, Borgias, and the novels of Anne Radcliffe. American playwrights, in particular, found that their audiences relished sensational love if it were non-American.

George Henry Boker wrote romantic dramas of Tudor England, Spain, Germany, and Italy. One of the most successful was *Francesca da Rimini* (1855) a blank verse tragedy with far greater vitality than Stephen Phillips's later *Paolo and Francesca*. It was revived in 1882, and in 1901. The play put chief emphasis upon Francesca and her husband Lanciotto. Francesca is the complete woman in love:

> Take me all,—
> Body and soul. The women of our clime
> Do never give away but half a heart.[19]

Almost equal to the Italian vehemence of Francesca is Bianca in Nathaniel Parker Willis's play *Bianca Visconti; or, The Heart Overtasked* (1837). Bianca is the victim of love in a different way from Francesca. She is married to a man she loves passionately but who, she thinks, does not love her. To gain this love and make him Duke of Milan, she poisons her brother, the right-

---

[19] G. H. BAKER, " Francesca da Rimini " in A. H. Quinn, *Representative American Plays*, New York, 1917, p. 374.

ful heir. She expiates by a dramatic death, as she places the crown on her husband's head.

Willis wrote another Italian play *Tortesa the Usurer* (1839) for which he raided *Romeo and Juliet, A Winter's Tale,* and *The Merchant of Venice.* The romantic lady in *Tortesa* is Isabella, the daughter of a count. She is beautiful enough to be the ideal of a painter, Angelo, and the proposed prize of the usurer, Tortesa. She is independent, resourceful, proud, heroic, and loving. As a character she is dwarfed by the part of Tortesa and the juvenile lead Angelo who seems rather more in love with his picture than with Isabella.

In Robert Montgomery Bird's play *The Broker of Bogota* (1834) the romantic lady migrated to Spanish America where she appears in the characters of Leonor and Juana. As this is a men's play the two women stay in the background. But they have the proper characteristics: they are dark and beautiful, they love violently, they are loved violently, and they suffer.

An unexpected locality for romance was colonial New England. *Superstition* (1824) by James Nelson Barker sets the romantic lady " in New England, about the year 1675." Contrary to the statements of the critics,[20] the play is not really concerned with the Salem witchcraft though there is talk about witches in it. It is really a play of a genuinely romantic lady, Isabella, who lives " in New England " in mysterious circumstances. She has a son, Charles Fitzroy, handsome, brave, and rash. In the end it appears that she had been " espoused in secret " by Charles II, that her son is the king's son, that her father is a regicide. Though she is accused of witchcraft, nothing comes of the charge. Charles Fitzroy, however, is hanged, not for witchcraft, but specifically because he had lived a life of " crime and profligacy " ending with " contemplated rape and murder " of which he was, of course, innocent. Isabella dies of grief after discovering her father. It was obviously impossible that a king's mistress, however much punished, should be allowed to live on happily, particularly in colonial New England.

[20] See e. g. A. G. HALLINE. *American Plays,* New York, 1935, p. 120.

An extraordinary opportunity for a contrast between the ideal of womanhood and the fascination of romantic beauty lay in the existence of two alien races in America, the Indian and the negro. Eventually Italy and Spain as natural sources for the romantic were bound to give out; the unexplored fields at home had the charm of novelty and the shock of two fighting issues, the treatment of the Indians and negro slavery.

The Indian heroine derives from Pocahontas. As an historical character she was an heroic girl who risked her life for Captain John Smith, married Master Rolfe, was accepted as a princess, had her portrait painted, and became a legend. She has all the attributes of the romantic lady except two: she was not celebrated for love and she married Rolfe with everyone's approval. In spite of her deficiencies, however, she became a favorite subject for plays, the first of the series being Barker's *Indian Princess* (1808), and the last Brougham's burlesque, *Pocahontas or the Gentle Savage* (1885).[21] There was really nothing to do with Pocahontas as a romantic figure, as the best of the plays *Pocahontas, or the Settlers of Virginia* by George Washington Parke Custis (1830) shows. She was too well-known and too respectable. By the time the romantic period was well under way, also, Virginia Indians had become old-fashioned. James Fenimore Cooper had set a new style.

The Indian woman who appears in the novels is directly descended from Pocahontas, but has been transformed into the romantic woman. As the heroine of a novel she falls in love with true romantic ardor but with one important difference; she never yields to a lover and she is never seduced. Even Mrs. Rowson, who was particularly susceptible to seduction, in a novel as early as 1798, *Reuben and Rachel, or, Tales of Old Times,* introduces an Indian girl, Eumea, who renounces a white man, saved by her from death, in these words:

"God of the Christians, make them forever happy. Wife of Reuben, thou are a happy woman, for thy husband is a man of honour. He saw

[21] A. H. QUINN, *Representative American Plays*, New York, 1917, p. 183.

the weakness of a poor unprotected Indian maid, he pitied her folly, but took no advantage of it. . . . Farewell," said she, enthusiastically clasping her hands, " do not quite forget the poor, poor Eumea." [22]

Indian passion on the female side is strictly Platonic. The reason is that the Indian girl's beloved must be a white man, and a white man of noble character. He, of course, would never seduce a trusting woman. Moreover, as an American hero he has a pure, white sweetheart whom he is fated to marry. The poor Indian girl is therefore doomed to self-sacrifice and a lonely life—unless she is fortunate enough to die.

The Indian heroine in fiction is best known through the character of Magawisca in Catherine Sedgwick's famous novel *Hope Leslie; or, Early Times in the Massachusetts.*[23] Hope Leslie and her sister Faith are English orphan girls of aristocratic birth who are sent to Massachusetts. They both fulfil all the requirements of the ideal girl. They are beautiful, intelligent, and good. But Faith is captured by Indians and for awhile disappears from the story. Hope grows up into ideal womanhood.

Her height was not above the medium standard of her sex; she was delicately formed; the high health and the uniform habits of a country life had endowed her with the beauty with which Poetry has invested Hebe; while her love for exploring hill and dale, ravine and precipice, had given her that elastic step and ductile grace which belong to all agile animals. . . .

[Her eyes] appeared gray, blue, hazel, or black, as the outward light touched them, or as they kindled by the light of her feelings. Her rich, brown hair turned in light waves from her sunny brow.[24]

The son of her guardian, Everell, falls in love with her, but he is captured by the Indians. He is about to be sacrificed on a high rock:

The chief raised the deadly weapon, when Magawisca, springing from the precipitous side of the rock, screamed " Forbear! " and interposed her arm. It was too late. The blow was levelled—force and direction given; the stroke, aimed at Everell's neck, severed his defender's arm, and left him unharmed. The lopped, quivering member dropped over the precipice.

---

[22] Quoted in A. H. QUINN, *American Fiction*, New York, 1936, p. 17.
[23] New York, 1842 (1827).   [24] *Hope Leslie*, vol. 1, p. 177.

Mononotto staggered and fell senseless, and all the savages, uttering horrible yells, rushed toward the fatal spot.

" Stand back! " cried Magawisca, " I have bought his life with my own. Fly, Everell—nay, speak not, but fly—thither—to the east! " she cried more vehemently.[25]

Throughout the book Magawisca though an inveterate hater of the white man protects Everell. Once she is imprisoned and condemned to death but escapes with his help. In the end she renounces him forever:

" The Great Spirit guide ye," she (Magawisca) said, and then, turning away, leaped into the boat, muffled her face in her mantle, and in a few brief moments disappeared forever from their sight.[26]

Hope's sister Faith reappears at the end of the novel, and marries an Indian, Oneco, who is the chivalrous young red man popularized by Uncas in Cooper's *The Last of the Mohicans*. But Faith has long been an Indian captive and besides has, in her captivity, become a faithful Roman Catholic.

A variation upon the romantic Indian woman appears in William Gilmore Simms's *The Yemassee* as Matiwan, the sympathetically pictured wife of an Indian chief. In everything except her complexion and " her long, black hair " she is the idealized wife and mother, beautiful, submissive, resolute, religious, faithful. She puts herself among the romantic women by her heroic killing of her condemned son to save him from losing the protection of his totem. When her husband dies, she dies, and Simms rises to an eloquence worthy of Thackeray:

She was unconscious of all things, as they bore her tenderly away, save that the Yemassee was no longer the great nation. She only felt that the " well-beloved," as well of herself as of her people, looked forth, with Occonestoga (her son), wondering that she came not, from the Blessed Valley of the Good Manyeto.[27]

The romantic negro strain had no such distinguished origin as was provided by Pocahontas. It was the inevitable result of the admixture of the black and the white races which began in

[25] Vol. 1, p. 137. [26] Vol. 2, p. 236. [27] *The Yemassee*, p. 441.

America with the introduction of negro slavery. Sooner or later there was bound to be difficulty as the black blood was gradually bred out of some individuals. The quadroon or the octoroon was certain to be beautiful for she was the offspring of the aristocratic slave owner and the most attractive of his slaves. As the slave owner's mistress she had a position far above that of the ordinary slave. She was usually well brought up, well educated, and well mannered. Undoubtedly her master often intended to free her. In spite of his good intentions, however, he frequently forgot to free her or was prevented from freeing her by legal difficulties.

To the abolitionists she was a figure of peculiar interest. She was beautiful, her emotions were presumably violent, she was unfortunate, and she was the prey of the passions of low-born slave buyers, in itself an occasion for emotional treatment. Longfellow's poem "The Quadroon Girl" gives a sentimentalized picture of the situation.

In the poem the Slaver and the Planter sit by the " still bayou ":

> Before them, with her face unpraised,
> In timid attitude,
> Like one half anxious, half amazed,
> A Quadroon maiden stood.
>
> Her eyes were large, and full of light
> Her arms and neck were bare;
> No garment she wore save a kirtle bright,
> And her own long, raven hair.
>
> And on her lips there played a smile
> As holy, meek, and faint,
> As lights in some cathedral aisle
> The features of a saint.[28]

In the end the Planter sells his daughter and her purchaser leads her away:

> To be his slave and paramour
> In a strange and distant land!

"The Quadroon Girl" is obviously not a "romantic lady." She is the sentimentalized dramatization of a figure in a naïve,

---

[28] *Poetical Works*, p. 22.

academic imagination. The real romantic lady with a touch of
negro blood was a much more complex creation. There are two
important examples, one from the beginning of the period and
the other from its end.

The first is Cora in Cooper's *Last of the Mohicans* (1826).
Here, in the standard manner, she is contrasted with her half-
sister, Alice, who has a " dazzling complexion, fair, golden hair,
and bright blue eyes." [29] Alice is loved by the hero, Major Heyward, and has an unimportant place in the story. Cora, however,
has the true romantic beauty. Her face showed " an indescribable
look of pity, admiration, and horror as her dark eye followed the
easy motions of the savage. The tresses of this lady were shining
and black, like the plumage of the raven." The only thing that
shows her racial admixture is " the rich blood that seemed ready to
burst its bounds." [30]

As is fitting to her type, Cora has great influence over men,
especially over Indians. Uncas obeys her instantly; a villainous
Indian, Magua, wants to make her his squaw. He has no interest
in the " ideal " Alice; he is willing to release " the light-eyes " if
" the dark-haired woman " will " live in his wigwam forever." [31]
Magua, of course, has no objection to her mixed race. Her difficulty comes from the fact that though she is almost white, she
can never marry a white man in the United States.

Her father, Colonel Munro, makes the difficulty clear:

" She (Cora) was the daughter of a gentleman of those isles (the West
Indies) by a lady whose misfortune it was, if you will, to be descended,
remotely, from that unfortunate clan who are so basely enslaved to
administer to the wants of a luxurious people . . . Ha! Major Heyward,
you are yourself born at the south, where these unfortunate beings are
considered of a race inferior to your own."

" Tis most unfortunately true, sir," said Duncan (Heyward), unable
any longer to prevent his eyes from sinking to the floor in embarrassment.

" And you cast it on my child as a reproach! You scorn to mingle the
blood of the Heywards with one so degraded—lovely and virtuous though
she be? " fiercely demanded the jealous parent.

---

[29] COOPER, *Works,* vol. 2, *The Last of the Mohicans,* p. 10.
[30] P. 10.   [31] P. 62.

"Heaven protect me from a prejudice so unworthy of my reason!" returned Duncan, at the same time conscious of such a feeling, and that as deeply rooted as if it had been ingrafted in his nature." [32]

When Cora is finally made prisoner by Magua, she leaves her sister with a nobly elegiac farewell. But she is not destined to make the complete sacrifice of actually becoming the red man's squaw. And though Magua threatens to kill her when she refuses to go further with him, her beauty is too much for the besotted savage. He lifts his knife again and again and drops it " with a bewildered air, like one who doubted." His difficulty is solved by " one of his assistants " who, since he is not in love with the romantic lady, can without a qualm " sheathe his own knife in the bosom of Cora." [33] The lady's dilemma is solved in a manner which became standard, by death.

One of the most famous plays of the end of the era, *The Octoroon* (1859) by Dion Boucicault, made the romantic character with negro blood the center of his composition rather than an incident as Cora is in Cooper's novel. He follows the regular pattern, however. Zoe, the octoroon, is beautiful and accomplished. She is well-educated and she has the manners of Louisiana. But she is a slave; though her father intended to free her, she was mortgaged with the other chattels. Zoe is in love with a young Southerner, George, who has been absent from Louisiana for years. She is subjected to one ordeal after another. She is forced to refuse the love of George because she is one-eighth negro; as McClosky, a villainous money-lender says in a soliloquy, " That one black drop of blood burns in her veins and lights up her heart like a foggy sun." [34] When the crisis comes and McClosky buys her at auction for $25,000 she drinks poison. Meanwhile McClosky has been killed by an Indian, but Zoe must die. She revives for a moment and ends the play with a speech to George:

When I am dead she (Dora) will not be jealous of your love for me, no laws will stand between us. Lift me; so—(*George raises her head*)—

---

[32] P. 96.   [33] P. 204.

[34] DION BOUCICAULT. "The Octoroon" in QUINN'S *Representative American Plays*, p. 444.

[76]

let me look at you, that your face may be the last I see of this world. O! George, you may, without a blush, confess your love for the Octoroon. (*She dies, George lowers her head gently and kneels beside her.*) [35]

Up to this point I have presented the romantic lady as she was conceived from one point of view by dramatists, poets, and novelists. Love is her whole existence, and the effect of her love upon herself and upon others follows a pattern which is relatively standard.

There were, however, two great writers of the period, Poe and Hawthorne, whose more complex imaginations produced characters which need special analysis.

Poe's romance was the romance of that dream world which is the artist's own creation and which is not concerned with social custom, fashion, prejudice, or pattern. His dream woman owes very little to any specific woman, though there is no doubt that some woman, particularly his wife, was identified for the time being with his dream. *Hawthorne*

His early poems present the dream woman as little more than a tenuous idea. The famous " To Helen " which has been identified with Mrs. Jane Stith Stanard, mother of Poe's playmate in Richmond, has hardly a specific reference in its fifteen lines. It is clearly a boy's poem. It contains not only no word of love, but not even one physical detail of importance. Helen is beautiful and she is statuesque. But that is all. The point of the poem is that she gets Poe dreaming of the golden, classic time. He has been restless, " weary," a " wanderer," " on desperate seas long wont to roam." Now her beauty has brought him home

> To the glory that was Greece,
> And the grandeur that was Rome.

His vague longings have focused upon the romantic dream of classic glory; with a boy's gratitude he identifies that glory with the woman who brought his imagination to a center. It is she whose hair is " hyacinth "; she whose face is " classic." She is Psyche, the soul-goddess from the holy, classic past.

Poe's other youthful poems are equally vague. The song in

[35] P. 458.

" Al Aaraaf " shows the romantic Ligeia as no more definite than a strain of music. She is impalpable, unlocalized, evanescent. The young Poe's romantic dream was of a time and place where he would " while away " a " little time with lyre and rhyme " where his heart would " tremble with the strings." Not even in his dream does he see any definite shapes. His dream world is one vast, enveloping, unlocalized emotion.

In his later poems Poe's dream woman becomes more definite, but only because she is someone lost or dead. Lenore in " The Raven " was " rare " and " radiant " but she has no more life than a whisper or an echo. Ulalume is " lost " in a vault in " This ghoul-haunted woodland of Weir." Annabel Lee has been " chilled and killed " and lies

> In her sepulchre there by the sea—
> In her tomb by the side of the sea.

Annie is the love of a man who is dead but speaks from his grave. Eulalie was " fair and gentle" and was " yellow-haired," but she, too, is dead. Lenore lies on a " drear and rigid bier." These dream women who were never much more than an emotion with a poetic name are mere characters in a dream play

> And the angels, all pallid and wan,
>   Uprising, unveiling affirm
> That the play is the tragedy " Man,"
>   And its hero the Conqueror Worm.[36]

In Poe's tales women are relatively uncommon, but they all share the evanescence of the women of the poems. Their evanescence is the result of a change which comes over them. They begin like Berenice, " agile, graceful, and overflowing with energy." But disease comes and they end as pallid creatures doomed to death, as corpselike as the shadows of an opium dream. Such creatures are Morella who died and returned to life in the person of her child who died again; Lady Madeline Usher, who was entombed in a cataleptic trance and arose from her vault; Eleonora

---

[36] EDGAR ALLAN POE, *Complete Poetical Works*, New York, n. d., p. 65.

who was the prey of an unknown disease and whose lover promised never to marry; Ligeia, who was beautiful and brilliant beyond all imagining but who died and inhabited the body of the woman who was the narrator's second wife.

All these dream women have the same characteristics. They are closely related to the man they marry; at first beautiful and healthy, they fall ill of a mysterious disease; they die and never pass from their husband's memory; if he remarries they drive out the personality of the second wife. It is no wonder that Poe's most thorough biographer, Mr. Hervey Allen, identifies the dream woman of the Tales with Virginia Clemm, Poe's girl wife who died of consumption and haunted Poe's memory as long as he lived.

The American writer who took the conflict of the ideal woman and the romantic woman most seriously was Nathaniel Hawthorne. On the one hand all his best moral judgments favored the good, blonde, submissive, religious ideal who kept one's house, bore one's children, and carried on the best New England tradition. On the other hand it could not be denied that there were dark, vigorous, ample women with powerful personalities and with a strange, disquieting, nameless influence. If one type were the ideal, then how explain the disturbance that the other type undoubtedly seemed to bring into the minds of good men? This disturbance apparently was like a poison, a sweet, provocative, subtle poison, but no less lethal than the bitterest and most corrosive draught.

This idea lies behind his allegorical tale "Rappacini's Daughter" in *Mosses from an Old Manse* (1846). The tale is set in Italy, the land of passion, "very long ago." A young man, Giovanni, has lodgings in a "high and gloomy chamber" overlooking a beautiful garden full of strange flowers and herbs. The garden belongs to an old man who walks among his plants as if they were "savage beasts, or deadly snakes, or evil spirits." He is assisted in his botanical work by his daughter Beatrice. She is the true romantic lady, "richly" dressed, "redundant with life, health, and energy." She tends the flowers like "one sister performing the duties of affection to another." But all the plants are violent poisons and Beatrice lives on their perfume. So poisonous is she that a bouquet which Giovanni gives her withers as she holds it.

Nevertheless Giovanni is wildly in love with her. No matter what he sees or what is told him, " it seemed an absolute necessity of his existence to approach Beatrice." He gains entrance to the garden and talks with Beatrice. The result is wilder love than ever. " Those tokens which he had hitherto considered as proofs of a frightful peculiarity in her physical and moral system were now either forgotten, or, by the subtle sophistry of passion transmitted into a golden crown of enchantment, rendering Beatrice the more admirable by so much as she was the more unique." [37] Then after a time Giovanni realizes that he, too, has absorbed the poison of the garden. A bouquet withers in his hand; he breathes upon a spider and the creature dies. He goes into the garden again and he is " affrighted at the eager enjoyment—the appetite, as it were—with which he found himself inhaling the fragrance of the flowers." In despair he offers Beatrice a powerful antidote which a friend has given him. His hope is that from " a poisonous thing " she will turn to an innocent and wholesome bride. But Rappacini's experiment with his daughter has been too successful, " the powerful antidote was death " and Beatrice dies at the feet of her father and Giovanni.

The meaning of this allegory is clear. Passion is poison; the attempt of the passionate to regain innocence is death. Beatrice like all other romantic women has no escape from her perverted nature. She must die.

Hawthorne was, however, too much of the artist and thinker to try to resolve the conflict of the ideal and the romantic in this rather naïve manner. In three novels, *The Scarlet Letter* (1850), *The Blithedale Romance* (1852), and *The Marble Faun* (1860), he tried to work out the problem in a way which would satisfy his exacting artistic and intellectual conscience. He began by concen-

[37] NATHANIEL HAWTHORNE, *Works*, 15 vols., Boston, n. d., vol. 2, p. 132.

trating upon the most powerful conception of the romantic woman in American literature, Hester Prynne in *The Scarlet Letter.*

Hester has all the physical attributes of the romantic lady:

> The young woman was tall, with a figure of perfect elegance on a large scale. She had dark and abundant hair, so glossy that it threw off the sunshine with a gleam, and a face, which, besides being beautiful from regularity of feature and richness of complexion, had the impressiveness belonging to a marked brow and deep black eyes. She was lady-like, too, after the manner of the feminine gentility of those days; characterized by a certain state and dignity, rather than by the delicate, evanescent, and indescribable grace, which is now recognized as its indication.[38]

Though her appearance follows the standard tradition, Hester goes far beyond the regular romantic conception as the book is worked out.

For one thing her romantic passion lies behind her. It is over when the book begins. She is alone, with neither husband nor lover; she has a child; she wears a scarlet letter A; she lives in loneliness; the only activity which her life knows is the activity within her own soul. What then is the romantic life which always belongs to the romantic lady? It is precisely the inner activity of her mind. By sinning she has won wisdom; she has won it not by the fact of her sin, but by facing the penalty for her sin. When she put on the scarlet letter not in boldness or defiance but in calm acknowledgment of her fault she rose into grandeur. Hawthorne takes pains to show that her sin and its acknowledgment have made her great. He contrasts her with the good women of the colony. They have never sinned; they are hard-featured, petty, narrow, and vindictive. Her wronged husband, Roger Chillingworth, is shrunken and pitiful in mind and body because he cannot enter into the grandeur of his wife. Her lover, the minister Dimmesdale, is "broken down by long and exquisite suffering"; his mind is "darkened and confused." When in the forest he faces his sin with Hester he rises to something of her greatness. The sunshine bursts forth in sympathy. "Love . . . must always create a sunshine, filling the heart so full of radiance that it over-

[38] Vol. 5, p. 73.

flows upon the outward world." [39] And when he stands upon the scaffold with Hester, admits his sin before all the people, and falls dying, then Roger Chillingworth utters final tribute to the greatness which the minister has learned from Hester, " ' Thou hast escaped me! ' he repeated more than once. ' Thou hast escaped me! ' " The romantic lady has not been overcome by her sin; she has rescued a soul from the devil's grasp.

In *The Blithedale Romance* Hawthorne was too concerned with contemporary problems to raise his heroine Zenobia to the level of Hester Prynne. Perhaps, also, Margaret Fuller, the presumed original of Zenobia, kept his imaginative creation too close to reality.

Zenobia Fauntleroy has the familiar romantic characteristics:

She was dressed as simply as possible, in an American print . . . but with a silken kerchief, between which and her gown there was one glimpse of a white shoulder. It struck me as a great piece of good fortune that there should be just that glimpse. Her hair, which was dark, glossy, and of singular abundance, was put up rather soberly and primly, without curls, or other ornament, except a single flower. . . . She was, indeed, an admirable figure of a woman.[40]

Other characteristics are " bloom, health, and vigor," " a mellow, almost broad laugh," " a fine, perfectly developed figure." But the romance of Zenobia comes not so much from her physical attributes as from her mind. Hawthorne speaks of her

noble courage, conscious of no harm, and scorning the petty restraints which take the life and color out of other women's conversation.

He also notes that

One felt an influence breathing out of her such as we might suppose to come from Eve, when she was just made, and her Creator brought her to Adam, saying, " Behold! here is a woman! "

To underline the character of Zenobia, Hawthorne introduces Priscilla, " the very picture of the New England spring; subdued in tint, and rather cool." She is " delicate, and virgin-like." He

[39] P. 243.   [40] P. 337.

speaks of Priscilla's slender and shadowy grace, and " those mysterious qualities which make her seem diaphanous with spiritual light." Priscilla is, in short, the ideal girl in contrast with Zenobia, the romantic lady.

The reader must expect, therefore, that Zenobia will be active and Priscilla passive. What tragedy there will be must happen to Zenobia. And it happens just because a naturally active woman is forced to take a passive rôle. Zenobia for all her vigorous mentality finds that she lives in a man's world. She herself states the " moral " of her story:

That in the battle-field of life, the downright stroke, that would fall only on a man's steel headpiece, is sure to light on a woman's heart, over which she wears no breastplate, and whose wisdom it is, therefore to keep out of the conflict. Or, this: That the whole universe, her sex and yours, and Providence, or Destiny, to boot, make common cause against the woman who swerves one hair's-breadth, out of the beaten track, Yes; and add . . . that, with that one hair's-breadth she goes all astray and never sees the world in its true aspect afterwards.[41]

Zenobia's crime had been that she had set a women's independent judgment against a man's; in the conflict she had lost. What would have been a defeat for a man is for a woman a crime which bears the punishment of destruction. Priscilla, whose life had only one purpose, identification with a man's will, secures happiness. Zenobia, following the regular pattern of the period, must die. She drowns herself. When her body is dragged out of the river all her romantic beauty has departed and Hawthorne ironically points out the ugliness, distortion, and horror of her end.

In *The Marble Faun* Hawthorne again contrasts the ideal and the romantic. Hilda is " the fair-haired Saxon girl " who lives in Rome in a tower room where she tends the Virgin's shrine. Doves hover about her as she leans from the window and she wanders about the pestiferous Roman slums protected by her innocence. Her angelic mind accompanies a perfect intellectual comprehension of art, and dwells in a healthy body.

[41] P. 573.

[83]

This power and depth of appreciation depended partly upon Hilda's physical organization, which was at once healthful and exquisitely delicate; and, connected with this advantage, she had a command of hand, a nicety and force of touch, which is an endowment separate from pictorial genius, though indispensable to its exercise.[42]

Miriam is the direct opposite to Hilda and is almost a complete example of the characteristics of the romantic woman. She was

so beautiful, that she seemed to get into your consciousness and memory, and could never afterwards be shut out, but haunted your dreams, for pleasure or for pain; holding your inner realm as a conquered territory, though without deigning to make herself at home there.

She is of exotic race, perhaps of Jewish blood; she has deep, dark eyes, " black abundant hair, with none of the vulgar glossiness of other women's sable locks." She reminds Hawthorne of Rachel or perhaps of Judith " when she vanquished Holofernes with her beauty, and slew him for too much adoring it."

With her physical beauty Miriam had the overpowering personality of the romantic lady, a personality which with no evil intentions subdues men to her will. But Miriam is no siren or Lamia-woman; she is not the romantic " femme fatale." Irresistibly she is drawn to a kindred spirit, Donatello, the Italian with the faun's pointed ears. Donatello is only partly a man; his mind is still undeveloped like a child's. His growth to maturity comes by association with the romantic Miriam whose vital personality has life-giving power. Because of her he commits murder and in that most awful of all sins attains complete manhood. With Eve the innocent Adam eats of the tree of knowledge whose fruit is death. But what he has gained by his sin!

" Is he not beautiful? " said Miriam, watching the sculptor's eye as it dwelt admiringly on Donatello, " So changed, yet still, in a deeper sense, so much the same! He has travelled in a circle, as all things heavenly and earthly do, and now comes back to his original self, with an inestimable treasure of improvement won from an experience of pain. How wonderful is this! I tremble at my own thoughts, yet must needs probe them to their depths. Was the crime—in which he and I were wedded—was it a

[42] Vol. 6, p. 74.

blessing, in that strange disguise? Was it a means of education, bringing a simple and imperfect nature to a point of feeling and intelligence which it could have reached under no other discipline? . . . Was that very sin— into which Adam precipitated himself and all his race,—was it the destined means by which, over a long pathway of toil and sorrow, we are to attain a higher, brighter, and profounder happiness, than our lost birthright gave . . . ? " [48]

Miriam thus reaches the climax of the career of the romantic lady. For she enters as no other woman had done into the very scheme of life. Her power is exerted toward a creation not of a mere body but of a soul, a creation on a scale as near God's as a human being can reach. The physical love which had been so completely the attribute of her predecessors, is in her refined to the infusion of her will into the mind of one as yet undeveloped. The physical tie which was the ideal consummation of previous women, with her becomes a psychic tie to be identified with the strange force which lifts man from the animal level to the angels.

All this, of course, in *The Marble Faun* is handled tentatively and half in shadow. The date was, after all, 1860, and it is doubtful whether Hawthorne's generation ever realized the heretical boldness of his imagination. As far as the novel was concerned, Miriam slips out of the story into mysterious darkness; she was no companion for mortal man, and Hawthorne did not know what to do with her. The ideal Hilda is happily married and returns to " breathe (her) native air."

Up to this point the romantic lady has derived her life from the romance of love, the romance of dreams, or, with Hawthorne, the romance of ideas. There is another source of romance in which, historically, women have had little concern, the romance of action. The era from 1820 to 1860 produced plenty of women whom the imagination of the twentieth century has made romantic, women who were leaders in education, journalism, prison reform, abolition, dress reform, and " women's rights." But they were not romantic in their own day. The women who gathered in 1848 at the " first convention in the interests of the New Woman "

[48] P. 491.

at Seneca Falls, New York, were not romantic; they were crazy faddists. They evolved none of the magic or mystery which is the indispensable concomitant of literary romance.

> The light that never was on sea or land
> The consecration and the poet's dream

shone on them long after their death when new generations evolved new romanticisms. The pioneer woman, that romantic creature who had to wait for the cinema for canonization, is unrepresented in the novels and plays of the period. All she achieved in her own time was one poem in R. W. Griswold's *The Poets and Poetry of America*.[44] "The Mothers of the West" by William D. Gallagher is a tribute to the women of Kentucky's "Dark and Bloody Ground." But it must be remembered that these mothers were long since dead and that pioneer Kentucky had had time to recede into the magic of romantic memory. A poem by Charles Fenno Hoffman "The Western Hunter to his Mistress" gives a highly romanticized picture of Far Western scenery but gives no indication of a real pioneer woman. And in Cooper's romantic novels of the West, *The Pathfinder* and *The Prairie*, there is no glorification of the pioneer woman.

When writers wanted the romance of action to include women, they turned to classical sources. The best example is William Ware's *Zenobia*,[45] a glorified picture of the half-legendary queen of Palmyra. Here was a figure who belonged to an exotic Asiatic country, who had great power, who moved with orators, generals, and kings, and who wore shining armor. It is characteristic of the era that Ware should stress "the diviner beauty of the emotions and sentiments which were working at her heart and shone out in the expressive language of her countenance."[46] But he also stresses the "gorgeous magnificence" of her armor, her dark hair, and her "marvellous union of feminine beauty, queenly dignity, and masculine power."[47] On the whole, however, the romance

---

[44] 8th edition, Phila., 1847.

[45] London, 1885. First published as *Letters of Lucius M. Piso from Palmyra, to his friends Marcus Curtius at Rome*, 1837.

[46] P. 61. [47] P. 317.

of Zenobia lay in the fact that she was a great leader of a wealthy city with the added pathos of her struggle against the strongest power in the ancient world.

The romance of the ancient world was reenacted for romantic America through the pages of an important historical work, Elizabeth F. Ellet's *The Women of the American Revolution*,[48] a collection of sketches of the heroines of the Revolution. In her preface Mrs. Ellet maintained that the success of the revolution depended upon " the sentiment pervading the mass of the people," a sentiment which " depended in great part upon the women."

It has often been pointed out that an important influence upon American thought was the tradition of Greece and Rome. One can see how naturally it formed a part of Poe's romantic ideas in " To Helen." Now one of the most romantic aspects of this tradition was the Roman matron like the mother of the Gracchi or Volumnia the mother of Coriolanus, brave, self-sacrificing, and patriotic. This romantic feeling produced Elizabeth Ellet's three volumes. In the preface she quotes admiringly a statement of a newspaper writer in 1780:

" 'Tis true, Cleander, no mean merit will accrue to him who shall justly celebrate the virtues of our ladies! Shall not their generous contributions to relieve the wants of the defenders of our country, supply a column to emulate the Roman women, stripped of their jewels when the public necessity demanded them? " [49]

Following this lead, Mrs. Ellet interprets the one hundred and fifty women, more or less, who appear in her volumes in Roman and Spartan terms. " Patriotic mothers nursed the infancy of freedom," she says. " Magnanimity, fortitude, self-sacrifice, and heroism " are common words. Their " fair hands " made flags; Washington praised the women as " advocates as powerful as they are amiable." The romanticizing of the mothers, previously existent only in the wish-thinking of mothers, themselves, had come at last to expression. From now on, though slowly, the American mother cult was to supersede the tyrannical hold of the philo-

[48] 3 vols., New York, 1848.   [49] *New Jersey Gazette*, Oct. 11, 1780.

progenitive male upon literature. Mrs. Ellet was doing her best. The mothers in her three volumes had " sprightliness, good sense, and benevolence "; " strong intellect, cultivated taste and refinement "; " heroism, fidelity, and piety "; " faith and devotion "; " firmness and resolution," and scores of other noble virtues. The steel-engravers reinforced Mrs. Ellet's patriotic romanticism, and the girl of the 1840's could study the heroic female faces with their impeccable steely complexions and their fashion-plate dresses, little realizing that in their old age, as mothers, they too would achieve romance.

In turning to the women of action in revolt from the soft, fair ideal of womanhood which was standard during the whole pre-Civil War era, Mrs. Ellet is practically alone. Her romantic interpretation of the Revolutionary women was, however, to be remembered later and was to be followed by a similar romanticizing of the women who were leaders of the great humanitarian movements of the century. In imaginative literature the vigorous, dark, passionate woman remained standard for romantic purposes for many years. Since life necessarily stressed the domestic virtues, romantic literature stressed the unusual. The compensation for the normal, good woman lay in the fact that however attractive her rival might be temporarily, in the end men would find her too disturbing to live with, just as they found that the " new woman " of action threatened too dangerous competition.

BOOKS FOR THE LADY READER, 1820-1860

by

Ola Elizabeth Winslow

THE average woman reader of the *Godey's Lady's Book* era is easy to find after a hundred years. She was also easy to find in her own day and uncommonly easy to please. When an enterprising publisher dared bring out the same book in two successive years under two different titles, hoping in the editorial preface that his "fair reader" would not mind, she kindly obliged, with the sequel that he repeated the deception and accordingly prospered. Magazine editors likewise dared borrow from each other with shameless regularity, reprinting month by month pieces which had proved popular. As a result, something resembling both a Gallup poll of current taste and a catalogue of stories and poems of the month and year can be compiled from the long list of duplications and near duplications which cancel out as the panorama of popular reading matter passes under review at the distance of a hundred years.

Along with the discovery that books and magazines for women were a profitable commodity and that women's taste might be easily manipulated to commercial advantage, came the earnest endeavor (chiefly feminine) to use the printed page toward mass conversion. Straightway the popularization of women's literature became to some extent a crusade as well as dividend business. Women were made the unsuspecting targets of a "read more and read better" campaign, launched and maneuvered by those who sought to prove that women had minds slightly feebler than men's but nevertheless minds, which might be safely used without robbing their possessors of that feminine charm which was the *sine qua non* of eligibility.

During the years 1820-1860 the banalities resulting from this new evangelism were spread over many thousands of pages, most of them beneath apology even as propaganda in a more or less worthy cause. If it were not for the leather and gold of the bindings, the delicately colored fashion plates, and sometimes the engravings, nine-tenths of these honeyed delights for a lady's " vacant " hours would be too insipid to seem even picturesque a century later. Making allowance for the laudable motives of their perpetrators does not redeem them. The author's approach to mysteries hitherto sealed is entirely too timid, the flattery of the reader too ingratiating, the dose too vanilla flavored. Yet this freight of printed matter is important to those who would read American cultural history through the tortuous windings of the mid-century, and important for the best of all reasons. It succeeded. As the average woman read these thousands of pages provided for her entertainment and moral improvement, she gradually changed her concept of herself and her whole mental outlook along with her silhouette. Popular literature always reflects current taste. In the years 1820-1860 it also shaped current taste. Therein lies its importance.

As one might expect, the small minority of those who thought for themselves, the Margaret Fullers, the Mary Moody Emersons, the Mary Lyons and Elizabeth Blackwells arrived at the same destination without benefit of campaign. They read what other intelligent people, both men and women were reading, and made no virtue of so doing. It was the rank and file who required time, gentle handling, and a variety of bait, politely dangled. They presently found it in all colors and flavors, swallowed it gladly and called for more. A new spirit was at work in middle-class America. A new prosperity was feeding aspirations for what was popularly called culture, a notion vaguely associated with the printed page. Books accordingly acquired a new importance in the life of the average American.

Using the typical middle class home as setting, one may take inventory of the several varieties of reading matter newly provided for women, each neatly sorted out and displayed in what custom decreed as the one most appropriate spot: namely, the bookcase, the centre-table, or the boudoir, with possibly the shelf by the lady's work-basket reserved for the current number of the *Godey's Lady's Book*. Of these four groups, only three are important to those who would read the signs of the times so far as women were concerned. Books for the boudoir require no pausing. Although more numerous than those in the other three groups put together, they were made out of the perennial romantic trash common to all ages of printing and have no special importance for the early nineteenth century. In each of the other three groups, however, the leaven of the time was at work.

Standard authors found sanctuary in the bookcase, a clumsy object requiring wall-space in every drawing-room of the period. With the introduction of steam power presses early in the century, it was no longer necessary to import standard British authors in order to have them. It was also possible for American editions of current British favorites to be issued almost simultaneously with the London editions, with the result that American publishers were flourishing and American bookcases filling up rapidly from the twenties forward.

Among the classical authors Shakespeare came first. "What is a library without Shakespeare?" exclaimed a woman writer in the *New York Mirror* for 1835, voicing the critical orthodoxy of the hour, and at the same time filling up one shelf (possibly the one on a level with the visitor's eye) in every American drawing-room. Not to possess an "elegant" edition of the "immortal bard," as he was invariably labelled, was not to belong to the cultured elect by the first of all specifications. To meet this demand as well as help to create it, more than thirty editions of Shakespeare's complete works were issued in America in as many years, together with numerous collections of his *Poems*, his *Beauties and Gems, Proverbs, Oracles, Laconics,* and *Pithy Extracts*.

To what extent Shakespeare was read by the women who dusted and arranged the numerous volumes purchased to honor him is harder to say, but there is no very reliable evidence that they had more than the merest conversational familiarity with the titles they so pridefully displayed. More probably their knowledge consisted chiefly in the epigrammatic giblets and hackneyed phrases distributed so plentifully up and down the columns of every woman's magazine of the period, used as sub-titles to popular fiction great and small, and as an inevitable ingredient of many lesser effusions which attained to print. " As Shakespeare says " was a safe preamble to any reflection on life, death, love, or any other profundity on the aspiring author's mind at the moment. Any woman who read the magazines written for her improvement might also have been able to call a brief roll of Shakespeare's " admirable sketches of the female character " which it was the fashion of editors to hold up for approval and emulation: Cordelia the gently firm, Ophelia the broken-hearted, Henry VIII's Katherine the deeply wronged, the quietly resigned, and according to one contemporary critic (undoubtedly a woman)

the most impressive portrait that poetical inspiration ever drew.

Beatrice and Isabella, according to this same critic, had unfortunately expressed themselves in language which could not be read; therefore they must be banished from the American parlor.

It is not likely that the average woman reader had done more than handle the other British classics usually enshrined in American bookcases, particularly Milton, who had been published in almost as many editions as Shakespeare, and Thomas Young, whose *Night Thoughts* was widely popular in illustrated editions. Both of these poets together with Isaac Watts in his *Divine and Moral Songs* and Bunyan in either *Pilgrim's Progress* or *Grace Abounding*, and probably both, made suitable Sunday reading for those who aspired so high among the sacred authors. Except for *Pilgrim's Progress*, however, most women contented themselves on the Sabbath with Felicia Dorothea Hemans, whose offerings were appropriately sorted for the purpose.

On the secular shelves they felt more at home, particularly with Scott, without whom no American library would have been even respectable. Before his death in 1832, bookcases displayed him in his poems and in separate editions of his novels; after 1832, in his complete works bound elegantly in red morocco. Some households had two editions, one for the bookcase and one to be read. In the verdict of various women who left record of their opinions, he deserved to stand with Shakespeare; in fact, they enjoyed him far more. Catherine M. Sedgwick, American novelist and a woman who usually talked sense on other subjects, wrote of *Kenilworth* in 1822,

I salute it with as much enthusiasm as a Catholic would a holy relic.[1]

Other women were equally enthusiastic, although less florid in their praise. When later Dickens eclipsed Scott in popular favor, women did not change their vote. Bulwer, who qualified for feminine editorial approval by never allowing "Guilt to be triumphant over Virtue," was also regularly welcomed to the bookcase, after each of his novels in turn had been read to pieces in the first American edition. Among current authors it was safer to honor only the British by a place on the shelves, but a few Americans were also present, notably Irving and Cooper. Neither was a great favorite with the women; they preferred tenderness to Irving's humor, and as for Cooper, he had made too many unkind remarks about American women.

If the lady reader had told the whole truth concerning her bookcase preferences, she would probably have confessed that to her the most exciting book in the whole collection was not a novel at all, but "Mr. Byron's Poems." She had read them, marked them with fern leaves at the "tender" places and committed choice stanzas here and there to memory. Editors of women's magazines and writers of pious essays urged her to separate the man and his life from his poems. He had lived sinfully and had offended God; she must not think on his sins, but she might read his poems. Perhaps she obeyed and perhaps not. An American edition "Embracing his Suppressed Poems and a Sketch of his Life" was in circulation and she may have satisfied her curiosity concerning it, but even the properly censored edition kept the drawing-room collection of "polite authors" from being too much an affair of awe and reverence.

[1] *The Life and Letters of Catherine M. Sedgwick*, ed. by M. E. Dewey, 1872, p. 118.

To the average woman, however, in her timid progress toward those realms which " did her softer brain perplex," the bookcase and everything in it yielded to the centre-table which stood in massive, marble-topped dignity in the precise center of every parlor or drawing-room of the period. In the cultural life of America the importance of this monstrous obstruction can hardly be overstated. For the woman whose great-grand-daughter would as a matter of course go to college, it was by all odds the most important piece of furniture in the house, although easily the ugliest. It held perforce many things and always too much, but unfailingly along with the *Bible*, the *Hymnal*, possibly *Robinson Crusoe* and an extra and particularly ornate edition of *Pilgrim's Progress* (Illustrated) it held at least two books directed almost exclusively toward the " gentler sex." One of these was the current literary annual, a collection of " blossoms " or " gems " culled (by a variety of mixed figures) from the garden of Parnassus or the seats of the Muses; the other was whichever of the more specialized gift-books corresponded to the family history at the moment: *The Lover's Gift, The White Veil,* or *The Marriage-Ring* for a new bride, *The Cypress Wreath* or *The Mourner's Chaplet* for a late bereavement. Neither of these varieties was ever purchased by the lady herself; it was always " bestowed," a book being, according to T. S. Arthur, one of the most prolific manufacturers of the centre-table sort, the ideal gift, since it could be both " given and received without violation of delicacy " and might in addition be also " a refining and elevating influence."

For these two reasons—the practical and the moral—the gift-book became one of the best sellers ever nominated by the American public and also one of the longest lived. First issued in 1825 in direct imitation of a British publication,[2] it quickly became almost phenomenally popular, and by the middle forties had reached a peak of favor which demanded more than sixty separate publications with each Christmas season. For another ten years the vogue suffered only slight diminution from year to year, then sharply declined in the late fifties and by the beginning

[2] *The Forget-me-not*, London, 1823.

of the Civil War was definitely a thing of the past. Examined in its more than thousand varieties during these thirty years of favor, this strange gallimaufry of literary titbits presents a revealing panorama of feminine taste for over a generation. Deliberately intended by their contrivers for the centre-table (although entertaining secret hopes of the bookcase) the literary annuals were meant to be displayed. They came in all sizes and styles and ranged in price from thirty-seven and a half cents to fifteen or twenty dollars. In their more ornamental varieties they were usually bound in leather, elaborately tooled and embossed with gold traceries in intricate and lavish patterns. As the vogue increased, enterprising publishers introduced greater variety by attempting bindings of velvet and silk, or more elaborately still, of glazed *papier maché* inlaid with mother of pearl or imitation gems of various colors. Although distinctly inferior and decidedly more gaudy than their British prototypes, these books as a *genre* were quite the finest books yet made in America, a fact which for purely patriotic reasons added materially to their sales value.

The first American title was *The Atlantic Souvenir*, published by Carey and Lea of Philadelphia in the Christmas season, 1825, and continued under the same title for seven years. In spite of the spirited competition which this publication quickly induced and the deluge of British annuals which followed, Carey and Lea's sales leaped from two thousand in the first year to ten thousand several years later. Other publishers were even more successful. The longer lived of the gift-book serials were *The Pearl, or Affection's Gift*, of Philadelphia, continued for ten years; *The Hyacinth, or Affection's Gift*, also of Philadelphia, for eleven years; *The Token*, of Boston, for fifteen years, and *The Rose of Sharon* of Boston, which held the record for eighteen years of continuous appearance under the same title. The editorial fondness for changing titles with each holiday season and the publisher's habit of reissuing the same book under changed names make the record of longevity somewhat misleading, for under whatever title, the literary annual was essentially the same book.

As any array of titles chosen from the available thousand might suggest, gift-books were keepsakes to be fingered admiringly, displayed on the corner of the centre-table and always shown to callers, filled with rose petals in private moments and at the end of the year, after the successor had arrived, consigned to a special shelf in the bookcase. Titles also suggest the hodge-podge of the contents: *The Ladies' Casket of Gathered Thoughts, Flora's Interpreter: or, the American Book of Flowers and Sentiments, The Album of Love*, dedicated to "those who have already learned to love, and to those who have yet to love," *The Wreath, a Selection of elegant Poems from the best Authors*. Floral names were easy favorites, having the obvious advantage of furnishing suggestions for cover decoration: *The Rose* (usually of the moss variety), *The Lily of the Valley, The Passion Flower, a Gift of the Heart, The Iris, The May Flower, The Hyacinth, The Violet, The Mignonette, or the Graces of the Mind*. Precious stones of all varieties were a close second: *The Opal, A pure gift for the holy days, The Ruby, a Token of Friendship, The Gem*. If the title permitted, title and presentation plate were in harmony; one wrote the lady's name in a miniature wreath or garland or pictured mirror. If the title did not permit, some other device was supplied; *The Atlantic Souvenir* used a sunburst; other volumes showed lilies bending in a heart shaped formation, scrolls, books lying open at blank pages, for without the name of the giver the gift-book lost half its meaning.[3]

The elegant "embellishments" which adorned all such offerings probably had more to do with their popularity than any other of the conventional ingredients. Literature and art should go hand in hand, one editor remarked in his preface, and according to contemporary standards, they usually did. Illustrations cost the publisher considerably more than the literary matter, but he willingly paid the price, distributing his steel and copper engravings, and often hand colored plates, lavishly throughout the

[3] For bibliographies of American gift-books, see Frederick W. Faxon, *Literary Annuals and Gift-Books*, Boston 1912; Ralph Thompson, *American Literary Annuals and Gift-Books*, New York, 1936.

volume. The engraver usually did his work better than the artist whose frequent bad technique not even the alleged elegance of his concept could quite hide. One critic's remark (probably Edgar Allan Poe's) that the engraved left hand of a certain lady resembled nothing so much as a turnip, was unfortunately more true than it was unkind.[4] Examination of the embellishments in any dozen gift-books will show various turnips and other vegetables, in kind.

Subjects for illustration were determined by the literary matter of the volume, poetic effusions having first chance at engraving honors. If the subject of the piece were sad, so much the better. A soldier's or lover's or sister's farewell had power to raise lumps in the contemporary feminine throat, and in the publisher's calculation, there was no more desirable criterion of choice. He gave orders for literature and art to join hands at this point, paid the bill and threw himself on the mercy of posterity. Rural scenes, made romantic by remoteness, over picturesqueness or lonely simplicity were also great favorites, particularly under such titles as " The Morning Walk," " The Evening Walk," lovers almost invariably just coming into view or disappearing in the distance. Felicia Dorothea Hemans' contribution labelled " The Woodland Brook " in *The Rose* of 1847 is a completely typical handling of rural scenery " tinctured " with romance. The concluding stanza reads,

> Then haste three onward, gentle brook,
> And tell thy pleasant tale
> To her—the maid of sweetest look
> That dwellest in the vale.

All brooks sang such songs and told such tales in the gift-books, and rural scenery as pictured must be sentimentalized to match. So were most other subjects chosen for illustration: sleeping children, un-American looking ladies who stood pensively at case-

---

[4] *Graham's Magazine,* Nov. 1841, XIX, 250. Poe was editor of the magazine at the time. The engraving in question appeared in *The Gift,* 1842. Annuals appeared in November or December and were always dated for the following year.

ments, were crowned May Queens, or entered a room just in time to see their pet canary in the jaws of their pet cat.

Once in a while illustrations were given a timely slant. *The Boudoir Annual* for 1847 used as frontispiece an engraving by Sartain entitled " Poland," in illustration of a poetic piece " Lament for Poland " beginning,

> Alas, crushed land! what unavailing tears
> Have fallen, and still must fall from manly eyes,
> When thy sad fate, Sarmatia, wakes the song!
> When shall the sword be stayed?　How long—how long?

It is interesting to note that although Columbia, according to the poet, heaves for Poland " the stifling sigh," her sympathy is somewhat qualified by the belief that Poland's fate is just, " 'tis sternly just," since within her borders

> The trampled rights of subjugated man,·
> The peasant faint with unrewarded toil—
> The serf that mourns his violated child—

are also part of the contemporary picture.

A few annuals and many more specialized gift-books were composed entirely of poetry but usually prose pieces predominated, poetry, as one editor put it, being intoduced only " to relieve the monotony."　Until the late forties most of the more popular American poets were represented in nearly every collection: Poe, Bryant, Longfellow, Emerson, Holmes and Whittier, but as the vogue began to subside, they withdrew one by one, leaving the field to the lesser fry, chiefly Nathaniel P. Willis and Samuel Woodworth for the men, and Lydia B. Sigourney, Frances S. Osgood, Lucy Larcom and Hannah Gould for the women. Without this quartet of singers with Felicia Hemans representing the British, gift-books of all varieties would hardly have been possible.　The verses of any one of these women are almost indistinguishable from those of the other four, that " respectable mediocrity " so often announced by editors being their common denominator as well as their zenith.　But since the gift-books were intended for an audience of women, " respectable mediocrity" was considered high enough. Editorial standards must be moral before they were literary. "Not a line in this book will cause a Christian to hesitate," was the safe boast of Mrs. Sigourney in her *Religious Souvenir* for 1833, although her standing among lady moralists was such as to render all such assurances unnecessary. In the comfortable belief that "literary elegance and Christian instruction may happily coalesce" she continued to pour forth "her seraph spirit in bursts of undying song." The critics knew better, of course, even in the 1830's, but the critics were not making the gift-books.

Specimen titles chosen from any table of contents provide suggestion for what was assumed to be the elevating, purifying and softening influence of poetry, more often called "poesy." From *The Ladies Wreath* of 1837 may be culled Hannah Gould's "The Moon upon the Spire," "The Empty Bird's Nest" and "Worship by the Rose Tree"; from *The Bouquet*, 183-? "The Blind Flower Girl's Song," "The Mother's Lament Over her Sleeping Child," "The Unwilling Bride," "The Cottage Immigrant's Farewell," "The Crusader's Return," "The Dying Soldier" and "Marius Among the Ruins of Carthage"; from the *Young Lady's Offering* of 1848, "Evening Prayer at a Girl's School" and "Disenchantment," beginning,

Do not ask me why I loved him;

from *The Book of Pearls*, 1849, "The Early Dead," "Love in Sadness," "The Country Graveyard" and "The Maiden's Vow"; from *The Boston Book* of 1837, "Elijah's Interview on Mt. Horeb." Innocent poetry all of it, as the *Advice to Ladies* column decreed all verse for fair ones should be.

Moral essays were sometimes included, but usually prose tales took up by far the greater amount of space. These qualified as "romantic" by virtue of remoteness from American reality or by the unmitigated tragedy of the ending, usually both. One issue of *The Rose* (1847) takes us in Tale I to South Africa and "The Wrongs of Amakosa," an African chief who in making a last minute escape leaps aboard an overloaded pinnace which straightway upsets, engulfing him in the " raging surf." In Tale II we go to Norway to share the adventures of a strange mariner who disappears in a maelstrom. Another tale entitled " A Peep into Negro Land," chronicles the experiences of the first white woman to visit the " Gaboon " via a jungle, a " romantic creek " and other avenues of inaccessibility. Once she has reached this strangest of all strange places she is feasted elaborately, flowers are showered upon her, the hem of her garment is reverently touched by the kneeling throngs; most amazing of all, she returns unscathed, although witnessing the deaths of multitudes as she goes. Other pieces in this same volume take us to the palace of a Persian sultan, the hospice of the monks of St. Bernard, and purgatory. Anything, it would seem, which would waft the thoughts of the lady reader far from Boston found a port of entry at this editor's desk. So with other annuals likewise. Even the familiar name Philadelphia, appearing in a list of illustrations for *The Centre-Table* of 1860 cannot be trusted. We read in the opening descriptive paragraph,

Philadelphia, the city represented in our picture, was an ancient town of Turkey, in Asia, in Natolia.

According to Strabo, its history had begun in 1097. It is comforting to note that the next illustration, labelled Albany, is really Albany.

The model for all such extravagance was the English annual, almost as popular in America as the native stock. American publishers were forced to compete with tales of Austrian assassins, warriors who strode on stone ledges clad in Highland plaids, castle goblins, nocturnal separations and nights in the catacombs. The Americanized versions of these Old World marvels are the brightest gems in native caskets, although for different reasons than the jewellers supposed. The fact that some of Poe's tales appeared in these same collections is of more than passing interest in connection with his own continuing interest in the grotesque and arabesque.[5]

[5] His *The MS Found in a Bottle* appeared in *The Gift, Philadelphia*, 1836; *Eleanora* in 1842; *The Pit and the Pendulum* in 1843; *The Purloined Letter*, 1845.

It was inevitable that extravagance and over-sweetness would presently cloy the appetite. In *The Ladies Cabinet Album* of 1837, at the very heyday of the annual, comes a protest from within. The volume is bound in red morocco, cupids on the fly-leaf as usual. The tales provide the usual romantic variety: Hungarian gypsies, kelp-gatherers, Greek lovers, bereaved sisters, a deaf postillion, a maniac, a sibyl, a fugitive, a lover's leap, broken hearts and last words. Only a quilting party carries hint of the American locale. Yet in a brief piece entitled " Woman " and signed *Traveller*, are these words,

Woman has so long been called an angel, that it may be deemed profanation to intimate she is a human being; and she has so long been addressed in baby-phrase and softened tones, that to speak to her in the language of common sense, may be to forfeit her esteem, and to fall under the condemnation of those who profess to adore the sex.

Her mind, the Traveller goes on to say, has been enervated to display " ' female loveliness,' ' amiable weaknesses and lovely defects ' "; her education has been shamefully neglected; she is afraid to store her mind lest she be called " masculine."

When shall she be permitted to approach the tree of knowledge for herself?

She is not even allowed to enjoy " tolerable health."

My fair readers must pardon me [Traveller concludes] if I speak an unfashionable language—truth is often unfashionable.

This clear-cut protest, of interest chiefly because of the harbor it found, epitomizes as well as any current statement the newer notion of woman's needs and capacities as they were already being championed by the forceful pens of both men and women. The making of this view current among average women readers without robbing them of their traditional womanliness was the peculiar problem and the eventual achievement of the woman's magazines between the thirties and sixties.

Women's magazines were no novelty even in the 1820's. Since

the turn of the century there had been dozens of brief and sporadic attempts to hold a reading public composed of women; some had lasted three months, some six or even a year, but none had succeeded. Fine print, poor paper, absence of illustrations or any sign of elegance, scrappiness of content—all these may have been contributing causes to failure, but possibly no one of them was the real cause. Sarah Josepha Hale may have been eminently right when after eleven years as editor of *Godey's Lady's Book* she attributed her own large success not to an editorial policy but to a single purpose and that moral; namely, "to do good especially to and for our own sex." Other periodicals, numerous as the stars, as she said, "have come and gone; we remain." As she saw it, other editors had made the mistake of trying to amuse when mere amusement was not enough. It took moral purpose to float a woman's magazine in America. She and Louis A. Godey, owner-publisher, had made no secret of theirs from the beginning.

By the time of this confession, however, Mrs. Hale had been editor of two magazines, had nineteen years of experience behind her, and had learned many things about her public. Chiefly she had learned to throw a veil over her didacticism at times and to make compromises with middle class taste while she was trying to elevate it. In her first venture, the *Ladies' Magazine* of Boston, she had been somewhat too deeply earnest, too eager for immediate results. Month by month she had admitted to her columns lengthy and humorless arguments for the respectability of female talent and equally lengthy proofs of woman's influence on human history; she had sponsored unpopular causes such as woman's right to participate in charity fairs and to collect funds for the erection of Bunker Hill monument. In the face of spirited opposition she had printed Emma Willard's widely ridiculed program for woman's education, and had been the target of criticism, both for the views and the printing of them.

Even so early in her editorial experience, however, she had usually known when to shift her course. In the issue for August, 1830, she had printed a letter of protest purporting to come from a subscriber who signed herself Letitia. She wrote,

Why do you not make it more amusing, more spirited and fashionable—I mean have pictures and descriptions that will improve the taste in dress, and not be eternally harping on "education" and the "domestic duties" and all the rusty fusty acquirements that go to make up the most tiresome of all vulgar characters, a good wife?

Then abruptly changing her tune, Letitia, who was no doubt Mrs. Hale herself, announced that after talking with her own grandmother and learning that ladies long ago had behaved very differently (not read novels at all or trilled the piano) she had decided to keep all the numbers of *The Ladies' Magazine* in order to astonish the ladies of the 1930's by the record of how their sisters in 1830 had been so bold as to contribute to Bunker Hill monument, establish Infant Schools, hold Ladies' Fairs and give "the work of their own fair hands to the charity. (I myself made two butterflies and a nun)" Letitia announced, her protest forgotten. Having thus (as she thought, tactfully) justified her own previous policies as well as supplied motivation for a change, Mrs. Hale straightway added fashion plates and music to the monthly offerings of *The Ladies' Magazine*.

Later, as the forty year editor of *Godey's Lady's Book*, she rationalized her policies in similarly obvious ways whenever a crisis occurred. When the venture was only three years old and success not yet assured, she printed a piece from the pen of her stout ally, Harriet B. Stowe, in which Jupiter himself was called upon to boost the subscription list. Mrs. Stowe's hand was heavy, and her humor mirthless, but the ladies got the point. Unrolling the after supper scene in the great drawing-room of the gods, which shone like "a galaxy or the New York streets by gas light," she presented the Olympians in relaxed mood and posture: Apollo stretched out on a gold and purple couch in well fed comfort, Juno occupied with a new sandal pattern, Minerva reading the *North American Review*, her elbow resting appropriately on a volume of Euripides, Juno knitting in a corner, the Graces discussing with Aurora cloud designs to be displayed on the morrow, Jupiter smoking his celestial weed, one puff of which "had more wisdom in it than a whole presidential message." Discussion played about the *Godey's Lady's Book* which Mercury had brought from Philadelphia in the current number. Minerva considered it light; Juno, a waste of time, since she had no kind opinion of "lady authoresses." When criticism had gone for enough, Jupiter pontifically ended debate by decreeing, "The book is worthy the patronage of you all. It goes to all the fair ladies of the continent." The climax was hardly worthy the *mise en scène*, but such matters did not worry either Louis A. Godey or Mrs. Hale. Blunt tactics worked with the constituency of the 30's and 40's, as they well knew.[6]

In her monthly broadcasts from "The Editor's Table," quite the most interesting department of the magazine to later readers, Mrs. Hale revealed that she knew her difficult problem precisely. In a word, she was obliged to find a safe middle course between two extreme views: one a belated eighteenth century view of the elegant female who had wept, fainted and clung through lesser English fiction and its American imitations for two generations; the other, the new concept of the "new" woman who shamelessly cultivated her mind, had opinions, pronounced hard words correctly and didn't care if she did. The first kind of woman had no connection with American reality in the mid-nineteenth century or at any earlier time in American history. The weeping, fainting, clinging female could never have survived the rigorous 1770's, let alone the days of King Philip; therefore as a heroine of fiction she was altogether romantic and altogether acceptable. The intellectual woman was still something of a Gorgon. The less said about her the better. If Doctoresses and Mistresses of Instruction were to be accepted at all by the rest of their sex, it would be because when the time came for them to emerge, they would do so wearing their black silk as fastidiously as the veriest coquette. It was exactly this compromise which Mrs. Hale was able to translate into print, taking forty years in which to do it. During all this time she led her public so gently they hardly knew they were being led at all. Bristling with independence herself, capable of

---

[6] The piece is entitled "Olympiana" and occurs in the June number, 1839. Mrs. Hale had become editor in 1836.

public life, she was also a model housewife, a Sunday School teacher and a perfect lady according to the current model.

Her willingness to advance slowly was her chief distinction as the leader of a somewhat reluctant army. For every two steps she advanced she took at least one step back, and whenever the marchers were tired, she suggested that they all play a game, thereby forgetting they were not on a picnic but a crusade. Her fashion plates were triumphs of tact as well as of Parisian styles, Americanized. To the last issue belonging to her forty year editorship, along with her little sermonettes on domesticity, woman's influence and the twenty best ways to please a husband, she continued to give hospitality to verse and fiction as banal as that of the gift books at their worst. In fact, many of the pieces fall to a lower level. The publishers of annuals could solicit their material; editors of magazines must occasionally flatter their subscribers by printing so-called " original " pieces, born of nothing save the itch for imitative composition. To some extent balance was restored by the contributions of Hawthorne, Lowell, Poe, Lowell, Emerson and other popular American authors, whom Poe himself was later to excoriate in the very columns of *Godey's* as " The Literati," but mediocrity was the rule.[7]

Much of the fiction which covered the largest number of pages in each issue was addressed frankly to young women still in the romantic chapter of their lives. This period, according to a piece which Mrs. Hale printed, began at fifteen and lasted until twenty-one. During these years a young woman was privileged to drawl the " drawl pathetic," love the moon, write in a liliputian hand-writing and read " Mr. Byron," provided only that from twenty-one to twenty-nine she lapsed into common sense. (One may note in passing that not even in print did a young lady cross the line into her thirties).

A plot analysis of the hundreds of tales which filled *Godey's* pages for forty years discloses a somewhat different definition of romance from that most commonly illustrated in the annuals.

[7] These articles appeared in a series extending from May to November, 1846.

Heroines named Marietta, Kathleen and Rowena were still omnipresent; also heroes named Algernon, Clarence, Percival and Gerald, or any two of these in combination. But Effies and Emmies had also arrived. They hired out as seamstresses, governesses or housemaids until such times as their simple charms were appreciated, when with great speed and lasting happiness they married the only son of their mistress who was invariably the widow of the town millionaire. This feminine counterpart of the poor boy who climbed the easy ladder of success and landed in the White House is in almost every issue, along with the more shopworn tale of the faithless maiden who dropped dead at the altar because she removed a ring she had sworn never to remove, or of the faithful maiden who drops dead under identical circumstances, when a messenger gallops up just in time to save her from the perfidy of a worthless bridegroom. Another favorite theme of the newer romance is the beautiful sacrifice of the older sister who discovers a few days before the wedding that her younger, and always more attractive, though always far more helpless sister has stolen her bridegroom from her. The scene is usually an arbor. Invariably she accepts her hard luck, becomes a school teacher, a visitor of the sick or a distributor of tracts, and when in due time she dies, the village has never known such a funeral. Other young women give up all to go as missionaries to foreign lands or find themselves married to rakes and drunkards whom they usually reform. If not, they love them to the last, the very last, and are sometimes rewarded by the words, " If only I had lived differently," spoken as the eyes close in death.

Since to Mrs. Hale the moral was more important than the plot, such pitiful incentives to tears probably cost her fewer pangs than she deserved to suffer, yet a study of her magazine over a period of years suggests not only that she deliberately printed such twaddle when she might have had better, but also that she knew exactly what she was doing when she chose it. This was the standard Sunday School story of the hour, and a large proportion of her one hundred and fifty thousand subscribers were mentally at the Sunday School age. She was speaking to them exactly where they lived and providing a diet on which approval of the magazine would thrive. Besides, when they turned the page, there would be the Editor's Table, the seasonal homilies, the health talks, the lives of great women who had molded history, the recipes, and in gradually increasing proportion, the tales of the American Revolution, of log cabins on the border of the prairie, of fresh air and green fields. In printing the Sunday School stories she was throwing a sop to the frailty of the frailest, just as she had done to other groups when she introduced the fashion plates and the pages of popular music.

When she spoke in her own person or through the articles she printed from Mrs. Sigourney, Mrs. Stowe and her other co-editors, she rang the changes on her dearest themes until no one could have missed them. You have a mind; cultivate it. Home is woman's proper sphere; stay in it. Woman's influence is profound; exercise it. Health is attractive in a woman; therefore, watch your diet, get plenty of fresh air and exercise, and above all things, wear your India rubbers when it rains. In her continual emphasis on domesticity she was not trying to belittle what Elizabeth Blackwell, Lucy Stone and other strong-minded women had done, nor was she trying to make all women into mere housewives. She was trying to define the place of the intelligent woman who belonged to the majority, not the place of the one woman in a thousand who would step out of the pattern because she must. Always conscious that she was speaking to the multitudes, not to the gifted few, she was more concerned to raise the level than to deal with the exceptions. In fact, she had little to say to the exceptions. For the thousands her common sense advice had a salutary effect in an uneasy time. The majority did not wish to be Elizabeth Blackwells; they wished to marry, stay at home and train their children. She assured them that was the best thing a woman could do, only she would do it far better if she grew up mentally and learned to use the mind she had. Her flat-footed strictures against the artificiality of the fashionable education were also comforting. The majority wanted their daughters to be ladies, of course, but when they stopped to think about it, the ability to play the harp, trill in seven languages and perform all the curtsies from " the slight bend to the low obeisance" did not help much with the housework. Mrs. Hale pricked the bubble and they were secretly glad of it.

But by no means did she leave her adoring public where she had found them. By her patient counsels, her ability to speak the language of the average woman without condescension, her unfailing politeness to her public, Sarah Josepha Hale and a few other intelligent woman editors and writers, notably Catherine M. Sedgwick, novelist, had done something that the militant women who were marching under banners far ahead of the procession had not been able to do. They had also done something that Emerson and Walt Whitman could not possibly have done for the same audience. They had stripped off layer after layer of romance and moonlight from the literature of the average woman reader, helped her to plant her feet solidly on the American earth, and to like what she found when she opened her eyes and looked around her. The most intelligent step in this long process was the decision to go slowly, substituting sensible details one by one for previous romantic absurdities. The combinations were often ludicrous, but the very young and very fragile heroines who continued to die beautiful deaths in the fiction pages no doubt cut the mortality tolls somewhat. By such steps fiction came gradually closer to reality.

Presently came the covered wagon era and the case was won. Instead of mooning over tragic wedding journeys, lover's leaps, heiresses who married dragoons or seamstresses who caught the millionaire, a whole generation of brides mounted not a charger or a steed but an Indian pony and rode away beside caravans of prairie schooners to lands more new and strange than the pictured orient or the gypsy's retreat. What the fashionable school and the *Ladies' Manual* had taught them about the art of being an " equestrienne" or stepping into a carriage with " measured action and premeditated grace " did not help much when it came to fording a river. Truth had at last become stranger than fiction, even in America, and far more interesting.

Books for the lady reader had taught her some things she would need to unlearn: namely, that books spell elegance and are an ornament to taste and beauty, whether they adorn the centre-table or lie open in the snowy hand of the great lady who acts the frontispiece; also that books are for a lady's "vacant" hours (a strangely persistent notion); most of all, that a lady requires special books at all. Presently she would learn to take her culture straight, or at least straighter, but this Bowdlerized elegance had put her on the path. In quite different ways the leather and gold keepsakes and the everyday wisdom of the women's magazines had helped to make a new woman of her. A century later these sentimental confections and pious preachments invite an easy mirth they do not quite deserve, but at least one may say they had met a need of their time and met it constructively. Perhaps that is more than will some day be said concerning certain of their successors whose alleged "glamour" begins with the cover design.

THE ROMANTIC INTERIOR

by

Roger Gilman

IF we wish to know the Romantic house in its truest and most appealing expression we must look for it in the Gothic cottages and villas that were built from the early thirties to the late fifties. A few of them linger on, picturesque reminders of a bygone fancy, half-hidden among the subdivisions on Staten Island and up the Hudson Valley; in Brookline, New Bedford and Newport; around Philadelphia and Baltimore. They were never really numerous and they now are rare. Their parlors and libraries hardly exist. But they can be reconstructed from the text and the engravings in old books of design; occasionally from later photographs. Yet scarce as they were, they represented in visible wood and stone the poems and tales and all the aspirations of the Romantic Era; they were the pioneers of that Gothic tendency which has continued in church and college architecture to the present day.

The earliest interiors of importance are to be found in the houses designed by the architect, Alexander J. Davis. They are also the most successfully Gothic, the most intensely Romantic. Davis was by nature an artist. He began his architectural career by making lithographs of buildings, such as the Boston State House. While still in his twenties he made such a beautiful drawing of a project for the Connecticut Capitol that it earned him a partnership with its architect, the successful Ithiel Town. Within three or four years he was designing such important commissions as Glen Ellen near Baltimore (1834) and the old New York University.

Although at one time he was a sort of silent partner of the famous Andrew Jackson Downing, assisting him in making the designs for some of his cottages and villas—and correcting where necessary their author's mistakes—he was an architect in his own right, with one of the largest practices of his day.

Glen Ellen was Davis's most striking design, although it was the first great house of the Gothic Revival. In Davis's masterly sketch of the plan (*see* Pl. IX), showing by convention the design of the ceiling decorations, we can still visualize its grandeur—the vestibule with coffered ceiling, the central dome, the vast drawing room with two fireplaces, the intricate Gothic vaulting of the great alcove. How far removed was the dissymmetry of these great apartments from the customary central hall and four main rooms of all Georgian houses. How strange for the visitor to find the staircase off at one end, no longer the principal feature. And how exciting to pass from an ample vestibule into a lofty rotunda, and then into a six-sided bay, two stories high and lighted by tall traceried windows. Here was indeed a break with all former tradition, a flight into romance.

In the Herrick house on the Hudson, a truly "castellated mansion" in the glowing phrase of the day, we can sense from the plan itself that shadowy dimness that was so much craved by Romantic writers. Here we should find ourselves in a hall shadowed first by a porte-cochère, then by a porch, and lighted only by narrow turret windows at the head of the staircase. Or we should grope through the dusk of a huge circular parlor, thirty feet in diameter, whose only windows give on a twelve foot verandah. No wonder that Davis labels this the "umbrage."

In the house built for William J. Rotch of New Bedford in 1845, and now restored, we gain an excellent insight into a villa of quality. The plan centres about an entrance hall with four Gothic arches. Opening off this hall are the drawing room and sitting room, each enlivened by a Gothic bay with mullioned windows. (*See* Pl. Xa.) Behind it are the library and dining room, each with an alcove. It is an interior very different in feeling from any colonial house; its Gothic arches and door mouldings, its lancet windows and latticed panes, create an old-world illusion that must once have seemed the height of romance.

As to the furnishings of such a house, we must reconcile ourselves to the fact that they were not Gothic. In part they were inherited pieces, American variations on Sheraton or on French Empire; in part they were contemporary, with the exaggerated outlines that we loosely call Victorian. There were, it is true, some chairs made with pointed arches in the back, and occasional beds and bureaus with tracery panels outlined in black walnut. But the carefully restored interiors of Irving's "Sunnyside" are almost pure Georgian; the completely preserved drawing-rooms of the Harrall mansion at Bridgeport are pure Louis-Philippe. The accompanying marbles, porcelains, bronzes and glass ranged from the school of Canova to Early Tiffany.

Yet the Romantic householders were by no means disturbed by these inconsistencies. In fact, anyone who cares to glance at Silliman's "World of Science, Industry and Art at the New York Exposition of 1853" will readily concede that consistency at that time had no value whatever.

Among all the influences that produced the Romantic villa, none was so potent as the writing of Andrew Jackson Downing. By his persuasive style, his blend of romance and democracy, and his numerous designs he crystallized the Romantic ideal of the house in the country. That ideal is firmly lodged in the thinking of the average home-builder today. Downing describes it for us at length, and although his phrases are somewhat sentimental and quite out of date, his picture has enchantment still. "In this house there should be something to love. It must not look all new and sunny, but show secluded shadowy corners. There must be nooks about it, where one would love to linger; windows, where one can enjoy the quiet landscape at his leisure; cosy rooms, where all fireside joys are invited to dwell." And his romantic soul has always in view the English cottage type: "its beautiful home expression, its thorough comfort and utility, and its varied form to accommodate modern habits."

Fortunately for us, he is quite specific in his directions for such a cottage. (See Pl. Xb.) Its size he defines as such that it can be cared for by the family. For the woodwork he prefers painted graining; "it is cheaper than natural finish, easier to clean, and it makes the house look furnished." (Now at last we have the reason for its popularity!) For the walls he recommends a tinted whitewash, or papers in new patterns, " Gothic, Italian, or Grecian "! Some of these have only panels and cornices printed on them; others present the appearance of oak wainscot. The floors he would prefer stained, but he admits that carpets are universal. For pictures he urges us to avoid all colored prints of the ordinary type—can he refer to Currier and Ives?—but to have only engravings after ancient or modern masters, " such as may be found at Goupil's in New York." (No modern sneers on that score, at least). For curtains: chintz, or printed cotton, or moreen; but they are to be hung from a moulded cornice with a lambrequin. Evidently a cottage was a pretty formal affair.

The villa, according to Downing's second section, was the home of the most leisurely and educated class of citizens. It was fairly large, requiring the care of at least three servants. It was Romantic in character: " Nature and art both lend it their happiest influence, amid the serenity and peace of sylvan scenes; . . . enriched without and within by objects that touch the heart and awaken the understanding." It was truly Victorian: " a house where beauty, taste, and moral culture are at home."

The Gothic style of the villa consisted in a prevalence of vertical lines, ornamented with bold and deep mouldings, and a use of pointed arches for all important openings. (*See* Pl. XIa.) But Downing really had much sense. He warned that the commonest error of decorators was to render their apartments " too elaborately Gothic, everything tending to the high pointed arch, only fit for cathedrals, and bristling with crockets."

The ceilings he says must be from 12 to 14 feet high: " Height always gives an expression of dignity, so the Gothic styles should have the highest ceilings." In the choice of paper-hangings he felt it necessary to warn even the most leisurely and educated class that a good deal of taste was requisite. They were to avoid " all flashy and gaudy patterns, such as imitations of church windows, magnificent carved work, pinnacles, etc." But in the best taste were flock papers, made to imitate woven stuffs, such as silk or worsted; or fresco-papers, with suitable cornices and moldings.

And what color schemes complete his interior? The hall and staircase should be of a cool and sober tone, grey, stone-color or drab. For the floors, there should be marble or ceramic tiles, such as browns enriched with patterns of blue. The drawing-room walls should be light. "Gilding," he says, "should be sparingly used; very delicate tints, such as ashes of roses, pale apple-green, have a more chaste and satisfactory effect." We will pass by the dining-room, "rich and warm," and the library, "comparatively grave," to have a look at the boudoir. But here Downing, for once, weakens: "It is essentially the ladies' apartment, which may be colored and fitted up with any variation of coloring that their fancies may dictate."

His summary of the human qualities in his Gothic villa is worth considering more carefully. It will reveal to us how much our present conception of a home belongs to the Romantic Era. Downing wrote, ninety years ago: "The great beauty of this style, when properly treated, is the home-like expression which it is capable of. This arises mainly from the chaste and quiet colors of the dark wood-work, the grave though rich hue of the carpets and walls . . . and the quiet, domestic feeling of the library and the family circle. Those who love shadow, and the sentiment of antiquity and repose, will find in it the most pleasure."

Our older generation may see here little that they would be willing to give up, but the younger set are already objecting to the quiet domestic feeling of the family circle and the sentiment of antiquity. And those who are turning modern want to demolish the shadows, the dark woodwork, and the rich hues; they would leave nothing but repose.

It was a strange thing that American architecture, after nearly two hundred years of continuity, should turn thus sharply aside. We may well ask ourselves what causes there were within the art itself for such a change of taste. And what influences played upon the architects' minds that conceived these exotic plans? What above all induced the owners to propose them—or to consent?

The Gothic style came to us from England, as our traditional styles had come in the days of the colonies. To understand its character and its vigor, its beginnings in England should be briefly reviewed. Before 1820, the Romantic spirit, lingering on from the previous century, had been renewed in a cult of the picturesque and the middle ages. Publishers, like Britton who brought out some seventy works, and artists, like Turner, had created a sort of nostalgia for castles and ancient manor-houses. Sir Walter Scott had made the people of the Middle Ages seem human, their castles seem livable. His own mansion " Abbotsford " seemed the authentic proof.

After 1820, this interest turned from the sentimental to the historical. Almost every year some book appeared, classifying the buildings, reproducing their plans and their traceries for architects' use, or supplying designs for " rural cottages and villas " of old English types. Gothic churches and country houses began to be built; a religious awakening added to the enthusiasm. By 1830 the Romantic spirit was finding expression in architectural literature, in antiquarian societies, and in numerous buildings.

In America, these activities had been reflected at first only in a few churches with Gothic windows. But they had prepared the American mind for its own essay in Gothic that was soon to follow.

The date of 1830 may be taken as our starting point. In that year two young men began their architectural practice, and each was to be a leader in the Gothic movement.

Richard Upjohn arrived from England, bringing a sound training in the style, several books—on which he had lavished almost his last shilling,—and a zeal fired by religion. Five years later he was building " Oaklands," a Tudor mansion in Bangor, Maine, and several houses around Boston. Nine years later he received the commission for Trinity Church, New York, a landmark in American Gothic. Through him the English influence entered directly.

Davis, by contrast, was a young New York draftsman who had attained an early success with his lithographs of buildings, and had then spent two years working in the Greek Revival. Why did he turn to Gothic, and how could he produce, in 1837, such a design as the vaulted Dining Room for the Paulding villa? (*See* Pl. XIb.) Was his medievalism an inheritance from his father, the editor of "The Theological Review," who must have been in touch with the religious leaders in England? Or was it a home where the romances of Scott were ready at hand? Or shall we be more factual and lay it to his own artistic temperament, his habit of drawing buildings picturesquely, and working in lithograph, that most picturesque medium? At least we know that in his working sketches the picturesque was always present, in trees, clouds, bright lights, dark shadows.

Downing, the third leader, came somewhat later. He passed his young years under the influence of Nature, as a horticulturalist and a naturalist who roamed the Hudson hills. In the houses of wealthy friends he met English travelers from whom he absorbed the cult of the picturesque and the rustic cottage. By his writings, first on gardens, later on cottages and villas, he captured the American imagination. Thus again the English revival was introduced by personal contacts.

A powerful influence was that of the English architectural books, which were of course current here. There were also the English "Gentleman's Magazine," which gave much space to Gothic subjects, and the "Architectural Magazine," with its illustrations. The well-stocked architectural library of Ithiel Town in New York was another source of inspiration and a centre of culture.

But the clients? How did they come to risk their money and their social standing on such adventures as Glen Ellen, or even the modest Rotch house?

Some of them no doubt read these same books, for architecture was still a current interest among those " leisurely and educated classes." All read the Romantic American authors. Irving, for example, who charmed them—as he charms us still—with his sketch of an old English manor-house in " Bracebridge Hall." Or

Poe, who loved to create vivid word pictures of splendid apartments, vastly romantic in effect despite their French upholstery.

Once upon a midnight dreary, while I pondered, weak and weary,
Over many a quaint and curious volume of forgotten lore—

    *   *   *   *   *   *   *

This and more I sat divining, with my head at ease reclining
On the cushion's velvet lining that the lamp-light gloated o'er,
But whose velvet violet lining with the lamp-light gloating o'er
               She shall press, ah, nevermore!
                        —*The Raven*

Some of the clients, as Mr. Lewis Mumford affirms, may well have found their newly mechanized cities so unendurable that Romanticism became a necessary refuge. Again, they may have been bored with the austerity of their former residences, in the mode of the Early Republic or of the Greek temple. But to create a villa in the Gothic style—and perhaps by such independence to figure as men of taste! And to live in a romantic scene! Like Mr. N. P. Willis, for instance, at " Idlewild " on the Hudson, whose architect could envision it thus: " The position is exactly such a one as a medieval knight would have selected for his strong-hold, and a little imagination may easily transmute the simple domestic cottage into the turreted and battlemented castle."

But there existed another cause, more fundamental, although unconscious. Underlying all tendencies, receptive to all influences, pulsed the romantic American soul. Some of its dearest desires were fulfilled by the subjective qualities of the Gothic style. We recognize them still: the love of variety, the impatience of restraint, the individuality, the sentiment. Even the idea of liberty was born of romantic political thinking. And as we realize more clearly this temperament of ours, we perceive that the Romantic spirit did not depart from the American house with the passing of Gothic windows and arches. It persisted in the pseudo-medieval manner of Eastlake, in the wayward variety of the Queen Anne, in the individual preferences for Italian or French at the end of the century; it lingers still in the sentiment of our Early American revival.

EARLY AMERICAN GOTHIC

by

Agnes Addison

A HUNDRED years ago in the annual exhibition of the National Academy of Design, Thomas Cole exhibited a painting entitled The Architect's Dream, which William Cullen Bryant described as " an assemblage of structures, Egyptian, Grecian, Gothic, Moorish, such as might present itself to the imagination of one who had fallen asleep after reading a work on the different styles of architecture." [1] Such structures were to be seen in this country not only in the painting of a romantic artist or in an Architect's Dream. Before 1840, in Philadelphia, one might see an Egyptian jail designed by Thomas Walter, a Grecian bank inspired by Nicholas Biddle, a Gothic country house designed by Latrobe and the Moorish Academy of Natural Sciences which Strickland originally built as a Swedenborgian Church.

The period of American architecture which parallels the Romantic Movement in literature is that of the Classic Revivals, especially of the Greek Revival from 1820 to 1860. While the majority of the most admired buildings of that period were Greek revival, the classic models were not the only ones to be copied. The catholicity of taste which became so evident later in the century was already beginning to show itself. Eclecticism was to be found in some buildings of the first half of the nineteenth century, also, even though it was decried by men of pure and chaste taste. Mrs. Trollope's Bazaar in Cincinnati combined Gothic windows with Ionic volutes [2] and a Synagogue in New York [3] had a Tuscan portico with four fluted columns and a neat Gothic tower without a spire.

[1] LOUIS L. NOBLE, *The Life and Works of Thomas Cole, N. A.*, 1856, p. 286.
[2] CHARLES A. MURRAY, *Travels in North America*, 1839, I, 204.
[3] *New-York Mirror*, vol. VII, no. 12, 1829.

A story which appeared in the *New-York Mirror* of September 15, 1838 confirms both the catholicity and the eclecticism of the period. It is a humorous tale which pokes fun at these propensities. The hero, Thomas Jefferson Montagu " was really a very accomplished man " and " had always felt an innate desire for a country life smouldering within him, like spontaneous combustion in the heart of a haycock." So he goes to the country and chooses a bare, bleak hillock for his cottage site and tells the innkeeper of his choice, who says " that darned ugly hill " is called Cat's Back. T. J. Montagu responds " Ugly hill! Why you have no idea of the sublime and beautiful. It is the most delightful location I have ever seen in New England." " A very few days brought an architect from the city, and the best parlour of the inn was filled with drawings of Spanish cottages, French hotels, Italian palaces, Grecian temples, Egyptian pyramids, Swiss shantees and Highland shealings." After forty ground plans had been made, " With the purest and most classick taste, the artists and their employer selected for their model a temple. . . . The Model was Egyptian with the addition of green blinds, Chinese gates, Indian verandahs, Gothick windows, Corinthian columns and a purely American roof, which formed altogether a beautiful specimen of the composite order of architecture."

The bulk of building both urban and rural, however, was of that type now called rational and which contemporary critics considered to be of no architectural style. The majority of buildings were purely utilitarian as befitted a young and not too wealthy country. Only the civic and ecclesiastical buildings received unnecessary architectural adornment and private dwellings of men of wealth who considered themselves, also, men of taste.

The Classic revival buildings were as much specimens as the Egyptian or Gothic buildings of the same period. That is what they were called—specimens—in the books and journals of the period, and the very word suggests their uniqueness. That the cult of the classic was stronger in these decades than that of the Gothic is well known, but the latter is not to be ignored completely. The vogue for the Mediaeval which became so widespread in the middle of the century had its beginnings in the previous decades.

Since the Romantic Movement is the topic for discussion, the Gothic Revival is the aspect of early nineteenth-century architecture which shall be considered, even though other styles were being employed and the period is generally called that of the Greek Revival. The reason for our interest in the Gothic is that one of the major characteristics of 19th-century romanticism was an enthusiasm for the Middle Ages. The Age of Enlightenment on the whole had considered the Middle Ages as barbarous times, full of superstition and bigotry, with a crude literature and an old-fashioned architecture, from which the men of taste averted their eyes, even though a certain number of them continued to live in late Gothic chateaux or Manor houses and worshipped in a mediaeval parish church. The eighteenth-century dilettante with his love of variety and febrile curiosity looked with affectionate amusement at the quaint, untutored efforts of his mediaeval ancestors and played with sham-ruins with the same delight as with a Chinese pagoda or a Roman Tempietto. The rococo interest in the Gothic was fostered by writers on taste who advocated the sublime and the picturesque as aspects of the beautiful (Burke, Kames, Uvedale Price, Knight, Allison) and by a widespread enthusiasm for Shakespeare and Spenser and early ballads. Then the Middle Ages became the age of chivalry and romance, largely owing to the writings of Sir Walter Scott, an era of true Christian faith and even of political freedom as exemplified by the Magna Charta, the mediaeval Bill of Rights. The Middle ages could be even cited by the growing Feminist Movement as the period when women had property rights. A great deal of the passion for the past in the romantic period centered itself about the Middle Ages and in those distant centuries. The Romanticists found precedent for many of the innovations which they wished to have in the present. As the mediaeval cult was so important an aspect of Romantic period, it is naturally the Gothic aspects of architecture which are most closely linked with romanticism.

That Gothic continued to be built and the old structures repaired in Europe is, of course, well known, and it is for that reason that Goodhart-Rendell prefers to call the nineteenth-century Gothic, the Gothic Survival. That mediaeval features in Colonial architecture are to be found, as in Parson Capen's House in Topsfield and St. Luke's Church in Smithfield, Virginia, has often been noted. The seventeenth-century colonial building continued the mediaeval tradition. In the eighteenth-century Colonial architecture which was largely influenced by Wren, Gothic forms became almost negligible, but Wren, himself, and his followers in this country, managed often to retain the mediaeval silhouette in parish churches with the towers and spires.[4] In decoration mediaeval forms were still sometimes employed; repercussions of Chippendale Gothic or Batty Langley orders. Fiske Kimball cites the Miles Brewerton house in Charlestown, South Carolina as a house of 1769 which is finished with Gothic and Chinese detail.[5] An ogee arch appears in the mantlepiece of Grayhaven Manor in Maryland. An advertisement in the *Maryland Gazetteer,* March 5, 1761, offers " stained paper for rooms in the Gothic and Chinese Taste." In the South Carolina and American General Gazette for October 25, 1774 " Plaistering and Carving in Stucco in all its Branches, either in the Modern or Gothic Taste " is advertised.[6] And the great patron of architecture, Thomas Jefferson, went so far in 1771 as to write among his Notes for a " Burying Place " at Monticello, " In the center of it erect a small Gothic temple of antique appearance." [7] So even in the eighteenth-century colonies, the Gothic was not completely ignored.

The history of Gothic forms in American architecture becomes more important from the Federal period until the present. The first period may be called that of the Early American Gothic,[8] from

[4] See essay on " Christ Church " in C. G. CHILDS, *Views in Philadelphia,* 1827-30.
[5] *Domestic Architecture of the Colonial Period,* 1922, p. 138.
[6] PRIME, *Arts and Crafts in Philadelphia, Maryland and South Carolina,* pp. 274, 290.
[7] RANDALL, *Life of Jefferson,* I, 60.
[8] This phrase is used in an article on " American Architecture," *North American Review,* XLIII, p. 369. The reference to this article was found in *Domestic Architecture of the Colonial Period* by Fiske Kimball, who cites the author as H. W. S. Cleveland, p. xvii.

1788 to about 1840, which parallels the beginnings of the Romantic Movement. The second period, from 1840 to the Civil War, is the period which Mr. E. M. Upjohn calls the Mature Gothic Revival. Five influences developed it and differentiate it from the earlier phase of the Gothic Revival. These are a more archaeological approach, more knowledge of mediaeval construction, the Ecclesiological Society, Ruskinian aesthetics and the use of continental styles. This, in turn, was followed by three decades of Victorian Gothic, in which Eastlake played an important role. The fourth period is that which Rexford Newcomb calls Neo-Gothic, from 1892 to the present, and which is an important style today as a visit to suburbs, schools, colleges and new churches testify.

The first period of the Early American Gothic has been condemned since its very beginning. The contemporary advocates of the Classic Revival scorned it as departing from the canons of pure and chaste taste. The latter builders in Gothic styles condemned these early buildings as being gimcrack and not showing a true understanding of Gothic construction and design. But also there were advocates of the style and buildings, especially ecclesiastical, which appeared despite the comparative dearth of information about the architecture of the Middle Ages.

The Gothic forms which were employed in this period were inspired by English mediaeval architecture and were used either by Americans who had travelled in Europe like Dr. Bard or by Englishmen and Frenchmen who had migrated to this country, as Latrobe and Godefroy. For the first buildings and designs in the Gothic, the source was personal, either direct or under the influence of an Englishman as in the case of Mills and Strickland who worked under Latrobe. The War of 1812 seemed to cause a slight lull in the use of mediaeval forms, but in the twenties with the importation of Britton's " Architectural Antiquities " and a little later of Pugin's " Specimens of Architecture," Gothic seemed to take on a new lease of life.

One of the first accounts of Gothic architecture to be written by an American was directly derived from Britton and Pugin. This account is to be found in " Elements of Technology, taken chiefly from a Course of Lectures delivered at Cambridge, on the Application of the Sciences to the Useful Arts," Boston, 1828, by Jacob Bigelow, M. D., Professor of Materia Medica, and late Rumford Professor in Harvard University. Jacob Bigelow (1786-1879) was born in Boston, went to Harvard, received his M. D. from the University of Pennsylvania in 1810, returned to Boston in the next year, began to practice, and became a professor in Harvard Medical School. He was a great botanist and wrote the " American Medical Botany " in three volumes, " Nature in Disease," and a history of the plants of the vicinity of Boston. He was a leading member of the Horticultural Society and started Mount Auburn first as an arboretum and then as a cemetery. Combined with his medical and botanical knowledge was a great enthusiasm for all the arts and especially architecture. Dunlap in his account of A. J. Davis writes that when in 1827, Davis went to Boston to make architectural drawings, he met Dr. Bigelow whose " beautiful models of architecture and private collection were opened to him " and through whom he was able to read at the Athenaeum which at that time had the " only respectable library on the Fine Arts." [9]

So Dr. Bigelow had several connections with the Gothic Revival in the late 1820's. His book " Elements of Technology " was reviewed in the April 1830 number of the " North American Review," the foremost quarterly in the country, the American equivalent of the " Edinburgh Review." The reviewer justly begins by saying, " The word Technology gives but an imperfect idea of the contents of this volume," which is really a compendium of the history and techniques of the arts, both practical and fine. The portion of the review which is of special interest is that which deals with Mr. Bigelow's short account of the Gothic which the reviewer calls " the poetry of architecture, the most curious and the most imposing of all the styles—the Gothic architecture, which, notwithstanding the fastidiousness of the southern taste, will long continue to command the admiration of the northern nations, with the wild songs and irregular dramas of the romantic school of

[9] WILLIAM DUNLAP, *History of the Rise and Progress of the Arts of Design in the United States*, 1834, vol. II, p. 409.

poetry." After this burst of enthusiasm for the architecture and literature of the Middle Ages, the reviewer continues, "On this part of the subject, it would have been well if Dr. Bigelow had been more full. There is no part of the history of the art, so little known in this country, indeed there is hardly a branch of any art so little known, as different modes, the different eras, and the best examples of Gothic architecture; and there is certainly none more fully deserving and more sure to reward inquiry." It would seem that the reviewer is not adverse to the introduction of Gothic.

Dr. Bigelow himself writes, " In edifices erected at the present day, the Grecian and Gothic outlines, are commonly employed to the exclusion of the rest." Which is an interesting comment to be written in the late 1820's in this country. He continues, "In choosing between them, the fancy of the builder, more than any positive rule of fitness, must direct the decision. . . . In general, the Grecian style, from its right angles and straight entablatures, is more convenient and fits better with the distribution of our common edifices, than the pointed and irregular Gothic. The expense, also, is generally less, especially if anything like thorough and genuine Gothic is attempted; a thing, however, rarely undertaken as yet, in this country. But the occasional introduction of the Gothic outline, and the partial employment of its ornaments, have undoubtedly an agreeable effect, both in public and private edifices."

Dr. Bigelow devoted in all four pages to mediaeval Gothic and illustrated the style by an engraving of the exterior and the interior of York Cathedral and a side view of Westminster Abbey to illustrate buttressing, and on another plate gives details of mediaeval piers. Of the style in general he writes that it " is peculiar and strongly marked. Its principle seems to have originated in the imitation of groves and bowers under which the Druids performed their rites. Its characteristics, at sight, are, its pointed arches, its pinnacles and spires, its large buttresses, clustered pillars, vaulted roofs, profusion of ornaments, and the general predominance of the vertical over the horizontal." Since his information as he indicates in his bibliography is derived from Britton and from Pugin, it is more advanced than that of most of the contemporary builders in the Gothic style.

In the thirties, the English books on architecture were still eagerly imported. In Richard Upjohn's account books there is the entry for " Jan. 6, 1836. To Monroe and Francis for a Britton's Christian Architecture $15." [10]

That Pugin and Britton were studied carefully can be observed in the " Essay on Gothic Architecture " by John Henry Hopkins, Bishop of Vermont. This small book illustrated with XIII Plates and a frontispiece was published at Burlington, Vermont in 1836 and is considered to be the first American work to be wholly devoted to Gothic architecture. Hopkins made some of the illustrations himself from the plates of Britton and Pugin. Sometimes Hopkins's lithographs give more of the Gothic feeling than the engravings in Britton, as for example the frontispiece of Blackfriars cross at Hereford. He evidently drew free-hand and adapted and modified to suit his artistic spirit; he put another figure in the cross at Winchester and a head on the second figure on the cross at Leighton Buzzard. Hopkins Plate I is Pugin's Plate II, the South doorway of Tattershall Church, and he introduces a cusping into the corner ornament, while the cusped center of a quatrefoil becomes a square. The moulding also is simplified. A study of the Hopkins illustrations makes one realize how far removed from the originals the Gothic adaptations in America were and makes one marvel that so many pleasing Gothic designs were executed, despite the lack of first hand knowledge or photographs of the models. That early American Gothic was so linear and detailed seems in large measure due to the engravings with which the architects and builders were working.

Not only in the illustrations was Hopkins indebted to Britton and Pugin but the glossary is directly taken (save for one emendation) from Willson's glossary in the " Specimens of Gothic Architecture." His idea of the origin of Gothic, that it was to be found in Solomon's Temple is, however, his own. But his history of Gothic is otherwise taken from Willson's essay. Hopkins, also, even as A. J. Davis, went to the library of the Athenaeum in Boston to gain material for his book, which, however, is not all library

[10] E. M. UPJOHN, *Richard Upjohn*, 1939.

learning. Hopkins had, himself, designed Trinity Church in Pittsburgh in the winter of 1823-24 with the aid of Britton and an English architect of the name of John Behan who was in Pittsburgh at that time. Therefore most of his chapters are very practical, for as he says, " Utility, not fame, is my object." How helpful and practical he is can be seen from his remarks on pinnacles. " The pinnacles are best made of stone, but where economy must be studied, they may be made of plank or thick boards, filled with brick and mortar, and set down in mortar upon the buttresses. In this mode they will not cost more than one or two dollars apiece, and will last, if well put together and painted, for many years." It is only when he comes to the Concluding Observations, in which heating is considered that he loses patience with " the effeminancy of our day " which could not revert " to the practice of our ancestors, who used no artificial heat whatever in the house of God."

Several of the illustations are original also; Pl. III shows the Chancel for St. Paul's Church, Burlington, Vermont. Pl. IV and VII are original designs for a plain village church. Pl. V and VI are of Trinity, Pittsburgh. Pl. IX is for a small cathedral—with the body of the church taken from King's Chapel and the tower from Fonthill. Pl. XI and XII give elevations and working drawings of a simple church. It is extremely interesting work and repays perusal.

Bishop Hopkins was very proud of Trinity and it still stands a very pleasing monument to his zeal. Hopkins in 1866 on the occasion of his Golden Wedding Anniversary wrote an " Autobiography in Verse " in which, his memory mellowed by age, he wrote:

A bright and prosperous course
Began forthwith, and in the month of May [1824]
My kind Masonic brethren came to lay
The corner-stone of our new buildings, planned,
In Gothic beauty, by the rector's hand,—
The first attempt throughout our country known,
Which had that style of architecture shown.

While undoubtedly Hopkins' Trinity Church was the first example of Gothic in Pittsburgh, that style had already been used in New York, Baltimore, Boston and Philadelphia for churches and also for domestic and civil architecture.

The church in New York which first showed the influence of eighteenth-century English-Gothicisms, especially those of Batty Langley, was Trinity Church on Broadway. The first church had been burned in the great fire of September 21, 1776 which destroyed about a thousand houses or a fourth of the city. It was not until 1787 that the Corporation could plan to rebuild the church. In the following year a committee reported " that a sufficient sum of money could be borrowed by the corporation upon interest, for the purpose of rebuilding Trinity Church. The plan adopted by the Vestry was one which had been proposed by Dr. Bard, and drawn by Mr. Robinson." [11] The corner-stone was laid in 1788 and the church completed in 1789. (*See* Pl. XII.)

Dr. Samuel Bard was a vestryman of Trinity Church in 1788 and so it is natural he was interested in the rebuilding of the edifice. Despite the fact that he was a medical man, and now known as the first president of the College of Physicians and Surgeons of New York, and for his book on obstetrics, his heredity and natural tastes made him a fit person to propose plans for the church. His maternal great-uncle was Dr. John Kearsley, the physician of Philadelphia who is known for his architectural interest and his plans for Independence Hall and Christ Church. Dr. Bard himself was an ardent botanist and encouraged horticulture and agriculture, especially after he retired to his country estate of Hyde Park in Dutchess County, New York, and one of his great pleasures from early youth until his death in 1821 was to draw botanical specimens, so it is known that he was skillful with the pencil and brush. He also studied in London and Edinburgh (1761-66) and made a tour of Europe, beside being a prisoner of war for a year in Bayonne Castle. He had had opportunities to study Mediaeval architecture and that he was interested in the current English vogue for the picturesque can be seen in a letter which he sent his father

---

[11] WILLIAM BERRIAN, *An Historical Sketch of Trinity Church, New York*, 1847.

April 1, 1764. " I heartily wish I could be with you at laying out your grounds, as I imagine I could be of some assistance. . . . From what I have as yet seen, I find those the most beautiful where Nature is suffered to be our guide." Later the same year he writes that he has been reading " Lord Kames's late work and recommended it to your perusal, especially that part of it relating to gardening and architecture, before you go on in improving your place on the North river." The next year when he learned that his father was putting up a paper-mill, he visited those in the neighborhood of Edinburgh and sent his father " a draught . . . of the mash-tub, etc." [12]

The church which Dr. Bard proposed may be seen in the drawings of J. Evers and A. J. Davis and exact information may be learned of it from the *New-York Mirror* of July 14, 1827. The article in the *Mirror* says " The style of the building is plain Gothic." The interior had a " gallery supported by square panelled columns directly over each of which rises a clustered Gothic column to the roof." The windows were pointed and that at the west end was one of the largest in the United States. " It is Gothic, with three compartments and contains 1039 panes of glass." In general plan it was a rectangular meeting-house type, 104 x 72 feet, with a steeple at the east end 180 feet high. The entrance was at the east end and protected by a circular porch of true Batty Langley style supported by paired quatrefoil columns banded at the third points and surmounted with a low dome surrounded by a parapet ornamented by quatrefoil openings and pinnacles. Similar forms crown the square tower from which rises a plain spire. The doorway itself seems to be pointed and surmounted by a cavetto moulding. A word should be said about the pinnacles of which there were sixteen in all for they show a characteristic of early American Gothic, which is to have plain pyramidal pinnacles sans crockets and finial. The Mature Gothic Revival as shown in Upjohn's Trinity Church (1839-1846) is complete with crockets and finials.

Benjamin Henry Latrobe was responsible for much of the Gothic

[12] JOHN MCVICKAR, *A Domestic Narrative of the Life of Samuel Bard*, 1822.

of the first decade of the nineteenth century. In 1805 he made two sets of designs for Bishop Carroll for the proposed Baltimore Cathedral. One was Gothic, the other Classic; the latter was chosen and is still standing, one of the noted buildings of Baltimore. Of the Gothic designs submitted April 16, 1805, Latrobe wrote: " The veneration which the Gothic cathedrals generally excite by their peculiar style, by the associations belonging particularly to that style, and by the real grandeur and beauty which it possesses, has induced me to propose the Gothic style of building in the first design submitted to you. . . . I submit the choice to you entirely, having myself an equal desire to see the first or second erected, my habits rather inclining me to the latter, while my reasonings prefer the first." [13] The revival of Gothic is so often linked with emotionalism that it is noteworthy that " reasonings " made Latrobe prefer the first. If the reasonings had been followed, the Cathedral would have escaped two criticisms, one of which appeared in the *New-York Mirror* of May 15, 1830, when St. Patrick's Cathedral, Mott Street, New York, was illustrated and described as a " magnificent gothic superstructure," and when completed, " No church in the United States (the Cathedral in Baltimore excepted) will then compare with it in capacity or elegance. In point of style we think it superior to that of Baltimore; indeed, the gothic order seems to be the fittest for religious edifices." The other appears in the October 1836 number of the *North American Review*. A description of the Cathedral is given in which it is said it has some resemblance to the Pantheon. " It is of the Grecian Order, with arched windows. We think the Gothic would have been more appropriate."

The church which is generally called the first of the Gothic Revival and which has always been admired, especially by Mrs. Trollope who calls it " a little bijou " [14] and by Dunlap who refers to it as a " beautiful Gothic chapel," is the chapel of St. Mary's Seminary in Baltimore. One would like to connect the use of

[13] *Architectural Record*, 42, 540-50. "Latrobe's Designs for the Cathedral of Baltimore " by FISKE KIMBALL.
[14] FRANCES TROLLOPE, *Domestic Manners of the Americans*, 1832, 1927 ed., p. 172.

Gothic there with the Romantic Movement in Europe, for the Sulpicians under Father Nagot who came out from France had for a fellow-passenger René de Chateaubriand, and it would be pleasant to think that they eagerly read " Le Génie du Christianisme " and noted the sentence, " on ne pouvait entrer dans une église gothique sans éprouver une sorte de frissonnement et un sentiment vague de la Divinité." At all events they retained their connection with France by employing Maximilian Gòdefroy who taught drawing at the Seminary. The original design is still to be seen in the Maryland Historical Society, and the Church itself is still standing, the original cost of which was $35,000.[15] (See Pl. XIII.)

The interior has been more altered than the exterior, but the whole building is in an excellent state of preservation. Godefroy planned to have a tower and small spire. Robert Carey Long built one in 1840 which was more Gothic than Godefroy's design. It was taken down in 1915. In comparing Godefroy's drawing for the façade and the building as it is today, one notes that engaged clustered piers with classical necking and Tuscan cap frame the sides of the first story instead of a decorated Gothic buttress, that the Rose window in the second story is larger and the six niches on either side are empty and the statues which Godefroy sketched were never made. The row of statues is reminiscent of the Gallery of Kings to be found in French cathedrals. Godefroy may have intended to have the twelve apostles, although the sketch makes them look like late Greek orator statues. The pinnacles, sans crockets, which Godefroy designed are lacking. It does have pointed arches for the doors and that of course was a primary importance. The second story is a false front and supported by flying buttresses at either side, which undoubtedly are the first employment of that form and a very structural one, although not very conventional.

The furnishings of the interior have thrice been changed, in 1842, in 1861 when the public was no longer admitted, and in

[15] Historic American Buildings Survey, Md. 13, Library of Congress.

1916 when the present choir stalls were erected.[16] The main form of the interior still persists with pointed arch arcade, supported by clustered piers, ornamented below the necking with acorns and topped with acanthus leaf capitals and the depressed barrel vault terminating in a semicircle at the end, decorated with mouldings simulating transverse and diagonal ribs. Of the interior Mrs. Trollope wrote that it has a " touching and impressive character. A solitary lamp, whose glare is tempered by delicately painted glass, hangs before the altar; the light of day enters dimly, yet richly, through crimson curtains; and the silence . . . had something in it more calculated, perhaps, to generate holy thoughts, than even the swelling anthem heard beneath the resounding domes of St. Peter's."

Since the other aspects of the Gothic Revival before 1840 must be noted, the discussion of ecclesiastical architecture will be curtailed. The Federal Street Church in Boston, designed by Bulfinch in 1809, should be mentioned. The writer in the *North American Review*, 1836, considered it to have the " lightest and most graceful steeple in Boston " and continues, " We believe the Federal Street Church is the first attempt at this style in Massachusetts, and one of the first in the United States." [17] Strickland designed St. Stephen's Church in Philadelphia in 1823.[18] Mills notes a Gothic design for Christ Church in Baltimore and for February 14, 1830 has the entry, " The Gothic Church which I designed built at Winchester, 40 x 60 ft. cost $5,300." [19] By 1823 there was a Gothic church in Mobile, Alabama.[20] By 1836, there were Gothic churches in Gardiner, Maine, Arlington, Vermont, Troy and Albany, New Haven and Hartford,[21] an example of Carpenter's Gothic in Cambridge, Massachusetts, where Harvard University used to hold its Commencement exercises,[22] and at least five in New York,[23] only

[16] CHARLES VARLE, *View of Baltimore*, p. 47.
[17] *North American Review*, Oct., 1836, p. 369.
[18] CHILDS, *op. cit.*
[19] H. M. PIERCE GALLAGHER, *Robert Mills*, 1935, pp. 174-5.
[20] Goodwin and Haire map in P. J. HAMILTON, *Colonial Mobile*, 1910.
[21] GRENVILLE MELLEN, ed., *A Book of the United States*, 1836.
[22] Architect, Isaiah Rogers, 1833, according to old printed church record.
[23] *New-York Mirror*, and *Ladies Literary Gazette*, vols. 4-9, 1826-31.

one of which shall be mentioned, namely St. Thomas' Church at Broadway and Houston Street, which was built of marble and brown freestone in 1824-26 from drawings by Josiah R. Brady, architect. It was 113 by 66 feet and the windows contained " rich stained glass from the manufactory of Mr. Brewerton." The *New-York Mirror*, which had the excellent habit of illustrating and describing Public Buildings in New York, says " This church exhibits the best specimen of the gothic style of architecture in the city," and also, " The beauty of the structure and the novelty of the style of architecture served greatly to attract the public attention to it," and the sale of pews increased accordingly. Which is a specific example of the value of the Gothic Revival to the Church of England. Besides the really pleasing qualities of the church itself, it is of interest as being an example of the work of Mr. Brady, who Dunlap says was the only architect in New York at the time and in whose office in just those years of 1824-26, Alexander Jackson Davis was working.

In 1836 it was written, " Thus far the Gothic order, where it has appeared in the United States, has been almost exclusively appropriated to churches." [24] While that is so, Gothic had also been employed in domestic and civic buildings.

The first use of the Gothic for domestic architecture in Philadelphia was the country house of Mr. Crammond who purchased land along the " banks of the romantic Schuylkill " in 1799 and employed B. H. Latrobe to design and supervise the erection of the house. It is now destroyed, but something of its character may be learned from the engraving published by C. G. Childs in 1828, who describes it succinctly. " The style is Gothic, with a portico front and rear, supported by eight columns each. It presents a length of seventy-five feet, and is well adapted in the arrangement of the interior for a gentleman's residence." Its gothic features were pointed arches in the upper story windows and in the doorways in the low flanking towers of the facade. The use of hood mouldings throughout and a touch of the picturesque cottage

[24] *North American Review*, XLIII, 361.

style is given by the scallopped bargeboard under the eaves.
(*See* Pl. XIVa.)

Before the decade was out, in the city of Philadelphia itself a Gothic Mansion was built. It was torn down in 1853 but soon after it was completed an engraving of it by Robert Mills appeared in the February 1811 number of the *Port Folio*. The owner was Mr. John Dorsey, who is mentioned by Dunlap for his design of a Gothic house in Chestnut Street. Since Mills made the drawing of it, it is thought that perhaps he aided Mr. Dorsey in his complicated design. It was sold in 1811 to Godfrey Haga and soon became Mrs. Rivardi's Boarding School and Academy;[25] hence Dorsey's Gothic Mansion is not only one of the first Gothic town houses, but also one of the first examples of Gothic used for an academic building. Dr. Bigelow mentioned the pleasing effect obtained by a restrained use of Gothic in domestic building, but we have no examples of domestic Gothic until the 1830's when it became quite popular, and examples such as Glen Ellen (1832), just outside Baltimore, and other designs by A. J. Davis are well known.[26] Davis was described to Dunlap as passing "hours in puzzling over the plan of some ancient castle of romance, arranging the trap doors, subterraneous passages, and drawbridges, as pictorial embellishment was the least of his care, invention all his aim."[27] His youthful pastime stood him in good stead, for he became one of the most popular and successful architects of the Hudson River Gothic.

Washington Irving's picturesque country house at Tarrytown-on-Hudson is one of the best known examples of the 1830's. Irving himself in his " Sketch Book " had done much to encourage the appropriate attitude of mind to enjoy the Gothic. His description of " a tomb on which lay the effigy of a knight in complete armor " is a good example of the romantic idiom and attitude toward the Middle Ages. "It was the tomb of a crusader: of one of those military enthusiasts, who so strangely mingled religion

[25] JOSEPH JACKSON, *Encyclopedia of Philadelphia.*
[26] *Metropolitan Museum Studies*, V, pt. 2, pp. 183-233, Sept. 1936. "A J. Davis and the Gothic Revival " by EDNA DONNELL.
[27] DUNLAP, *op. cit.*

and romance, and whose exploits form the connecting link between fact and fiction; between history and the fairy tale. There is something extremely picturesque in the tombs of these adventurers, decorated as they are with rude armorial bearings and Gothic sculpture. They comport with the antiquated chapels in which they are generally found; and in considering them, the imagination is apt to kindle with the legendary associations, the romantic fiction, the chivalrous pomp and pageantry, which poetry has spread over the Wars for the sepulchre of Christ." [28]

Nevertheless, despite his appreciation of the picturesque, when in 1835 he bought Van Tassel's farm, which he had already made famous by the " Legend of Sleepy Hollow," he wrote that he was going to make of it a "Dutch Nookery." An English architect, George Harvey, who lived nearby, was entrusted with the remodelling and the result had stepped gables and hood mouldings. It was satisfactory and Irving moved in to Wolfert's Roost, as Sunnyside was called until 1841, in November 1836. [29]

Gothic was used occasionally in various types of public buildings before 1840: in a State House, a bank, educational institutions, Masonic temples and prisons.

The State House is the old capitol of Georgia at Milledgeville, which was built between 1804-7 by General Jett Thomas (1776-1817) and remodelled after a fire in 1835. Knight [30] writes that " under the supervision of General Jett Thomas, the handsome Gothic structure [31] which became for more than sixty years [1807-1868] the home of the General Assembly of Georgia was erected. The original cost of the structure was not in excess of $60,000; but extensions were made from time to time, and the finishing touches were not applied until 1837." (See Pl. XIVb.)

It is now used as the Georgia Military College and is in good

[28] From essay on Westminister Abbey, *Sketch-Book*, 1848 ed., pp. 214-15.
[29] PIERRE IRVING, *Life of Washington Irving*, III, 77-92.
[30] L. L. KNIGHT, *Georgia's Landmarks, Memorials and Legends*, 1913, I, xxxiv, 960; II, 347.
[31] FISKE KIMBALL in his *American Architecture* says that it was remodelled in the Gothic style in the 1830's. The historical notes accompanying the photographs in the H. A. B. S. (GA-137) in the Library of Congress give no information as to whether Knight or Kimball is correct.

repair. The walls are brick covered with stucco, the skyline is crenellated. Most of the upper story windows are pointed with hood mouldings. The doors and windows of the lower story have labels. The square central tower, crenellated and ornamented at the corners with pyramidal pinnacles without crockets or finials was put up in 1835 after the original cupola with a clock had been destroyed by fire. The tower is the least successful part of the building, and otherwise it is a very pleasing and satisfying example of a castellated mansion.

Jett Thomas is an example of a contractor who acted as architect. He, also, speculated in real estate. He purchased one of the first lots in the future town of Athens, and constructed Franklin College there. While he was building the college, "Dr. Meigs [the president] gave him access to the library, and devoting what little time he could spare after a hard day's work to mental culture, he acquired the love of books which made him in his time a man of wide information." He was an officer in the State Militia and was made a General for his bravery in action in the War of 1812.

The Gothic bank was erected in 1809 at 4th and Chestnut Streets, Philadelphia. Robert Mills tells of it in his unfinished autobiography. "Among the buildings executed by the author in Philadelphia was the Bank of Philadelphia, a modern Gothic structure—the design of Mr. Latrobe—a work of the most intricate and difficult character to execute from the novel forms of the vaultings and great span of arches in the center hall, all of which were built of solid masonry and made fireproof." [32] An early Gazetteer of Pennsylvania has the following remarks, "The banking home of the bank of Philadelphia is also from a design of Mr. Latrobe. It is in the Gothic style and covered with stucco imitating marble. The building has its admirers but does not receive the general approbation of the citizens."

The first educational institution of importance which used Gothic, albeit a very plain Gothic, employing only pointed windows and pyramidal pinnacles was Kenyon College in Ohio, which

[32] GALLAGHER, op. cit., p. 159.

was built between 1825-27. The money for the college was raised by Bishop Chase in England between 1823-5. Hinton illustrated it in his "Topography of the United States," so that it became well known both in this country and England. A. J. Davis's building for New York University (1833-36) was another early educational building of some pretensions. A contemporary wrote of it, "The new building for the University, which is of the Gothic order, has some striking merits; and, though far from perfect, is still very interesting as the first remarkable specimen of a style, which has been but lately introduced into this country." He then commends the use of Gothic, criticizing four of the Harvard buildings as "vast brick barns," and the fifth for having wooden Ionic pilasters, so he concludes that "The New University at New York is on this account [viz. use of Gothic] vastly handsomer than any college building which we have seen in the United States." [33]

The first Gothic Masonic Hall was built in Philadelphia on Chestnut Street west of Seventh by William Strickland. So within eight blocks on Chestnut Street by the end of 1810, there were three Gothic buildings, but not for long for it burned in 1819. Both Boston and New York followed suit with Gothic Masonic Halls. The Boston building faced the Common and had small spires which according to a critic, stuck up like asses' ears. [34] The New York Hall (1825) was more admired and was illustrated in Hinton's Topography. It had a 70 foot façade, four stories high with an elaborate ogee arch over the doorway, pointed windows with tracery, two circular windows with quatrefoil design and one wheel window in the top story. The silhouette was crenellated and relieved by four pinnacles which did have crockets and finials. No wonder the *New-York Mirror* of September 26, 1829 wrote of it with enthusiasm. "Its style of architecture is purely gothic, without the least mixture of any other order; copied from the most approved classical models, with original appendages, by our celebrated artist, Hugh Reinagle, esq."

[33] *North American Review*, XLIII, 361-2.
[34] *Ibid.*, p. 364.

The use of Gothic architecture for prisons was introduced into this country by John Haviland, an Englishman who settled in Philadelphia. The Eastern Penitentiary (1825) in Philadelphia was immediately admired both for its arrangement for solitary confinement and for its architecture. At Auburn, N. Y., Gothic was also used. Thomas U. Walter in his first important commission, the Philadelphia County Prison (1832-35) was influenced by Haviland in his use of the castellated style but showed his originality by designing the Debtors' Jail and the Women's Section in the Egyptian mode. Haviland's prison was illustrated in Childs' "Views of Philadelphia" with the following comments: "The design and execution impart a grave, severe, and awful character to the external aspect of this building. The effect which it produces on the imagination of every passing spectator, is peculiarly impressive, solemn, and instructive." Half a page on the writer with seeming inconsistency states, "This Penitentiary is the only edifice in this country which is calculated to convey to our citizens the external appearance of those magnificent and picturesque castles of the Middle Ages, which contribute so eminently to embellish the scenery of Europe." (See Pl. XV.)

Thus it seems that a study of American architecture up to 1840, as illustrated by Childs, Hinton, Mellen and the *New-York Mirror,* as well as of the buildings which are still standing, convinces one of the truth of such statements as that of Dr. Bigelow, of 1829, " In edifices erected at the present day, the Grecian and Gothic outlines are commonly employed to the exclusion of the rest," or that of 1836, " Meantime, the Grecian and Gothic styles, neither of which is discoverable in the earlier architecture of the country, are beginning to appear in every village." [35] And it is hoped that this study shows that even as the Romantic Movement was affecting all other aspects of American life, it was, also, affecting architecture and bearing fruit in examples of Early American Gothic.

[35] *Ibid.*, p. 359.

THE BEETHOVENS OF AMERICA

by

Lubov Keefer

On June 12, 1821, Berlin lay prostrate before Weber's *Freischütz*. In the breathless and spellbound audience sat a handsome, open-eyed lad of 12, here to see the world, with some symphonies, operas, and Greek translations to his credit, Felix Mendelssohn. In Vienna this most perspicacious, laziest, and best humored of composers, Rossini, had just tossed off his *Donna del Lago*, en route to a new work, the *Semiramide*. Beethoven, totally deaf, was bridging the abyss from illness and ingratitude, dying patrons, fickle audiences and negligent publishers and performers, to him "above the stars" in the *D Mass* and the *Ninth Symphony*. In that year Franz Schubert, whose genius had been deciphered only by a few: Sonnleithner, and Vogl and von Schönstein, finally succeeded through the valiant intervention of amateur singers, in publishing his *Erlkönig* by private subscription. Recovered from his great triumph at Oedenburg, Liszt was about to embark for secluded study in Vienna, a key to the conquest of the world. From Lucca to Parma and Genoa and on through the hemispheres led the blaze, lit in that year by Paganini's wizardry. Was this fiend of the G string mortal or the Evil One? As yet free from his hypnotic power, Robert Schumann, hidden in the cellar of a Zwickau bookstore, was penning exalted poems à la Jean Paul Richter and Rückert. In Paris, Berlioz, the flameheaded, was sacrificing anatomy and *materia medica* on the altar of women and song; in Roncole Giuseppe Verdi ran ecstatically after every organgrinder of the village, and in Leipzig, Richard Wagner, ten months his senior, was forgetting the world in the Odyssey, a stepping stone to *Der Freischütz*.

On February 10, 1821, the city of Philadelphia was all agog.

A treat was in store for the patrons of the new Walnut Street Theatre: the first taste of a Melodrama, entitled *The Child of the Mountain*, or *The Deserted Mother*. Its composer was Anton, or, as he preferred to be called in the land of his adoption, Anthony Philip Heinrich. Of the forty years of his life, only a negligible share had been spent in the Quaker City. Born in Schönbüchel, near Schönlinde, in northern Bohemia, just across the German border, he was raised from infancy by an uncle, a well-to-do merchant. Driven by Wanderlust, Anthony visits, when still a youth, Italy, France, Portugal, and parts of Spain. At the outbreak of the Napoleonic débacle he packs, as best he can, his beloved Bohemian glass, buys himself in Malta a Cremona violin, and sets sail to the new world, to start here anew his business career. While he fiddles and directs the orchestra of the Philadelphia Southwark Theatre—a labor of love—his entire fortune goes in the Austrian financial crash. With his wife, a Bostonian " of superior personal and mental endowments," he revisits his home, and sits in at the sessions of the " waltzing " Congress. By 1816 he is back at the *City of Fraternal Love*, alone. The journey proved too much for the wearied mother. Toni, the baby, is left behind in Schönlinde. Now, at 35, the indomitable Heinrich becomes American. He changes his first name, and starts the study of the violin in earnest. In the poetic metaphor of his compatriot and biographer F. A. Mussik, befitting so weighty a decision: " Mit diesem betrat er nun als Concertist and Compositeur seine neue Laufbahn and legte dagegen Merkur's Handelsstab auf immer nieder." (Upton, William Treat, *Anthony Philip Heinrich*, New York: Columbia University Press, 1939, p. 2.)

How proud Anthony was to be admitted into the cénacle which numbered among its melodists the revered Alexander Reinagle (he had just died in Baltimore), the broad-visioned Charles Hupfeld; Raynor Taylor, the wit, and Benjamin Carr, publisher, producer, conductor, and composer! Jointly through the medium of the *Musical Fund Society* and Reinagle-Wignell ménage, and alone, they were as indispensable to the cultural uplift of the Quaker City in its campaign against the fig-leafs of propriety as

James Hewitt and Victor Pelissier to New York, Van Hagen to Charleston, and Gottlieb Graupner to Boston. No mean achievement was this. In Philadelphia had lived Francis Hopkinson and James Lyons, the first native musicians. Franklin, Freneau and Thomas Godfrey were residents of the city. Here Robert Fulton worked as draftsman, and Copley became enamored of the Italians. The city sheltered Thomas Doughty, landscape artist, and William Rush, pioneer American sculptor; of portraitists, Henry Benbridge, Matthew Pratt, and Gilbert Stuart; of actors, Wood, Warren, the Jeffersons, Frank Blisset; of vocalists, Wignell, Mrs. French, Mrs. Ostinelli, Mrs. Burke, "the most famous American singer," mother of Joseph Jefferson III. Here Benjamin West launched on his career as free painter and John Krimmel lent dignity to genre. Publishing prospered, with the beautifully illustrated *Columbiad* of John Barlow and Wilson's *American Ornithology*, which carried the reputation of native artistry far and wide.

Dear as these luxuries of the spirit were to Heinrich's heart, he was not to indulge in them. There came a call for him to direct the theatre—*The* theatre—at Pittsburgh, this time a salaried job. Undaunted, Heinrich makes the 300 mile cross-country journey by foot. Nothing is known of his stay in the dusty city, except that he soon lost his keep, and with a band of pilgrims, started out for the promised land of Kentucky. Nor are we sure by what sort of craft Anthony made his long way down the Ohio river. But his letters and compositions reveal that he was immensely impressed by the romantic grandeur and historic significance of the frontier country, the battleground of White and Indian: Limestone and Blue Licks. He arrives in Lexington in the fall of 1817, exhausted, penniless, and alone. Already on November 12, he announces the first of those Gargantuan musical repasts, so essential to the national and artistic consciousness of our ancestors. "The Grand Concert of vocal and Instrumental Music," unrolling with Beethoven's *Sinfonia con Minuetto* for full band, and closing with Haydn's *Finale*, with Glees, Adagios, Catches, Overtures,—both single and Grand, as middle courses, presents

Anthony as violinist and two-piano performer. Heinrich, the composer, was not yet born.

Just as Anthony was about to settle for a useful teaching career, fate claimed another sacrifice. He became desperately ill. With convalescence there came the growing conviction that music must be his salvation. A true romanticist, he puts himself under the guidance of nature. Seclusion in a Kentucky Log House was to bring not alone equanimity and peace, but the fruition of his latent powers. The creator comes into being. As the "basis of all his ensuing efforts," he chooses Collins' Ode, *How Sleep the Brave*. The stronger the fascination of providing a sensuous embodiment to the irresistible forces within him, the deeper waxed his attachment to the Kentucky forest. Suddenly a prey to some hidden impulse, Anthony leaves his hut, and takes up his abode at "Farmington," the estate of Judge Speed.

Soon his communion with streams and birds begins to yield opulent fruit. Many of his smaller works are joined in the ambitious *Dawning of Music in Kentucky*, or, *The Pleasures of Harmony in the Solitudes of Nature*, opera prima, copyrighted May 4, 1820. The following month, in Philadelphia, Heinrich prints *The Western Minstrel, A Collection of original, moral, patriotic and sentimental songs for the pianoforte, interspersed with airs, waltzes, etc.* In humbly dedicating "these firstlings of his Muse" to the citizens of the country at large, he professes "to be fully aware of the dangers which attend talent on the crowded and difficult road of eminence," but "rests confident that Justice will be done, by due comparison with the works of other Authors but who have never, like him, been thrown, as it were, by *discordant events*, far from the emporiums of musical science, into the isolated wilds of nature, where he invoked his muse, tutored only by *Alma Mater*."

It is a mystery to what purpose Heinrich retraced his steps to the Quaker City. Perhaps, it was the vanity of the artist, anxious to hear the plaudits attending the Walnut St. première of *The Child of the Mountain*. Surely, its protagonists, the *crème de la crème* of the old Chestnut St. Theatre, Mr. Durang and three of the Jeffersons, were well worth the journey. Manufactured specially for the occasion, the scenery was, if one can trust the program, of unusual lavishness: Gothic castles with resplendent thrones; rocks and tempestuous torrents, and in the midst of eternal snow, opulent flowering garlands.

Nor was the story to be overlooked. Virtue and depravity, the one symbolized by Albert, count of Tockenburg, and his lofty Vassals of exotic lineage, the other, by Furbino, were fighting a deadly issue. A single touch of local color was furnished by Zozo, the Negro boy. Scenes three and four were separated by a *Festive Dance* for the Ensemble, and a more elaborate *pas seul* for Miss Durang, while the intermission between the two last acts was enlivened by a *Grand March* and *Quick Step*, Heinrich's tribute to the Washington Guards of Philadelphia. As an epilogue, the orchestra, led by the composer's fiddle, gave a *National Olio, A Columbiad, intended as Overture to a new farce, never performed, called the Author's Night, or, The Bailiff's Outwitted, by H. M. Murtrie, M. D.*

How tempting it would be to pass on Heinrich's accompaniment to the collapse of the balcony in the cottage scene, or the " precipitation of Mother and Child to the Gulph below." Unfortunately, it is lost, except for a few instrumental episodes, borrowed from that earlier epic, *The Dawning of Music in Kentucky*. Fortunately, a large pack, some will say, too large, of Heinrich's music, survives. Fortunately too, the *Deserted Mother*, must have possessed more than its share of the " Will of expression," which dominates all the writing of Anthony, a style whose " vigor of thought, variety of ideas, originality of conception, . . . boldness and luxuriance of imagination, are the more extraordinary, as the author but a few years since, was merely an amateur and a prosperous merchant. There is versatility for the capricious, pomp for the pedant, playfulness for the amateur, learning for the scholar, business for the performer, pleasure for the vocalist, ingenuity for the curious, and puzzle for the academician. He seems at once to have possessed himself of the key which unlocks to him the temple of science and enables him to explore with fearless security the mysterious labyrinth of harmony." (*Boston Euterpeiad*, April 13, 1822). In Heinrich, the untutored, foreign born romanticist, there merge all the constituents, felt and enjoyed in the colorful subjective speech of Weber, Rossini, Wagner, Verdi, Schumann, Paganini, Schubert, and Berlioz.

How, if at all, does Heinrich's *Deserted Mother* approach the home-product? One of the strongest issues of romanticism, its very raison d'être, is nationalism. In the States musical aboriginal expression has been and promises well to remain, a sore subject. From its inception, American music has been so only in name, the whole process being that of assimilation, penetration rather than of production. For this, there could hardly be a cure. Yet, in many ways, Heinrich is a fervent nationalist.

His first title to his "Americanism" is the circumstance of German, rather than English, French, or Italian, parentage. In its formative years the latent musical genius of these shores had bowed to other races. The mother country was first to shower on her colony instrumentalists, singers, and composers. To Philadelphia, Boston, Baltimore, and New York came the Hewitts and Reinagles, the Carrs, Young and Raynor Taylor. Where could one find a truer London in miniature than Williamsburg and Charleston, where styles in song, concert, and ballad-opera were copied as alertly and eagerly as coiffures and petticoats? And with what verve did the British, swelled later by Adgate, Selby and Tuckey, well-born and once upon a time well-fixed gentlemen, organize and promote their favored mammoth brand of vocal and instrumental entertainment!

Then, just as Napoleon's brother came to woo a Baltimore belle, Rousseau and Grétry, Capron and Pelissier bid fair to take precedence over the *Beggar's Opera*, Arne, Atwood, and Shield. Some sporadic attempts to transplant Latin fare had been detected earlier. Already on June 12, 1760, Baltimore had been regaled by *Mistress and Maid* by "Per Golaise." Now New York follows suit with Rousseau's *Devin du Village*. Mehul's "Celebrated Overture to *Les Deux Aveugles de Toledo*, arranged for the pianoforte by T. Carr of Baltimore," is played by the *Musical Fund Society*.

Benjamin Cross introduces New York to a *Pastiche* of tunes concocted from *La Dame blanche, Massinello,* and *Fra Diavolo.* Boston stages Rousseau's *Pygmalion,* Norfolk Monsigny's *Deserter,* New Orleans Mehul's *Une folie,* Baltimore *A Concertante Nocturno* for oboe and piano. Grétry intrigues through *Zémir et Azor, Fausse Magie,* and *Richard Coeur de Lion*; Dalayrac through *Nina* and *L' Amant Statue.* " Pleyel " becomes a household term. Malibran bids her farewell in Boildieu's *John of Paris.* Now that French immigration began in earnest, many a marquis and count brought fine taste and ability to the ranks of theatre and concert orchestras. They left their imprint in Godey's, in the architecture of City Halls; François Gignoux's *Niagara by Moonlight*; in the programs, fairly brimming with the names of Dalayrac, Chateaudun and Rousseau; incidentally, the last complete crop of newspaper announcements.

" From Italy " becomes the pass in 1825, when Manuel Garcia gives New York his *de luxe* troupe in the resplendent Park Theatre. Rossini, whose *Barber of Seville* launches the glamorous season, is represented by four works; the next year, on May 23, the metropolis hears for the first time Mozart's *Don.* Something of its tension and luscious melodiousness must have escaped unscathed: it ran for nine nights. The belles begin to discuss the *utile* and *dolce* of the arts; their gentle lips learn the meaning of *bravo* and *bis.* They show signs of taste: hosannas are showered on the orchestra of the *Barber,* and the home-brewed *L'Amante Astuto* is hissed off the boards. Earlier already New Orleans had produced Paisiello's *Barber,* Heaven alone knows how. America was very fond of the perky coiffeur, and while Philadelphia listened to the *Deserted Mother,* New York was introduced to Mozart's *Marriage of Figaro,* à la Henry Bishop. Cimarosa and Paisiello are rulers for the moment: by virtue of the latter's favorite air, " Hope told a Flattering Tale," with variations for the harp by Desargues and of the former's Symphony for full band (*Baltimore American and Commercial Daily Advertiser,* 1820).

Soon, however, the audiences show symptoms of fatigue with the foreign fare and only " respectful information that Stoves have been erected, and Pipes distributed " has the power to bring the patrons back. This attraction failing, Garcia closes his doors, and sets sail for Mexico. The Italian régime is no more.

In all, American romanticism in music is conditioned by German temperament, technique, forms, and philosophy. German is its beginning, the *Collegium Musicum* of Bethlehem, Pennsylvania, where violins, gambas, flutes and horns resounded in concert at a time when New England and Philadelphia turned thumbs down on orchestra; where organs and trombones frightened away enterprising redskins, and where both Washington and Franklin were amazed at the high quality of " needlework, tambour, drawing, and music." German is its consummation—the ideology of the Brook Farm brotherhood. Its preludes are Händel's *Messiah* and Haydn's *Creation* salvaged by the Moravian adherents of Zinzendorf; its coda—the lofty heights of the *Choral Symphony; Muss es sein?—Es muss sein* as transmitted to Horatio Parker, John Knowles Paine, Edward MacDowell, and Charles Ives. The " Beethoven of America," this tribute paid Anthony Heinrich by the *Boston Euterpeiad* (April 13, 1822) has more truth than appears on the surface.

By a strange paradox, it is the German, or, as the case might be, English, French, Norwegian, or Italian resident of the United States, who hoisted highest the tricolor for the musical Independence of his new country.

The natives: Lowell Mason, William Bradbury, Thomas Hastings, Sylvanus Pond, Isaac Woodbury could afford to remain indifferent to the cause. If George Frederick Bristow and William Henry Fry, whose *Lenora* was the first native opera to gain a hearing in this country, thought the matter sufficiently grave to get on each other's nerves, they had a personal axe to grind. Frederick Crouch, historian of the Civil War and trumpeter of the Confederate army, could not help himself. None of them ever carried on so prolonged and spirited a campaign for the glory and the future of his homeland as the German, Anthony Heinrich. When first moved by the genius of music,—and no human ever took his God-given mission more literally than he,—

he produces a *Birthday to Washington*, some *Farmington Marches*, and the Minuet, *Hail, Columbia*. Legion are Heinrich's versions of the *Yankee Doodle* refrain. There are *Doodle Valses, Marches*, and, to crown all, the heroic *Yankee Doodleiad*, a worthy twin of the *Anarchiad, Democratiad, Guillotiniad, Porcupiniad*, and similar monsters. In medium, at least, it anticipates Beethoven's best manner; scored for string quartet, it demands of the first violin superhuman feats of doublestopping and castrato coloratura. Hardly a national incident, to which Heinrich fails to react: *Hail to Kentucky, Columbia's Plaint, the Young Columbian Midshipman, President Harrison's Funeral March*.

Indeed, the very pretext for expressing himself through the medium of sound was the determination to add to the fount of American harmony. "The fantastical drapery" of the *Western Minstrel* was a conscious one. "The many and severe animadversions, so long and repeatedly cast on the talent for music in this Country has been one of the chief motives of the Author, in the exercise of his abilities, and should he be able, by this effort, to create but a single *Star* in the *West*, no one would ever be more proud than myself, to be called an *American Musician*." (*Preface* to *Dawning of Music*.)

In a way, Heinrich could not lay claim to having first directed American music towards the National Road. That is as old as Hopkinson (1737-1791) and Billings (1746-1800), the natives, the first, the signer of the Declaration of Rights, the other, a destitute New England tanner. It is alive in Oliver Shaw's marches, *Bangor, Bristol, Governor Arnold's*. It animates Charles E. Horn's *National Melodies of America*, and George James Webb's *Ode to the 4th of July*. Charleston, Baltimore, New York, Annapolis, each and all made a thriving business on *Columbia, Independence of America*, alias, the *Ever Memorable 4th of July, 1776*. Splendid historical *Pantomimes, Glees, Catches, Pastorals, Ballets, Quicksteps* and *Quadrilles* were the utterances of joy for destruction of despotism and for the "Rights and Priviledges of America."

A deeper meaning was not looked for. The fireworks and

Columbiads were grafted on the eclectic compendiums of Russian, Turkish, and Greek Marches; Circassian, Hungarian, and Parisian Waltzes; on anything from anywhere, be it Mexican, Neapolitan, Swiss or Viennese, Tyrolean or Danish, Bohemian or from New Orleans. (J. Cole's *Catalogue* for 1829.) They stopped the show of *Araby's Daughter, Deserter of Naples, Highland Reel,* or *Peep into the Seraglio, Castle of Andalusia,* the *Gipsy,* of *Sicilian Romance,* and *Slaves in Algeria.* (Operas by Alexander Reinagle.) They are the *pièce de resistance* of *Incle and Yarico* (an adaptation of Shakespeare's *Tempest*) and of *No Song—No Supper,* of Goldsmith-Pelissier, a *Macbeth* with music by Locke; of Goldsmith-Pelissier's *Edwin and Angelina.* They enrich with cannon and seismic explosions the *Beggar's Opera,* the classic " which made Gay rich and Rich gay." [1] They are as legitimate in Nelson Baker's *Indian Princess,* as in Gottschalk's *Isura de Palermo,* or *Charles IX.* Dryden, Thomas Moore, Goldsmith, Burns, all become American, in a fashion.

And if that were not enough, enterprising impresarios add to *The Temple of American Independence* a display of " a view of the lower Broadway, Battery, and Shipping, taken at the spot," salutes, military files, and all the " uniform companies of the city, horse, artillery and infantry in their respective places" (*The New York Daily Advertiser*), the spectacle to be climaxed by an inside view of the Temple of Independence " as exhibited on the birthday of General Washington."

Hilarious salvos fell to the lot of John Hodgkinson, whose insatiable vanity could not obscure a phenomenal memory and staggering versatility, in his Boston appearances in *Adams and Washington,* and *Hail, Columbia.* The publishers, P. A. Hagen & Co., and Benjamin Crehore, instrument manufacturer of the Hub, made a specialty of patriotism: *Adams and Liberty, Adams and Washington,* and *Hail, Columbia.* Wonder-children in Charleston, Williamsburg and Baltimore enchanted their audiences with the *Battle of Lake Champlain and Plattsburg,* or, with the same

---

[1] EDWARD KREHBIEL, *Chapters of Opera*, New York, Henry Holt, 1909, p. 6.

acclaim, with *The Battle of Trenton*, a graphic *Overture,* picturing *the Army in motion, attacks, confusion, surrender, the grief of prisoners, and the Conqueror's Quickmarch.*

Woe to the traveller who would trust himself to the compass of this domestic muse. There is no perception of the differences of ethnography or temperament. Lafayette and the Morgan Volunteers; Napoleon and the United States Marine; the Boston Cadets; Jefferson and Adams; Military Ballads, Valses, Minuets; and Variations for flute, guitar, and harp are entirely cosmopolitan. From a purely musical standpoint they are as yet definitely inferior to *Charleston is Ours, Brave Men, Behold your Fallen Chief, When the Cruel War is over, The Battle Cry of Freedom, Marching through Georgia, We are Coming, Father Abraham,* born of a later conflagration. They are the sarcophagus not alone of nationality, but with a few exceptions, of music, truncated melody stubs, tinkly, dry. Their rhythms display an enervating monotony of dotted eights and perky sixteenths. Modulations are angular; atmospheric concern—nil.

Among the prodigious piles of *Quadrilles* and *Processionals,* paeons of glorious deeds committed for the glory of the Republic, in that maze of *gallops* and *variations,* Heinrich was one of the few to divine the deeper meaning of American patriotism. From his first stay in the Quaker City his new fatherland is for him the fount of political and artistic emancipation. Through every preface, every musical image, he underscores the integration of the two fundamental principles. America has given him the felicity of liberty. "America demands of me now that I should prove myself as worthy of her adoption." A resident of the New World deserves more, more truth, more justice, more respect, nay, even more humanity, than any other citizen.[2]

Freedom means the right to develop one's genius according to the dictates of one's heart. It means release from rules and prohibitions. It means the recognition of talent as the prime factor of the creative act. It means the fullest awareness of one's ego.

[2] Heinrich's Letter to John Sinclair.

Once more, the creed does not originate with Heinrich. In 1770, the very year in which another apostle of the immunity of the artist, Beethoven, saw the light of day, Billings, the first American to starve for the sake of music, proclaims his manifesto. Crippled and one-eyed, but aglow for Bach and harmony, he refuses to recognize rules of composition, maintains "that Nature is the best Dictator, for all the hard studied rules that ever were prescribed will not enable any person to form an *Air* any more than the bare knowledge of the four and twenty letters, and strict Grammatical rules will qualify a scholar for composing a piece of Poetry. It must be Nature; Nature must lay the Foundation, Nature must give the thought!" Something slipped, and Nature failed to supply poor Billings with the necessary cue.

Into the divine protection of Nature, Heinrich puts himself wholly. Each one of his heart-felt melodies must be born of loneliness, escapism. Each *Overture* and *Ballad* voices a warning against the pitfalls of the heartless city, as eloquent as the *Pastoral* or the *Freischütz*. An inner need dictates the long expeditions on foot into the Virginlands. "Come there a curious stranger, seeking amusement by foreign travel, stripped by capricious fortune of the wealth gained in traffic, I left the crowded cities and sought refuge in the wilderness of Kentucky, there to form, under the rafters of the log-house, the musical taste, which has been since my chief solace in life." [3]

What is Heinrich's nature? Is it the Mendelssohnian catching of moonbeams in ocean waves? Is it Beethoven's "aufgeknöpfte" rustic joviality of the *Pastoral*, the lyricism of Schumann's *Spring*, the thunderbolts of *Prometheus*, the serenity of Liszt's *Preludes*, or the orgiastic eroticism of *Gotterdämmerung* and *Tristan?* It is all that and more. It is the "matrix which receives the seed of the poet's purpose, and brings it forth fully formed" (Wagner). . . . It is friend and mother, teacher and lover. It is sublime, a law unto itself. To a solitary traveller the American forest extends faith, a fresh hold on life. It opens to him the sesame

[3] UPTON, *Heinrich*, p. 221.

of eternal truths. Like Siegfried, he is suddenly aware of a divine breath. He is reborn, a God.

As regards his *Wild Wood Spirit Chant*, one of the episodes which go into the making of the *Grand Chorus Canonicale, The Pilgrim Fathers*, he confesses: "There is no fact better authenticated than that poets heard, or feigned to hear, the voices of spirits and the music of the spheres, and men have always believed that myriads of beings walk the earth unseen to mortal eyes. But, whether that be truth or fable, the author had heard himself the genii of music in an American forest and although strange vicissitudes have chased him since, yet, the impressions of that ethereal music were no deception and he recalls vividly that by the help of sketching—scored upon that mystic ground in the state of Kentucky—then the favorite abode of Sylphs and Naiads—he has been able to note down that music on these pages as he heard from an invisible hand."

Niagara, the Eagle, the Catskills, an Ohio Prairie, the roar of avalanches, those are the forces which unravel to Heinrich the labyrinth of tortuous melody and bold flaming modulation. Of his *Western Minstrel* he says, that "the firstlings of his Muse" were drawn up in the wilds of the frontier country, where "the minstrelsy of nature, the songsters of the air, next to the other virtuosos of the woods, have been my greatest inspirers of harmony and composition." Himself Heinrich envisages all along as a wild, primitive troubadour, a child-savage. Nature is his meat and drink. He loves every stone, every hill of his chosen fatherland. He loves its people, its colors, for he loves its spirit. The landing of the Mayflower Heinrich sees as the unlocking of the golden gates of freedom, whose genius resides in the vast American woods. This cult animates the *Catskills*, a duet for piano and violin. It pervades the *War of the Elements* and the "Capriccio grande for full orchestra" *Thundering of Niagara,* supreme among Heinrich's works in the contrast between graceful lyricism and dramatic zest. It adds pungent flavor to this towering edifice, with its syncopation of woodwind and violins set against the steady march of the tutti, punctuated by fortissimo interjections of triangles, cymbals, and tambourines. It gives dignity to the flowing polyphony and rhythmic interplay of the *Jubilee*, "a grand national song of triumph, composed and arranged for a full orchestra and a vocal chorus." It dictates the brilliant fireworks of the *Wild Wood Spirit's Chant*, or *Scintillations of Yankee Doodle*, this, a "national heroic fantasia, scored for a powerful orchestra."

He fears no man. Divination, intuition, are his deities. "If Bohemians are able out of mere pebbles to fashion the finest glass (one might even say gold), why should not I, too, simple creature of nature that I am, be able, to produce something sublime." [4] Heinrich's fountain-head of inspiration, and his crowning triumph is the American Forest. Now sunny and joyous, now moaning, now enraged, it is ever new. He met it first, homeless and ill. And she took him in her fold.

> Far in the West, an endless wood
> Sighs to the rushing cataract's flood—
> 'Twas here a humble log-house stood,
>   To fame unknown:
> There first loved minstrelzy I woo'd,
>   And woo'd alone.
>
> The thundering fall! The bubbling stream,
> Murmuring midst stones, and roots between;
> Where Nature's whispers for some theme
>   To inspire my lay—
> Trilling appeggios thro' my dream
>   With wild sweet play.
>
> He came—a wand'ring, wayward Child;
> A Native flower, free and wild;
> With ardor fierce!—with feelings mild;
>   'Tis Genius' boon,
> Then swept his Minstrel Lyre—and smiled;
>   For fear had flown. [5]

---

[4] Letter to Mussik, August 18, 1840.

[5] Presented in the Farewell concert, words and "items" by William Edson, in which Heinrich represents himself in the last verse, musically in the characters of "Melancholist," "Enthusiast" and the "Romantic" and terminates with a "flying Cadence."

Never is nature as bountiful as to the weak, the beaten, the downtrodden. "A wand'ring, wayward child," Heinrich seeks its blessing for each of his cataclystic effusions. With admirable determination he underscores the circumstance that every single one of his chefs d'œuvre has been built on frustration, loneliness, fatigue, despair, melancholy, and starvation, of both mind and body. Once Nature reaches out its hand of friendship, the victory for liberty is assured, for the moving melodies with which she regales her solitudes are the luminous messengers of right.

Whatever our reactions and estimate today of Anthony Heinrich's talent, and they are bound to diverge, by his contemporaries he was hailed as a great genius. Some isolated voices objected to the " difficulties in which his writing is intrenched " (*Boston Euterpeiad*, April 13, 1822), to the " eccentricity mixed with the real spirit of his compositions" (*Scrap Book*, p. 1194), some compared his course to a comet rather than to a " regular planet," but those were few and far between. From Boston and Philadelphia to London and Berlin, Heinrich's name was holy. From every corner of the Universe, from every profession, every channel of activity there came warm testimonials to his usefulness.

In unison, the critics laud the freshness, the spontaneity, and originality of Anthony's musical ideology. From Waverley House John Braham, Britain's most distinguished songster, congratulates Anthony on the wildness, the uniqueness of his language in the *Stranger's Requiem*, and voices his conviction that his " musical effusions" would not disgrace Beethoven. Throughout, in the life-sketch of F. J. Fétis' *Biographie Universelle* (1842), of von Schilling's *Encyclopedia*, in the flattering offers from painters, literally besieging him for a sitting, in the acclaim of thousands who hear him play and conduct, there sounds like a red streak the dogma that Heinrich's genius is more sublime for being self-nurtured. Washington Irving in a letter (February 28, 1842) gives thanks for the sincerity of the Lament, *The Maiden's Dirge*.

If Heinrich, at a time when Beethoven was yet a closed book to France and Italy, was saluted as his peer in Kentucky and New

York, it was because the listeners were alive to the supreme "boldness, individuality, even sublimity" of his creations. How comprehensive the gamut of his expression! How suggestive his imagery! How infinite the form, "from a waltz or song up to the acme of chromatic frenzy!" (*Boston Euterpeiad,* August 1823.) With what fervidness do they rhapsodize over the onrush of Heinrich's crescendos, the quivering modulations, the tender cantilena! They laud the uniqueness of his designs, and delight in the circumstance that his subjects are "chosen apparently more to please himself than others. In all his compositions a rich and visionary fragrance breathes through them, uncommon and delightful . . . the luxury of wand'ring thoughts and visionary fears." They are enraptured by his determination to forsake the vain pleasures, and to discourse in "nature harmonies and distant echoes of eternal songs, from harps seraphic and immortal tongues."

He gives his former fatherland the first musical embodiment of New World idealism. From Potsdam, Humboldt, aged 88, sends a token of gratitude, for the gift "tief-gerührt von dem Walten der Naturkräfte, anmuthig und grossartig wiederzugeben." What Heinrich himself cherished as the loftiest approbation was the message from Heinrich Marschner, another arch-romanticist, and second to none in "Schrecklichkeit" in opera and symphony. Marschner rejoices that "the German school of music is so worthily represented in America. . . . Character, originality, and solidity, appear through your works; and nowhere do you imitate the inflated exhibitions of superficiality and shallowness, perceptible in many modern Italian, and alas! also in French works of the present day. . . . The originality, and deeply poetic ideas developed in your compositions, repay the painstaking to master them. (Hanover, May 10, 1849.)"

One could go on and on. Let us select but two examples: one from Mrs. M. E. Hewitt, American; the other, from the pen of Benjamin Gough, of England. Both are written to Heinrich.

How shall we crown the minstrel,
Who had brought us from the wild,
The melody that nature
Taught her free-souled mountain child!

They twined for him of Teos
The myrtle and the vine;
And the never-fading laurel
For the Chian bard divine.

And of old in tuneful Provence,
Where the monarch wore the bay
They gave the golden violet
To the victor Minstrel's lay.

But for him, who with the pilgrims,
Knelt in spirit on the sod,
While the full heart's prayer, like incense,
Went up to freedom's God;

Who, amid the swaying forest,
'Mong the old primeval trees,
Learned the glorious song of liberty
From the voices of the breeze,

While fame shall give his minstrelsy
To the world, in after days,
Let's crown him proudly in our heart,
With the deathless meed of praise.

(May 6, 1837.)

Say what is music? Is it not the thrill
That sorrow checks not—death can never kill,
That dwells in thunder's deep and awful voice
And makes the coral gales of spring rejoice;
The poesy of sounds—the rich—the wild—
Creation's herald—Nature's loveliest child!
The symphony of Heaven—the dropping myrrh
That steals upon the soul when breezes stir. . . .[6]

If one is tempted to devote so much space to Heinrich, it is
because he himself has spoken so vehemently, through word and

[6] *The Musical Enthusiast*, Respectfully inscribed to A. P. Heinrich, *London Morning Advertiser*, August 25, 1831.

music. The issue of American talent and the defense of liberty add color to the career of another visitor, Ole Bull. To the indigenous composer, facing in Ole's opinion, insurmountable odds, he sends encouragement. A reward of $1000 shall crown the most deserving delineation of a strictly domestic theme, since "the national history of America is rich in subjects both for the poet and the musician." Like Anthony, he gives homage to *Niagara* and the majestic *Solitude of the Prairie*. Here, he lives his theory in *Oleana*, the ill-fated *New Norway* of Pennsylvania, "consecrated to freedom, baptized in independence, and protected by the mighty flag of the Union." Bristow's (1825-1898) prolonged controversies with the Philharmonic, and the subsequent success of his opera *Rip Van Winkle* are merely incidents of a course, barren in loftier abstractions. With others, as with Louis Antoine Jullien, the great popularizer of all music, regardless of source or calibre, the backing of the native was a convenient pose, a humbug, perhaps, "the most splendid, bold, and dazzlingly successful humbug." Only one son of the Republic, the New Englander Asahel Abbot has honored in his oratorio *Waldenses* the New World races in their struggle for liberty. William Henry Fry (1813-1864) whose opera *Lenora* (adapted from Bulwer's *The Lady of Lyons*) was produced at the Chestnut Theatre, Philadelphia, 1845, and revived eighty-four years later in New York by Otto Kinkeldey and the *Pro Musica*, fought his battles with his pen, in the *New York Tribune*. Heinrich alone gave all of himself to American Nature and Liberty.

Heinrich's *Bird as Prophet* is the *Ornithological Combat of Kings*, an imaginary tournament between the Condor of the Andes and the Eagle of the Cordilleras. It was a commissioned job, sponsored by the Vienna *Concerts Spirituels*, and Anthony goes the whole length of a magnificent unwinding of his powers: "The Conflict in the Air . . . the Repose . . . the Battle on Land . . . the Victory." Commensurate with the gigantic subject matter is the medium "the more stringed performers, knowing their parts, the better." . . . As apotheosis Heinrich appends excerpts from Wilson's *Ornithology*. Bits of realistic anatomy enliven a humbler species, *The Migration of American Wild Passenger Pigeons.* It may be that *St. Francis walking over the Waves,* and the *Prologue* of the *Walküre* splash and foam more violently, than Anthony's *New England Feast of Shells, a Divertimento pastorale oceanico.* That, a stupendous mural, marshalled in by Home *Adieus of Departing Nymphs and Swains,* and *Fanciful Curvetings of the Mermaids in the Ocean Surf,* dying away in a morendo of the *Romantic Love Feast,* the *Sacrifice of the Shells,* vulgate *Clam-Bake!*

Those, however, are innocuous bumps in a route of such tremendous earnestness and integrity as Heinrich's. The love which he gave this country is not sham. He speaks from the heart, when he tells of the agony with which he contemplates parting with the *Land of the Free.*

> And I love thee, Columbia, with patriot zeal,
> Thy soil ever dear with my blood I'd defend,
> Should a foe to thy freedom dare step on the shore,
> Thy shore, which is always the Emigrant's friend.
> Then blame not the sigh that will sometimes arise
> For the land of my birth as a thought lingers there:
> Yet no clime but my own, would induce me to roam,
> From a country so free, and from daughters so fair.[7]

In his highly seasoned, exotic, and voluminous correspondence, extending from Paganini and the Mayors of towns of both continents to President Tyler, Heinrich invariably signs his name, as a minstrel-troubadour of nature. This laurel was bestowed on his, alas, bald head, by the " yelling, screaming, cheering, laughing, stamping " thousands who felt his appearance to be " the most remarkable, exciting, never-to-be-forgotten event."

The minstrel, the most beloved metaphor of the sentimental years, is concocted of two strains: Storm and Stress,—the " becoming "—and genteel cloying nostalgia, the " being." That it was a smooth mixture is attested by the large number of astonishingly excellent ballads which do it honor. The dualism between the bloody exuberance of the battlefield and feminine amorous

[7] *The Bohemian Emigrant,* presented at the Farewell Concert, Boylston Hall, Boston, April 29, 1826.

[156]

languor is the axis around which they revolve. Among the best is John Hill Hewitt's *The Minstrel's Return from the War.*

John Hill was one of the half-dozen of talented progeny who had for father the accomplished Englishman, James Hewitt. Landing in New York in 1792, Hewitt Sr. did his duty for romanticism by projecting photography into music. The first of his huge aquatic celluloids was a ten movement Overture expressive of a *Voyage from England to America.* Whatever omissions in the direction of disagreeable propensities of the weather the scenes contained, were presently filled in the *New Overture, to conclude with the Representation of the Ship at Sea.* It must have been a cyclonic evening when in its première April 1, 1794, it shared honors with another tempestuous programatic pillar, Haydn's "Celebrated Earthquake" from the *Seven Words.* In the miniature *Farewell to Nahant,* and still more, in the *Nahant Valse,* James Hewitt foreshadows much of Chopin's graceful interplay of meters.

His offspring was even more protean. As song writer, editor, journalist, composer, playwright, officer of the army, John Hill Hewitt had a large following in Baltimore and the South. Written in 1825, the *Minstrel's Return from the War* is his first-born. So little did anyone, least of all his brother, a fellow-publisher, suspect the latent box office appeal of the lyric, that it was printed merely as a magnanimous gesture, minus the copyright, cheating its sponsors thereby of a round $10,000.

Schönberg, Neue Sachlichkeit and other doctrines have not silenced anything of the plastic tellingness of the *Minstrel.* Those trumpets fading away in the luminousness of the "indestructible soul" ring true today. That John Hewitt expanded toward greater rhythmic wealth and a bolder use of key can be derived from another Minstrel classic, *The Knight of the Raven Black Plume.* Strikingly akin to Mendelssohn's *On Wings of Song,* the Gallant Knight is by three years his junior.

Of the many figures, refined and otherwise, spreading their lustre on the American Ballad, none is drawn with such drama, fervor, and conviction, as the Minstrel. One looks in vain among the *Little Saylors, Little Marys, Old Arm Chair,* and *Highland*

Songs for his peers. They contain something of the energy, the pace, and the breadth of the Republic. Clothed in medieval garb, the troubadour is nevertheless an inherently American figure, the apostle of equality and fraternity.

The strain is foreshadowed in the *Minstrel Boy* (composer unknown) published by J. Carr in Baltimore. In some miraculous way the message breaks through the stereotyped and rigid 4/4 pattern, cuts loose from the superfluous turns and graces, to tell that:

> The Minstrel fell! but the foeman's chain
> Could not bring his proud soul under:
> The harp he loved ne'er spoke again;
> For he tore its chords asunder.
> And said: 'No chains shall sully thee,
> Thou soul of love and bravery!'

Among the most audacious is Heinrich's *Dying Trumpeter*, its magic thread winding its harmony from the trumpet's fanfares to eternal sleep. A quaint medievalism lends exotic charm to the naïve fermatas, apoggiaturas, and arpeggios of B. Carr's *Minstrel Knight*, for voice and harp. In a chiaroscuro of half-light and dim shadow is wrapped another, anonymous, vocal Duet, published in Baltimore by John Cole, *The Lady and the Minstrel*: How comes it, sad Minstrel, thy Harp's gentle tone is awakened by sorrow?

As accessory, the American minstrel carries with him some inoffensive tinkling contrivance; preferably, a harp; in its absence a guitar, domestic or else Spanish, or the lowly banjo. The Aeolian brand, that quintessence of transcendentalism, enshrined in a halo both by Jena and Brook Farm, had to wait for Emerson and the metaphysical rhetoric of the *Dial*. Unlike the Lyre of Hölderlin and the Schlegels, this harp is not a mere figure of speech.

In all, the romantic decades of the Republic appear to have been attuned to instruments of clear, high pitched timbre: bells, flutes—of all shapes, makes, and perforations—the flageolet, oboe, and guitar. But the real pride, alike of parlor and concert platform, was the harp. The harp accompanied and extemporised, it lamented, invented variations and embellished national and operatic airs, it played solo and in concert. It was the correct finishing touch for the honorable and pure child, the fashionable " demoiselle " of Godey's, and the sweet matron who wept over Mrs. Lydia Huntley Sigourney and pondered over Miss Leslie's *Seventy-Five Receipts, More Receipts,* and *The Human Body.* Even the onslaught of the pianoforte—the new pyramidical spinets, the Grand Uprights and Grand Squares, " equal to any celebrated importation from London, Paris and Vienna, and indorsed by Liszt and Thalberg "—was impotent to break the harp's spell, whether in the flesh or emblem of Elysian fields and bowers of Ambrosian brightness.

All the more glaring is the New World's disregard of the lyre, in older climes, the very incarnation of mystic yearning. How typical of the crudeness of the frontier country that Apollo, the renowned Greek dog of the famous Castle Garden, is called upon to display his exceptional prowess in mathematics and card-sleights-of-hand without the benefit of divine strings.

But has not the Land of the Free gloriously absolved its obligation to mankind by evolving the most heavenly of instruments, a device, so " saturated with peace and harmony descending like white doves from the world supernal " that it dissolves into nothingness in more robust times: the musical glasses. Perfected by one of the nation's most ingenious amateurs, Benjamin Franklin, whose practical mind foresaw the advantages for chord producing in a spindle, the " harmonica," forgotten today like the Werther pose, is the true spokesman of the Werther era. At the time when the *Jupiter,* the *Eroica,* and the *Western Minstrel* were maturing, the nectar of the musical glasses held both continents enthralled. Did not Christoph Willibald Gluck owe a considerable part of his London fame to the virtuosity with which he handled the liquid and spindle in concert, or to his own *Concerto for harmonica and orchestra?* Goldsmith's " fine Ladies " in *The Vicar of Wakefield* would talk of nothing " but high life and high lived company . . . pictures, taste, Shakespeare, and the

[159]

musical glasses!" Among the performers were Marian Davies and the blind Marian Kirchgessner, who prompted Mozart to write an *Adagio* and *Rondo* in C for harmonica, flute, oboe, violin and cello. Naumann honored the glasses by a dozen *Sonatas*; Beethoven, by an intermezzo for *Leonora Prohaska* of his friend Duncker. At Darmstadt, C. F. Pohl, master of the Grand Duchess Louise, was engaged specially for teaching and playing the instrument.

They kindled the fancy of Jean Paul and Wieland. Schubert writes of them: " The sensitive artist is if made for this instrument: his finger tips have bathed in the blood of his own heart; each tone is a beat of his own pulse." [8] Nocturnal and pensive, invoking in its altered chords of fourth and fifth, in its rubato and sliding, a fata morgana of dulcet fancies, the harmonica tantalized and transported into Elysium the susceptible souls of ante-bellum days.

Was it not marvellous to behold a set of crude vessels giving out the " most delightful melody and the most sublime harmony, without the assistance of wind, strings, keys, and mechanism? " (The *Federal Gazette*, Maryland, March 31, 1820.) What bliss to hear *Oh, Nanny, wilt thou gang wi' me* (by request), the *Robin Adair, How Sweet in the Woodlands, My Lodging is on the Cold Ground, Star Spangled Banner*, and a variety of the most admired English, Irish, and Scotch melodies " in a manner, showing utmost exertion and guaranteed not alone to give general satisfaction to all those who favor the artist, Mr. Cartwright, with their company," but also, to dispel the unfavorable impressions made by preceding virtuosos. What satisfaction to know that the harmonica has been authorized not alone by individuals, but the most " select audiences in London, Paris, the Universities of Oxford, Cambridge, Dublin, etc." (*Baltimore American and Commercial Daily Advertiser*, March 8-10, 1820.) Alas, the musical glasses seemed to have been subject to atmospheric conditions, and many an evening of celestial harmony had to be postponed until further notice.

[8] WILLIAM LÜTGE, *Die Glassharmonika, das Instrument der Wertherzeit*, Leipzig, 1925, p. 49.

So puissant was the hold of the musical glasses that had they been silenced there and then, the catastrophe could have wrought more grief than the loss of Orpheus's lyre. For generations the glasses were the sacred shrine, ministered in illness and trouble; to canines as an anti-epileptic narcotic, to belligerents as a palm of peace. It was in their domain to conjure convalescence and death, to evoke or suppress fainting, cramps, convulsions, and paralysis. Loreleyan, they eventually destroyed their hearers; many a member of the noble brigade of artists in Baltimore, Annapolis, and farther south, summoning the spiritual voices of the waters from three to seven p. m. for all of fifty cents, adumbrated the tragic fate of Schumann or Smetana. They either became insane, or, like Chopin and Schubert, died at the pinnacle of their powers.

Heinrich may have had a premonition. He steers clear of their lurid call. But he did anticipate another musical fashion. Is the presence of Zozo, the negro lad, in his *Deserted Mother* merely an incident? Is he part of the setting, a black spot in a sea of radiant light? Almost to the very day that the *Deserted Mother* was or was not pleasing the Quaker City (the play was repeated on March 7), up north, in New York, the *National Advocate* advertised an evening of Richard III, with " gracious accommodation of the whites by some gentlemen of color." Staged in the " African Grove . . . back of the Hospital " it made use of fashionable glees, minuets and ballads. The intensity of its climax, the stirring " gib me nother horse" was achieved by means of deafening rolls of drum and clarinet.

What was the ultimate fate of the Negroes? There is no telling. Had the Great White Way already then awakened to the Aladdin's Lamp of Harlem's syncopation and Blues? The hypothesis is justified, if only in part. Entitled *Sports of New York*, an illiterate pamphlet of Simon Snipe lists as the chief attractions of the Metropolis of 1823, a " Trip to the races with two appropriate songs " and an " Evening at the African Theatre."

But the great wave of quasi-African swing and saxophone was not yet. Not yet was Europe taken sufficiently aback by " the sudden shock, the brusque awakening, by that new school of rhythm, the new elements of sonority, the bringing into focus of percussion "[9] to sanction *Golliwogg's Cake-Walk* and the *Rites of Spring*. Not yet did jazz become an antidote for rosewater and absurd decorativeness. Not yet had the caravan of musicologists and victrolas advanced into the wilderness. Not yet had the Black celebrated his revenge over his oppressors. Not yet was there any suspicion of the pathos and the poignancy of the songs of labor and of play. Even the minstrels, the first exploiters of Negro humor as seen by objective eyes, were not yet popularized.

Even Heinrich with his keen perception of the latent developments in the direction of nationalism, did not give the Negro more than passing attention. They interested him merely as kind, primitive children. He enjoyed their company. In the forest stillness Anthony plays by the hour dirges and "Dead Marches" to his "poor departed wife" to the delighted black visitors. They cannot get enough of the plaintive airs; why, they pay for them!

The first Negro of the opera forms part of the equipment of the Drury Lane Theatre as far back as 1768, libretto by Isaac Bickerstaffe, music by Charles Dibdin. On native soil the stimulus is provided by a German, Gottlieb Graupner, who gave the *Gay Negro Boy*, with banjo, in character. So at least goes the story. If so, it stopped the show, namely, *Oronooko*, December 30, 1799, at the Federal Street Theatre, Boston. If true, it proved the kernel from which sprang the luxurious growth of American minstrelsy. At first they were gay, infectious in their laughter. Only rarely do they strike a lugubrious undertone, such as the *Lament* by Benjamin Carr, a sweet and mournful plea for pity for the poor, orphaned white. He has no wife to grind his corn, no mother to bring him milk. Later there came Thomas Rice, with tumultuous bravos for *Jim Crow*, and an insatiable thirst for more: still later the Big Four, Dan Emmett, Frank Brower, Dick Pelham, and Billy Whitlock, the *Virginia Minstrels*. They grew in size, following, repertoire, skill. Their guitars and bones, their

---

[9] MILHAUD, *French Music since the War.*

clowning and butts, their witticism and good humor, their hidden tear and their breathless dancing, their parades and posters, their wailing and crooning, became a real adjunct of American living. Who did not revel at *Zip Coon*, the *Big Sunflower*, *Old Dan Tucker*, or kept still to the frolics of their triangle and tambourine? And when George Washington Dixon gave the world *Betsy Baker* and the tender *Coal-Black Rose*, the dynasty of Cork and Satin troupes, and ascendency of the national in music was assured.

To them fell the first recognition of indigenous spontaneity and color, the first acknowledgment of talent and skill. And what an acknowledgment! America could not supply quarters large enough to house the Campbell, Bryant, Christy, or Elias Howe troupes. Barnum's *Museum*, the New York *Palace of Music*, Mechanic's Hall, all gave out. On and on they went. The British Isles were taken by storm. What matter if the spirituals and reels had little or nothing of the real Negro? They were novel, exotic, vivacious, up-to-date. They were swell entertainment. What is more, they performed a service for which the universal language of Carr, Hewitt, or Heinrich proved inadequate. They brought to Europe the first pungent taste of *My Old Kentucky Home, Old Dog Tray, Oh Boys,* and *Jeanie with the Light Brown Hair.* They were a wonderful propaganda for Foster— for a number of years E. P. Christy, the minstrel singer—was the official liaison officer between him and the public.

There was something in the Negro lyrics which went directly to the heart. By the middle of the century there was not a person in the country who did not know *Old Folks at Home.* " It is on everybody's tongue. Pianos and guitars groan with it, night and day; sentimental ladies sing it: sentimental young gentlemen warble it in midnight serenades: volatile young ' bucks ' hum it: boatmen roar it out stentorially at all times: all the bands play it . . . flute players agonize over it . . . the chambermaid sweeps and dusts to the measured cadence . . . the butcher boy treats you to a strain of it." [10]

[10] *The Albany State Register,* 1852.

John C. Dwight (1813-1893), the Germanophile, became alarmed. He warned against the African's hold, as detrimental "to the purity and dignity of American music," spoke of their skin-deepness, of their lack of genuine emotion or passion. It accomplished little. The minstrel songs survive the Civil War, and are crowded out only by the spicier swing of the World conflict.

Different is the case of the Indian. If Heinrich was not young enough to foretell the great vogue of African rhythm or to appreciate the Negro as a musico-ethnographic entity, the Redskin is Anthony's hero. It has been argued that Indian music is not truly American music, since citizens of the United States are not descendants of the first inhabitants of prairie and canyon as the Slavs and Finns are. What then is American? Certainly no review of romantic tendencies in music can pass in silence the cult of the Indian, the favorite leit-motif of Edward MacDowell and Cadman. Who knows when and why it was born? Were not the Pilgrims charmed and made uncomfortable by the melancholy amorous chants? Back in 1634, William Wood, on a visit to Plymouth and Massachusetts Bay reports on the weird Indian melodies: "Their musick is lullabies to quiet their children, who are generally as quiet as if they had neither spleens or lungs. To hear one of these Indians unseene, a good eare might easily mistake their untaught voyce for the warbling of a well tuned instrument. Such command have they of their voices."

England, not the home country, printed the earliest of Indian lays on record. Under the corrupted title of *Alknomook* it was announced as "the death song of the Cherokee Indians, an *Original Air*, brought from America by a gentleman long conversant with the Indian tribes, and particularly with the Nation of the Cherokees. The words, adapted to the air by a Lady," allegedly Anne Hone Hunter, better known as Haydn's hostess of *Solomon Symphony* days, and author of "My mother bids me bind my hair."

No wonder, the Chief was as British as kidney stew, or a Gilbert-Sullivan admiral. On crossing the ocean the song, changed to "The Sun Sets in Night" is woven into the opera *Tammany*, staged March 3, 1794, at the John Street Theatre, New York. It had everything in its favor: the Chief's name had been corrected; the score was prepared by James Hewitt; the libretto was the work of Mrs. Anne Julia Hatton, a sister of Mrs. Siddons; the hero, a noble chieftain, is burned with his love, the fair Manana, in a wigwam. It was put on with unusual magnificence, and acted with a definite flair. In those days the feeling between the Federalists and the anti-Federalists ran high. To the latter belonged Mrs. Hatton and the powerful Tammany Society. A violent controversy over the merits of the opera was the outcome. The anti-Federalists fondled their own; while their opponents denounced it in the *New York Magazine* as a "wretched thing," and William Dunlap, the erudite gentleman, who knew whereof he spoke, called it a "melange of bombast."

None of the music has been published. But the groundtone of the work appears in the prologue, supplied by another poet, R. B. Davis.

> Secure the Indian roved his native soil,
> Secure enjoyed the produce of his toil,
> Nor knew, nor feared a haughty master's pow'r
> To force his labors, or his gains devour.
> And when the slaves of Europe here unfurled
> The bloody standard of their servile world
> When Heaven, to curse them more, first deigned to bless
> Their base attempts with undeserved success,
> He knew the sweets of Liberty to prize,
> And lost on earth, he sought her in the skies;
> Scorned, life divested of its noblest good,
> And seal'd the cause of Freedom with his blood.

A less strenuous course was the lot of another quasi-Indian tune, published 1799 in William Beresford's *Annals of a Voyage around the World, but more particularly to the Northwest Coast of America*. One becomes now conscious of an "Indianization" of the subject matter. Among others, Dryden's *Arthur and Emmeline* is made more authentic through the interpolation of Zuni *Canoe Songs*.

Those naïve accents fade into air alongside of Heinrich's glorification of the Big Chief. Granted, Zozo was a piece of stage furniture, the Indian, the noble savage, is the most magnificent fiction of Anthony's fancy. He represents progressive stages in the great process of liberation; is the emblem of fairness, justice, breath of vision, spirituality, ceaseless aspiration, courage. Not a major opus of Heinrich's that does not pay tribute to the *Son of the Woods,* simple, mysterious, and proclaiming the vanity of all earthly things.

Like his twin, the Redskin of Fenimore Cooper, Heinrich's aborigine belongs, in the words of Mark Twain, " to an extinct tribe which never existed." The pedestrian, the every-day, is not for him. He dwells in celestial halls. Only as exception to a general rule, does Heinrich extend a realistic treatment to his Indian motives: Chipewa, Hopi, Blackfoot, Shawanee and Mingo, as in the *Treaty of William Penn with the Indians,* op. 35, Concerto grosso for full orchestra, or in the squaw dance in the *Landing of the Pilgrims.* Otherwise, each one of the annoyingly exotic Black Thunders, Shenandoahs, Pushmatahas, Tecumseths, Logans, are but a mask for the protagonist Heinrich, his own striving and frustration, a duologue between his own heights and depths. Like him they are sensitive to the whispers of elm and birch, like him, in love with liberty, aflame for a glorious chimera. Like him, they have no present. What a past is theirs! Emblazoned in chivalry and sympathy, it is a prophecy of a still more radiant future: the brotherhood of men of all colors and creeds.

Particularly pregnant with this imagery is the *Landung der Pilger Väter,* or *Der Felsen von Plymouth.* To think that the elated epic was conceived in " a desolate comfortless chamber, without any fire whatsoever . . . as also without the aid and solace of a pianoforte." Had such reinforcement been forthcoming, the world of magic melody might have been robbed of *Baletto indico nazionale,* a vociferous manifestation of squaw gratitude for white man's gifts, or of a *Fugue,* elucidating the Confucian wisdom of the great spirit Manitou. In more serene vein, an *Adagio tremolante molto agitato* transcribes the moonlit waves of the Gulfstream.

The Indian was tremendously useful to Heinrich. He made excellent orchestral fodder, and the list of instruments heaving and thundering in behalf of the melodramatic savage lives up to its source of inspiration. The Zunis and Hopis held out magnificent symphonic promise. Therefore only a few isolated items are scored for solo: The *Indian Carnival,* with *Camanche Revel, Sioux Gaillards,* and *Manitou Air Dance, Imoinda,* an Indian love song, and *Ne-La-Me* (Morning Star) " pianoforte and voice epitomes," but the bulk of aborigines go the full, unabridged, the romantic gamut of symphonic splendor. Cornet, bugle, strings, bassoons, drums, each choir floats the national brilliancy. *Pocohontas,* or, *Prize of the Wilderness,* later to win the commendation of the finished German virtuoso, William Sharfenberg, and *Pushmataha, Fantasia instrumentale,* written " under peculiar circumstances which have given it great wildness," demand super-Berlioz bands. Note the affinity with Beethoven: Anthony begs " that no decision on their merits be made, unless performed by a master."

It may be that Heinrich's run on Indian subjects was in a degree occasioned by Forrest's spectacular success in Stone's *Metamore,* or, *The Last of the Wampanoags,* at Park Theatre, New York, a great actor in a great rôle, or by the score of other favorites: *Pokota, the Red Men of the Wood,* in Wheatley's *Sassacus* or, *The Indian Wife,* and *Pawnie Chief, Onylda, Ontiata.* This does not detract an inch from the poetry and superiority of his romantic vision. It would be gratifying to report that Heinrich has produced another *Life for the Tsar,* or a *Peer Gynt* suite. Occasionally, one senses something of the breathless energy, the sweep, or the magnificence which Heinrich reads into the aborigines. Praiseworthy is his abstinence from superficial reproduction of unexpected stresses or downward leaps. The discovery of the pentatonic syntax had to wait another century. And if one agrees with MacDowell that nationalism is a penetration with the ethos of bygone cultures, rather than a photograph of rhythmic and melodic peculiarities, Heinrich's Chiefs are as true to the soil of Kentucky as *In the Indian Lodge,* or all of Cadman. Naïve touches are not wanting. In *The Manitou Air Dance* glissandos, runs, grace notes and trills, scored in the highest heights of the treble, are supposed to give the illusion of ether and its inhabitants. The unprepared changes from A minor to D minor and D major in the *Camanche Revel,* translate the daring of the redskins. Throughout there is a fine freedom of meter: transferred accent, triplets, pauses, tom-toms, suspensions.

Such was the mighty call of the Republic that Heinrich outshines his hosts in yet another phase of romanticism, the woeful. Its legitimate dwelling place is the ballad; less, the opera, and hardly ever the sonata. Not that awe-inspiring nocturnal tale of Bürger's which set the whole wheel going, is its prototype, but rather the simpler, homelier sing song of Loewe. However, if the American Song is built on German syntax, its sentiment is English: the moor, the sea, the Highlands. Never militant, bellicose, or blazing, it is entirely devoid of Storm and Stress. A future, no matter how sparkling, is not within its orbit. It feasts alone on reminiscence. It is a careful genteel fashion, where virtue never goes unrewarded. Its statement is the tear. Of sentiments only the every day is sanctioned, of emotions melancholy alone is considered ennobling.

Of this syrupy gloom the natives, John Hewitt, and Benjamin Franklin Baker, J. C. Baker with *Where Can the Soul Find Rest?* and William Clifton with *The Last Link is Broken,* voicing the motif of noble resignation and self-pity provide as redolent illustrations as the newcomers: Frederick William Crouch, with the beloved *Kathleen Mavourneen* and *That Death should sever two hearts that could have loved forever,* and the past master of the genre, Joseph Philip Knight.

What *Alexander's Ragtime Band* meant a generation back, what *Scatterbrain* and *The little Man who was not there,* mean today, the superbly saccharine ballad, saturated to a *Nevermore* of hopeless docility was to the disciples of Fitz-Green Halleck. For some years anything more pretentious, opera, oratorio or chamber music, no matter how flawless the execution, drew mediocre crowds. Of the seventy odd concerts in New York of 1839 ten were given over to sacred music, ten to operatic arias, six to instrumentalists, fourteen were mixed, but half had resorted to the "Weal and Woe." Elegies blossomed more lushly than the sentiments of which they sang. Fragile and innocuous as each of them was, they expanded into a tidal wave, an engulfing torrent, a national institution which crowned and undid composers and singers overnight. The Englishman Knight emerges as a national figure by dint of a single resounding elegy written on a stay of some months, *The Cradle of the Deep,* the aura of which even the famous *O Lord, I have wandered* by Henry Russell, British organist, singer and composer, was unable to dim. Russel stayed here nine seasons, a sufficient term to become the sponsor of *Mother Songs.* His chief forte were the paeons of ripe age: *The Brave Old Oak, The Old Sexton, The Old Bell,* a motif which he transfers directly to Stephen Foster. A reviewer in Boston wrote that the only item missing was *The Old Boot-Jack.* No artist was exempt from the fetters of this sobby vogue. Malibran, who fainted from emotion on hearing Beethoven's *Fifth,* chooses for her American Farewell, at the very height of her fame, not Boildieu, Mozart nor Rossini, but tearful trivialities.

Many were the tricks of the trade. To blacken the gloom still further, the composer frequently steps out to address his listeners in the first person, and to lay bare the emotional spasms which gave birth to his brain child. Heinrich is a confirmed devotee of this sort of frame for his laments, and merciless are the strokes with which he portrays his cold, hunger, privation, and loneliness. George J. Webb deepens the gloomy sentence of relentless death by a lengthy foreword, beginning: "Something more than a year ago, a friend of the writer, a young gentleman of fine intellect and of noble heart, was snatched by the hand of death from all the endearments of life, in a brilliant career of usefulness."

Nor were the singers blind to showmanship. After an especially heartrending recital by Russell of his own *Woodman, spare that Tree,* there rose from the audience suddenly an old gentleman to inquire tremulously amid general stillness: " Mr. Russell, tell me, in the name of Heaven, was the tree spared? " " It was, sir." " Thank God, I breathe again! " And pacified, the dotard sank back in his seat. More than any other memento of Victorianism, the ballad is a chronicle of American tastes and manners.

The grandiloquent elegies of Woodworth, Morris and Sargent, which had inspired Knight and Russell, " stood breast high in the common stream of sympathy " and remained the possession of the Republic long after the English had departed to their mother country. In parlor and dressing room, concert hall and church, were performed " not alone with power, but also with love " the plaintive dolorous refrains. Knight's setting of Thomas H. Bayly's *She Wore a Wreath of Roses*, where the heroine progresses from rosebuds to full blooms, and, finally, a widow's cap, was given in costume. A few years later, with Stephen Foster, these staples of song-mongery yield to something directly from the heart, and American balladry reaches its high for all times.

Judged objectively, from the perspective of reason and musical structure, the lament of Heinrich's day, was in the expression of the witty lady-editor of *Godey's*, " lamentable." Certainly, their musical freshness is the least constituent to account for their vogue. Hardly ever does the sentiment expressed in the poem engender fertilization of melody and rhythm. Always lean, the tunes not infrequently approach rollicking bits of doggerel. Cupids and Roses, dying brides, *Little Sailors*, and *Little Marys*, *Oh, the Sight Entrancing!* and *Oh! ye Dead!* fail even distantly to suggest the terror of the *Erlkönig* or the pang of *Gretchen am Spinnrade*. Take the two anonymous glees, printed by Carr in Baltimore—one of Ellen, " pride of howry Richmond Thames "; the other, with flute obbligato, of *Highland Mary*, a setting of Burns. That " pitying tear " which is the prerequisite of one and all, wets alone the rhymes. Even an artist of the stamp of B. Carr lets *Poor Mary* shiver for a departed soul in pitch black night to vivacious and perky arpeggios in F major. Even Heinrich follows the anguish of the *Broken Heart* with rippling merry

cadences. Well may the sob grow "pensive," "timid," "lonely,"
"dear," the barrel airs trickle their joyous rounds of appoggiaturas
and Alberti basses. The onomatopoiea is of the crudest: "Pit a
Pat," "Tink, tink, a tink, tink." Who would recognize Beethoven
in *Music, Love and Wine,* or *O Swiftly Glides the Bonnie Boat,* or
else Cimarosa, Haydn, Pleyel, Mozart, and Paisiello in still more
far-fetched adaptations, *The Manly Heart, the Parting Kiss, the
Knitting Girl* and *The Sweet Maid?* As late as the fifties Dwight
could not break loose from the odious task of thus "seasoning"
Adelaide.

Alone New England shows signs of revolt. In his *Hymns*
Lowell Mason (1792-1872) strikes a note of sincere yearning,
which is taken up by Thomas Hastings (1784-1872) of Middle-
boro, Charles Zeuner (1795-1857), Henry Kemple Oliver (1800-
1885), and James Webb (1803-1887). William Batchelder Bradbury's *Golden Series: Shower of Sunday School Melodies* and
Bright Jewels for Home make a fortune. Indeed, these sturdy
and enterprising New Englanders till the soil for the gravity of
Dwight and Margaret Fuller. To them is due the revival of
oratorio and sacred melody, which form so intriguing a phe-
nonmenon of the late twenties. In a vague way it may be seen
as a parallel to the rebirth of Catholicism with Schlegels and
Schleiermacher. Oliver's *Federal Street* and the *National Lyre;*
Mason's *My Faith looks up to Thee* and *From Greenland's Icy
Mountains;* Thomas Hastings' *Musica Sacra,*—all were related
and caused the temporary distaste for opera, and the lull in the
trivial. Cantata and Hymn are rulers, for the day. Sacred Societies multiply. Bethlehem, and the world at large are enriched
by the American-born Jacob Van Vleck (1751-1831), Peter Rick-
secker (1891-1873) and Francis Florentine Hagen (1815-1907),
and the Germans Georg Gottfried Miller (1762-1821), Johann
Christian Bechler (1784-1857), and Peter Wolle (1792-1871)
for whom colonial life had a religious purpose, and who were
able to give more genuine expression to the faith which they
bore than any European of the same age. Unsophisticated, sincere,
the vast out-put of the Bethlehem fraternity, presents a still virgin

source of the same romantic impulse which dictated Beethoven's *Christ on the Mount of Olives* and Berlioz' *Requiem*.

The *Baltimore American* carries the following editorial on June 9, 1820: "We are sensible, the generous, the humane, and the lovers of Music, will be gratified at the notice of the last rehearsals in St. Paul's Church of an *Oratorio* for charitable purpose." It mentions the high degree of perfection attained by the choir of the Church, and the superior endowments of the Ladies and Gentlemen, Amateur and Professors who are to assist. The enthusiasm was on the whole deserved, for not only did the program contain works by Händel, Haydn, and Martini, but the soloists included some of the outstanding musicians of the time.

The most sacred year on record in the history of America is 1823, and when July 2, 1829, there was announced a concert on musical glasses "in the spacious room, occupied by Mr. Cartwright, on Broadway, four doors below Fulton," the event was greeted as deliverance from the clutches of spirituality.

The belief that all men are brothers is the Bible of all true romanticists. No romanticist was more convinced of it than Heinrich, not even Beethoven. The cult began in the intimate outpourings of the soul between the ageing Goethe and Bettina, Wackenroder and Tieck, Schubert and Vogl, Beethoven and Waldstein, Schumann and Brahms. The result is a strong realization of one's mission and one's obligation to society. Nowhere was this service more sacred than in early America; nowhere was man ready to sacrifice and sweat for it more. Never does the ecstatic Heinrich wax as eloquent as when he is transported to testify to the divine charge of his calling. Rank and inequality in social station cease to exist face to face with ignorance and lack of taste in music. "Mein Gott in Himmel! de peebles what made John Tyler President ought to be hung! He knows no more about music than an oyshter!"

Societies for promotion of music, sacred, operatic, symphonic, or national; for the betterment of general taste, are as old as music in America. Wholehearted and portly, they served the communion of kindred spirits better than the platonic effusions of Schiller and even Beethoven. Among the earliest are the *St. Cecilia* of Charleston and the *Collegium Musicum* of Bethlehem. Without the latter there would be no *B-minor Mass* today. Hordes of others, with an honor roll only slightly less distinguished, have escaped the notice of the historian. Hanover, New Hampshire, Harvard, Fredericksburg, Dartmouth College, Richmond, Cincinnati, all of them brimmed with their *Uranian, Euterpean, Philharmonic, Choral,* and other euphonious groups, determined to sow the seed of musical culture in spite of fires, apathy, and none too ethical competitors. Of exceptional lustre is the *Händel and Haydn* of Boston which may have got herself born as early as 1814.

In March 1815, Graupner, the German, signs an invitation to consider the expediency of forming " a *Society* for cultivating and improving a correct taste in the performance of sacred music." In reality, he accomplishes more: *The Händel and Haydn.* Who cares whether or not the claim of the *Händelians* to the premières of *Messiah* and *Creation* is borne out by cold fact: theirs is the badge of honor in promulgating the choicest of European genius. Hardly a name that is not inscribed in their scrolls. Only in. New England could it be born, and what it gave, is attested by John K. Paine (1839-1906), George Whitefield Chadwick (1854-1931) Edward MacDowell (1861-1908) and the moderns, Charles Ives, Roger Sessions, and Roy Harris.

In its initial concert the *Händel and Haydn,* presided over by Thomas Webb, employed a chorus of 100, ten of them women, and an orchestra of 13. There were two *Musical Fund Societies*: one founded in Philadelphia, 1821; the other of Boston, 1847. Among the valiant *Davidbündler* of the earlier were Benjamin Carr, Raynor Taylor, Hupfeld, and Cross. Associated with Graupner in the *Händel and Haydn* were the very Ostinellis who helped out in the *Deserted Mother*; he, the best violinist in Boston; his wife, the daughter of James Hewitt, in her own right, a first-class organist, pianist, and singer. Asa Peabody and Thomas Smith Webb, George Webb and William Mason, each and all lent the best there was to give to the cause of musical education. New York whose *Philharmonic* was inaugurated with a splendid memorial concert to Daniel Schlesinger, the talented pianist, had to make larger concessions to the masses; suppers and balls were indispensable to the *Euterpean*, which ran for nearly half a century, and to the *Concordia*. Not so Baltimore. Membership in the lately identified and discovered *Harmonick Society* was at a premium. Select and decorous in tone, it was troubled infinitely more by whom to discriminate against than whom to admit. In spite of such exclusiveness, its members numbered 300; alongside of " professors " and publishers many of the city's leaders took its music with a vengeance: cigars, late-comers, and refreshments were taboo. They initiated lectures on the comparative merits of Mozart and Haydn. Eventually, a *Mozart Society* with its own *Mozart Hall* came into being.

Through these bodies America first learned to know Weber, Mozart and Mendelssohn. In 1831, Ureli Corelli Hill, a Yankee, possessed of much energy, shrewdness, pluck and self-reliance, directed the *New York Sacred Society* in Händel's *Messiah,* and a few years hence, in Mendelssohn's *St. Paul,* Beethoven's *Fifth* and Weber's Overture to *Oberon*. When Hill's career of usefulness was over, he took morphine.

Into this tumultuous maelstrom of activity the American musician was thrown. He had no middle road. What the German sought by instinct the American romanticist accomplished by necessity. From Moses Mendelssohn and Sulzer to E. T. A. Hoffmann and Wagner the Sehnsuchts-poets dream of a *Gesamtkunstwerk*. The artist had to become singer, actor, mime, player, not because such outlets interested him personally, but because the totality, the " Ganzheit " of his creation depended upon them. Of immediate contingency for such a varicolored sphere of interests there was little in Germany. In America such a need was axiomatic.

No matter what the latent poetic gifts of Schumann or Mendelssohn, no matter how sound the pianism of Beethoven, there was little or no opportunity for their fruition. How different the American scene! Hopkinson sets the style. The first matriculant in what is now the University of Pennsylvania, a leading lawyer, traveller, statesman, humorist, a controversialist who wielded a cogent pen, he is remembered as the first native composer. John Hill Hewitt is his peer: editor of the *Republican* of Greenville, South Carolina; the *Massachusetts Journal* of Boston; the *Baltimore American* and Washington *Capitol*. A composer of more than passing ability, he yet triumphs in a poetical contest over Edgar Allan Poe. And who could challenge the pictorial quality of the opening lines of the prize-winning *Song of the Wind*:

> Whence come ye with your odor-laden wings,
> Oh, unseen wanderers of the summer night
> Who, sportive kiss my lyre's trembling strings?

The singer turned poet in order to notify his patrons of a postponed performance, or of his recovery

> Hence, cough and cold, you threaten here in vain,
> Hoarseness, avaunt, Richard's himself again! [11]

They were born to versatility, these intrepid Van Hagens who undertook to cater to the spiritual uplift of their charges, and teach them every instrument in captivity, while their wives and daughters attended to their sartorial and culinary needs. Baltimore's *American and Commercial Daily Advertiser,* January 4, 1820, announces that Mr. Duclairack, having taught dancing, fencing and music at Georgetown College under the direction of Bishop Dubourg and Bishop Neale offers his services as instructor on the violin, flute, and piano—the terms $12.00. On February 8, of the same year, Signor Helene, " lately from Italy, the same who has played in New York with great applause on five different instruments *at once* " promises to play in the course of the evening simultaneously the Italian Violi, Pandeau Pipes, Chinese Bells, Turkish Cymbals, and tenor drum to the tune of *Lodoiska, Marseilles, Bonaparte Grand March,* and a *Hungarian Waltz.* A month later we meet Mr. Cartwright, performing on his " Grand set of Harmonic Glasses, which for melody, expression, and

[11] The *Baltimore American*, January 2, 1820.

sweetness of tone challenge competition," to the accompaniment of "philosophic Fire-Works" guaranteed to do their job without smoke or gunpowder. Later in March we come across a young gentleman, respectfully informing the public that he wishes to impart German Flute together with German grammar, "on the most accommodating terms, either at their residence or his own lodging."

At Niblo's on lower Broadway, between the house of Cooper and John Jacob Astor, where Irving worked on the *Life of Washington*, many of the vocalists owed the larger residue of their fame to their reputation as chefs. In turn, they guaranteed that "strictest attention will be paid to the literary and moral improvement of the scholars": [12] It speaks well for the openmindedness of the time that Raynor Taylor, as Lyons before and Dwight after him, could steal away some hours from the pulpit to partake in *The Flight of the Fancy* and risqué family skits as actor-singer, and play in Baltimore and Annapolis "the portable grand-piano." Charles Edward Horn (1788-1863) who came to Boston in 1847, was conductor of the *Händel & Haydn*, composer of operas, singer and publisher. The duties of Thomas Hastings (1784-1872) as associate of the *New York Normal Institute*, essayist, editor, and writer, did not keep him from producing the words to 600 hymns, the music to 1,000. A master on piano, horn, trombone, was Henry C. Timm (1811-1892) who settled in New York in 1835, and later conducted operas and played the organ in Baltimore. Let us not forget Heinrich and others, too numerous to mention.

In this *laissez-faire* society, teaching, playing, selling, conducting, preaching, all went hand in hand. Obviously, retailing pianos was hazardous, to say the least. The advertisements of instrument merchants are samples of refined oratory. On the occasion of removing his Music Store to 78 Market Street, Thomas Carr in Baltimore announces an arrival of Grand and Square Pianofortes in 6 octaves "made entirely on a *new principle* (combining more durability in the mechanism and strength of tone

[12] *Baltimore American and Daily Advertiser*, January 3, 1820.

than those formerly imported) and lately introduced by *Beethoven* and *Moschelles* in the principal cities of Europe." Vehemently they parade their wares: " squares in sweetness and uprightness of tones not equalled anywhere in the world, silverkeyed, silver-stringed; trumpets, bugles, oboes, flutes with nine keys made by the celebrated Koch of Vienna and now used and recommended by that eminent flute player Furstenau," violins, cellos, bridges, pegs, mutes, mouthpieces, strings, London-made fifes and pic-colos by Potter and Meltzer, wire of every size and description, auctioned off with kitchen pans, Madeira wine, herring, lard, tobacco, gold epaulettes, and once, at least, with a Presbyterian burying lot. But a real bond of some occult sympathy seemed to mutually attract sheet music and umbrellas. Who can divine the " why " of the mysterious magnetism? For the pairing of glees, catches, and first rate fiddles with " umbrellas of a superior kind made of the best senshaw " the world of music is indebted to a certain Roach of Baltimore, in 1820. Between 1825-1850 Boston specialized in these bilinear trades, in the houses of Ashton, Prentiss and Keith.

How these carriers of sunlight into the musical night survived, is a miracle. Their helpfulness was wanted in yet other channels. With the famine of instrumental fare in the Republic, the composer-performers willy-nilly turned publishers. With their own hands they printed and engraved, anywhere and everywhere: Graupner, H. Mann, and Peter Van Hagen (1796-1836), an excellent player on oboe and double bass, who conducted piano and organ classes, and led the band at the Federal Street Theatre in Boston, high up over " Warranted Imported Piano Forte Ware Houses," and later in spacious establishments bequeathed from father to son. What is more, they freely promoted music by their own " For the Gentlemen," Shaw's *Columbia Sacred Harmony* and *Instrumental Selections for the Schools*. That theirs was a real need, can be argued from the avalanche of instruction books, with and without a leader, for piano, oboe, violin, the Spanish guitar, flageolet, harmonica, whole-and-half-toned; and for tuning. Adaptations of the loosest kind, arrangements of Beethoven *Sym-*

phonies, Rossini, opera, and *Marches* were turned out by the thousand.

In New England, Bradlee, Samuel Parker, W. Oakes, J. A. Dickson; farther south, Hewitts, the Carrs, Meinecke, each kept a keen lookout for the latest morsels of domestic and imported fare. Vision they had galore, marvelous pluck and perseverance. If no dealers could be found to handle the printed product, they sold it on street corners, as did young Elias Howe, the farm boy, who established a large business in 1843. Francis Millet, a fellow-traveler of Lafayette, was composer, singer, violinist, organist, and yet did a thriving business as publisher. Was William Dunlap, his erudition in Mandeville, Lucretius, Leonidas, and Voltaire notwithstanding, as useful in awakening the common man to a higher sense of beauty than Heinrich, or yet, his namesake and compatriot, H. Christian Timm, virtuoso on piano, horn, trombone, and organ, leader of chorus and opera, writer of part-songs, and piano arrangements, and a *Grand Mass*, eventually, President of the *Philharmonic*! Let us give his due to the indefatigable Lowell Mason, Boston's native son, psychologist, lecturer, composer,—and this New World's contribution to the old—pioneer of music as a part of man's general education, in the public school.

But absorption in music claims its sacrifices. A sensitive nature, capable of savoring emotion, and of reproducing this emotion to others, is not necessarily immune from bids for popular favor, to wit the very *Freischütz*. Such has been the curse of romanticism in Germany, France, and Italy, that the sanction of the ego has led to the expansion of egotism and eccentricity. With the mutual approach and wedding of the arts in America, with composer, publisher and performer centered in one person, the abuses of showmanship were bound to soar. They did. In this branch of romanticism, the frontier country would in vain look for its peers. The Star system is intrinsic to these shores. The young Hallam's *Munro*, Thomas Wignell's *Darby*, and Shield's *Poor Soldier*, with its run of eighteen nights, are the humble beginnings. It is conceivable that the glowing reports of the physical attributes of Miss George and the invincible pulchritude of Miss Broadhurst,

Miss Melmoth and other stars of the *American, Hallam,* and *Reinagle-Wignell* troupes do not particularly deviate from the Old World technique. By the time of Heinrich exhibitionism is at full, mad swing. Heinrich, Jullien, Russell, Ole Bull, Jenny Lind, what a dazzling parade of tinsel and foppery!

It was enough to overwhelm a veteran like Henri Herz, " le bel Henri," who left France in 1845, "muni d' un bon piano, d'un sac de nuit, et d'une petite malle," but remained here six years, going as far as California, Mexico, and the West Indies.[18]

Herz is overawed, or says he is, by the size of the concert posters, the realism of the musical offerings, the mannerisms, the mammoth buildings, mammoth rivers, mammoth girls; the impromptu speeches, with which he, among others, was expected to regale audiences in a foreign tongue, and by his manager-shadow, a merciless dictator in all matters of diet, fees, schedule, and mode of living, who defined music as " the art of attracting the largest crowds and earning the highest profits."

What Henri did not see, is the American prodigy. He missed the Hutchinson ménage and the Bakers, born to New Hampshire, twenty-two strong, who disbursed their lachrymal repertoire with the expert aid of their young. No infant was spared the rigors of diligence, unheated halls, and nightly appearances before the lamps. There was something infinitely " attendrissant" about an entire " corps de famille" and the van Hagens and Hewitts Srs. were satisfied to play temporarily second fiddle, if only to illumine with more flashing glow the talented flesh of their flesh. Singing and fiddling began in the cradle. Not Paganini or Liszt, but alone Mozart is the peer in age of this army of wonder-children.

At the turn of the century the East, Philadelphia, Baltimore, Alexandria, Richmond, were all in a flurry over " Miss Marianne, five years old, eight months from Paris," the daughter of the harpist, Madame d'Hémard. Her " astounding powers, vocal and instrumental" shone nightly in Dezède's *Overtures,* Kotzwara's *Battle of Prague,* and *The Cottage Maid.* On the piano

---

[18] *Mes Voyages en Amerique,* Paris, 1866, p. 3.

Signor Masi, of Baltimore, was doing the *Battle of Lake Champlain and Plattsburg* and *Sonatas with flute obbligato* by Jadin. The Monumental City had in addition its team of Miss and Master Ewington, specialists in hornpipe solos and Pas de Deux.

New York could show other prodigies, Jamieson, Holloway, and the greatest of all, Louisa Lane, later Mrs. Henry Hunt. If a concert began at six in the afternoon, and kept it up till two in the morning, a real star would not contribute to it more than two or three ditties. Jenny Lind was treated with a veneration which continued in force to the days of the Civil War, when Essipova and Anton Rubinstein vied night after night with the huge *Combination Concerts of the Rive-King*, and *Donaldi-Rummel Concert Companies Consolidated.*[14]

Sensationalism in America, thinks Herz, can go no further. " L'imagination des artistes est à bout. On a tout essayé. On a donné des concerts costumés, des concerts en action, des concerts religieux, dansants, historiques, improvisés, sérieux, comiques, pyrotechniques, bacchiques, gastronomiques, et diaboliques!" With shivers Herz recalls a Boston musical soirée where an excruciating voice, unaccompanied, exhausted all the known repertoire of hymns of every creed and sect; a seance of musical virtuoso-spitting in Baltimore, and yet another, where Mephisto conducted an invisible orchestra with wild gesticulations and sardonic laughter. Another gave a surrealistic version of Noah's Ark. Fortunes were made by imitating the squeak of an angry hag. A charlatan of the first rank, Jullien conducted with studded baton from a crimson platform, edged in gold, with a fantastic gilt figure supporting the desk. One pianist showed off by playing scales and arpeggios with one hand, while with the other he threw kisses to the Baltimore belles; another, Henry Christian Timm, a player of rare sensitiveness, performed with a full wine glass on the back of his hand. Russell attracted crowds by distributing free passage across the ocean. Ole Bull played all four

[14] O. ORTMANN, " Musical Life in the Seventies," Baltimore *Evening Sun*, July 16, 1935.

strings of the fiddle at once, doing what Paginini himself would not dare.

No wonder that the periodicals launched a campaign against these abuses. To quote the *Pittsburgh Evening Chronicle* (1853): " And Signor Pound-the-keys for having rattled and splurged and hammered and tinkled and growled through three or four musical compositions with long line names, fills his pockets for one night's work with as many dollars as three-fourths of the community earn in the year, while the mustached gentleman who assists him by quavering, quivering, and shouting through three or four songs in as many different European languages, which is all gibberish to the audience, pockets half as much."

It is hard to gauge which conditioned which, but with easier money and more comfortable transportation, exhibitionism on a scale unknown in Europe was multiplied. What a leap from the meagre half-dollars, admitting a gentleman and two ladies, to those resplendent honorariums, later in the century! The memorable New York Philharmonic Concert which first gave the *Finale* of Beethoven's *Symphony in D*—the earliest Beethoven movement heard on this side, charged $2.00. So did Garcia on the occasion of the debut of the illustrious Signorina Malibran, afterwards Madame de Beriot, when regulations concerning the direction of carriages and "heads of horses" on Broadway were in order. Both, the Castle Garden Huerta, in his farewell evening of guitar ensembles, and the Park's *Barber of Seville* charge prohibitive prices by 1825. Then, as now, opera was first of all a social event. " Never before has such an audience been assembled—pit and boxes filled to overflowing . . . lower circles occupied by elegant and well-dressed females . . . no unsightly bonnets . . . detracting from the array of beauteous and smiling faces, decked in native curls." Once at least a box for a single night of opera retailed at $6,000. If one is to believe Herz seats cost $6.00 a piece. [Odell, *Annals of the New York Stage*, N. Y., 1928, III, p. 183.]

That bizarre team, Jenny Lind and Barnum, of the Big Tent, undertaken so as to disprove the humbug and the belief that the latter's capacities did not extend beyond " Tom Thumb," exhibiting a stuffed monkey-skin or a dead mermaid, earned well over a thousand in spite of the Swedish nightingale's more than generous contribution to charity (1810-1880). A humble hatter runs into a gold mine when he pays several hundred to hear her sing. Ole Bull the Herculean fiddler who could silence his strings in the faintest of calandos, and was pronounced the superior of Vieuxtemps and Paginini, built his *Oleana* from the king's ransom collected during his first American tour. On the second, chaperoning the world's most advertised prodigy, Adelina Patti, he sweeps the entire country, straight to the Golden State, in his victorious march. Louis Moreau Gottschalk (1829-1869), the earliest of the matinee-idols, with a tinge of Jew, Creole, and Parisian, singled out by Chopin and Berlioz as "king of pianists," was approached by Barnum with an offer of $20,000 a year, and expenses. Every woman's heart was set aflutter by his fiery playing, and his nonchalant pose. New York, the West Indies, South America, were fighting for a scrap of the white gloves which he invariably wore on the platform, and took off with utmost deliberation, one finger at a time.

Gottschalk fell a victim to the megalomania, which is so typically a current of romanticism. His death in Rio de Janeiro was brought about by a monster musical festival, participated in by 800 musicians, with reinforcement by bands of army, navy and the national guards.

If distending orchestral means *ad infinitum*, and a stress of coloristic values can be accepted as common denominators of romanticism, Heinrich and Jullien are more intrinsically romantic than Beethoven, Schubert, Liszt, and Berlioz. Where else but in a capitalistic clime could the mammoth parades of the indefatigable Selby, Tuckey and Adgate take such firm root? Their enthusiastic disciples are Carl Lenshow and Carl Bergmann, conductors of the Germanian Society, the earliest of the well trained orchestral bodies to take their technique seriously. An addict to the craving for impressiveness was Louis Antoine Jullien (1812-1860). From his father, a band master, and later, in Paris, from Halévy and Le Carpentier, he learned a lot about the subtleties of orchestral timbre; still more about the intricacies of box office call. When, in 1853, he disembarked in New York, already a celebrity, all the newspapers carried stories of the " monster ophicleide exhibited on Broadway," and of a drum brought over by several steamboats, of such immense proportions that it required a player at each end. His orchestra, "complete in every department," was ready to hurl some 1200 "grand compositions of the grand masters," Beethoven, Mozart, Mendelssohn and potpourris of questionable merit on unsuspecting listeners.

In order to do justice to his motto: *Music for the Masses,* Jullien resorted to rather original devices. Not the water or air, not the *Rheingold* or *Flying Dutchman,* or *Waldesrauschen* is the Leit-Motif of realistic romanticism in America, but the more dynamic of the elements *Wotan's Farewell*—fire. Many a brilliant musical image has been brought into being by the fire-engine. Jullien, for one, staged lovingly *Firemen's Quadrilles,* symphonies of deafening fortissimos in the violins, doubled by a *Domestica* of splurging waterhose, broken glass, and the inferno of angry flames.

Carl Bergmann, cellist and conductor of the Germanians and Philharmonic, responsible for the best reading of *Tannhäuser* and *Midsummer Night's Dream,* paid his homage to realism in his Suite, *Broadway.* From Castle Garden to Barnam's he led the ear-splitting brass band, to form a climax in a *Firemen's Parade:* machine, bells, whistles, and a vociferous combat between two rival fire Companies. To lend the event a more theistic foundation, a church organ and Turkish patrol swelled the harmony. Odell records a New York benefit for the Fire Department Fund, June 24, 1826, where music, a showing of banners, and an elegant engine pouring water on a house enveloped in flames, were the preliminary stages to the impressive Finale—a Stalinesque figure of the Fireman.

But the real Wotan of the orchestra is Heinrich. By some uncanny felicity of thought, he anticipates all the grandiose schemes of Berlioz, of the *Requiem,* the *Te Deum,* the *Funeral Symphony* and the *Song of the Railway* with their armies of participants. Heinrich's seismic, dynamic, "becoming" approach has been dictated by nature, "but not by that Nature, whose quiet idyllic grace possesses us all unconsciously. He has sought out Nature in the workshops where she produces her mighty works, where great bridges of rock are thrown across streams: where rivers, broad as seas, flow out of undiscovered sources over hundreds of miles to the ocean itself; where great falls plunge with a deafening roar to the depths below, and the tornado, with its crashing strength lays bare the impenetrable secrets of the primeval forests." [15]

Nietzschean is every drop falling from Heinrich's fertile pen. No patience had he with "Butterfly effusions," no sympathy for negligence, smallness, for players who "remained strangers to their parts." With each one of his Promethean Sagas his daring grew. Possessed of a truly Wagnerian conviction of his genius, he solicits for his *Jubilee* of 1840, a national *Song of Triumph*, scored for Herculean orchestra and chorus, the support of the most exalted patrons. Years are spent in drawing up a *Who's Who* of official Washington. He pesters Paginini for an audience, corresponds with Jenny Lind.

"Numerous and powerful," Heinrich's symphony, consisting of all the available professors and volunteers "upon scales of grandeur, seldom equalled in his or any other country," was not idle daydreaming. It existed, the child of the labors of B. Carr, Charles Hupfeld, and the *Musical Fund Society*. His orchestra, of which the newspapers spoke in a hush, was as follows: six double basses, six violoncelli, 8 violas, 24 violins, primo and secondo, 4 trumpets, 4 horns, 1 cornetto, 1 bombardo, 1 ophicleide, 1 serpent, basshorn, 3 tromboni, 1 contrafagotto, 1 fagotto, 2 oboes, 3 clarinetti, 1 petite-clarinette, 2 flauti, 1 piccolo, timpani bass, and side drums, tambourine, cymbals, triangle, gongs.

As a colorful personality, Heinrich is the peer of Beethoven, Berlioz, and Wagner. His attachment to his daughter Toni is no less pathetic than Beethoven's hunger for love, or Berlioz's

[15] F. A. Mussik, *Skizzen aus dem Lebendes sich in America befindenden, A. P. Heinrich*, Prag, 1843, pp. 18-20.

impassioned wooing of Henrietta Smithson. Through his idiosyncrasies, his foibles, there shine the inviolable integrity and honesty of his work. His friendships with John and Lucy Audubon, the Sneeds, John Howard Paine, Jonas Chickering, disclose as potent and many-sided a personality as the Brunswicks and Breunings deciphered in the ill-mannered Beethoven. Extravagant Heinrich could be on occasion as Russell, as grotesque and morose as Stephen Foster, as temperamental as Charles Zeuner, as complex as Ureli Hill, as nearly mad as Jullien, but poseur and mountebank, he refused to be.

But the Baroque, stars, Barnum, musical glasses, the championship of Negro and Indian, evaporate into air next to America's deep, dynamic faith in music as a weapon for emancipation of the spirit. For the torch " held by that queer miasmatical group of lunar phenomena, in which philosophy, self-culture, politics, art, social reform and religion, were all mixed up and felt to be, in some vague way, the same thing," [16] had been lit by none other than Beethoven. In part a by-product of nature and temperament, in part a revolt against Puritan Orthodoxy, transcendentalism was an Utopia, a dream built on German ideals. From Jacobi and Kant, Wackenroder and Tieck, Herder and Novalis, did Brook Farm acquire the entire dogma of its trust in individual reason as correlative with Supreme Wisdom: Goethe, Schiller, and Rückert, translated over and over again by Charles Brooks; John Sullivan Dwight, musician, minister; and Margaret Fuller, spread the " philosophical idealism with its indwelling Godhead that exalted man to the divine and transferred a mechanical universe into the dwelling place of divine love." [17]

Jamaica Plain, Groton, Boston were enraptured by Bettina, " from amid whose golden or moonlight waves arose thoughts like green islands, thickly scattered, born to tell us the secrets of nature, unclouded visions of innocence." (*The Dial.*) Brook Farm dreamt of Italy with Wackenroder and Tieck, and held

---

[16] Van Wyck Brooks, *America's Coming-of-Age*, New York, 1930, p. 70.
[17] Vernon Louis Parrington, *The Romantic Revolution in America*, New York, 1927, p. 317.

out a gauntlet to conventionalism with *Lucinda*. Everyone searched for the blue flower, listened fervently to the Aeolian harp. They slept in the fields with *Sternbald*. With him they sang, and imitated the lark and nightingale. Music was love; love-music, freedom, unending "becoming," genius. They scorned with Herder system and rule. They shed tears over *Meister* and the *Wahlverwandtschaften*. They shuddered at *Kater Murr* and the *Mad Kappelmeister Kreisler*. They knew by heart Schlegel's

> Durch alle Töne tönet
> Im bunten Erdenraum
> Ein leiser Ton gezogen
> Für ihn der heimlich lauschet.

and Tieck's,

> Liebe denkt in süssen Tönen
> Denn Gedanken stehn zu fern.

From Novalis they learnt that "all method is rhythm. If one has perceived the rhythm of the world, one has also comprehended the world. Every human being has his individual rhythm. . . . Genuine mathematics is the real element of the magician. In music mathematics appears as a revelation, as creative idealism. Here it is authorized as a heavenly ambassador to mankind. All enjoyment is musical, and accordingly, also mathematical."

They discovered a new world of Orphic mysteries in Bach with E. T. A. Hoffmann: "There are moments when the musical properties of numbers, nay, the mystic rules of counterpoint, evoke an interior horror. Music! with a mysterious awe, even fear, I call you! Thou in sound expressed Sanscritta of nature!"

Here, in prim, orthodox New England, the exalted metaphysics of the early German romanticists work a revolution. Its vestal is Margaret Fuller, whose seeking for truth, self-truth, leads her on to a contemplation of nature's divine harmonies. Tieck, who has embodied so many Runic secrets, had opened her eyes on herself, has made her a wonderful bird singing in the forest, had kindled her sympathy for the oppressed in Russia and Greece. Novalis she adores, also Jean-Paul. They should never be profaned by the mob—Margaret shares their heavenly tunes only with the élite.

To illustrate the supremacy of the human spirit in the face of insurmountable obstacles, Margaret Fuller takes as example Beethoven, Beethoven harassed by grief and affliction. To her smug, bigoted, provincial New England she tried to prove that man was not made for society, but society for man, by the example of music, timeless, compounded of past and future.

> Most intellectual master of the art,
> Which, best of all, teaches the mind of man
> The Universe, in all its varied plan—
> What strangely mingled thoughts the strains impart.[18]

Beethoven proves that the only "hope for man was grounded on his destiny as an immortal spirit and not as a comfort-loving inhabitant of the earth or a subscriber to the social contact."[19] The contemporary opera showed her that knowledge, bare fact, not accompanied by a corresponding deepening of the sources, was apt to vulgarize rather than ennoble the spirit: the *Fifth*—the rôle of fantasy in igniting the divine spark. Disappointed in her love for James Nathan, she invokes Beethoven.

Once more, as with Herder and Novalis, true music is pure, a law unto itself, scorning the scaffolding of word. Margaret reads *Die Ideen zur Philosophie der Geschichte der Menschheit.* (Herder.) She sings her ode

M. FULLER—*Instrumental Music*

> The charms of melody, in simple airs,
> With human voices sung, are always felt;
> With thoughts responsive, careless hearers melt,
> Of secret ills, which our frail nature bears—
> We listen, weep, forget. But when the throng
> Of a great Master's thoughts, above the reach
> Of words and colors, wire and wood can teach
> By laws which to the spirit-world belong—
> When several parts, to tell one mood combined,
> Flash meaning on us, we can ne'er express,
> Giving to matter subtlest powers of mind,

---

[18] M. FULLER, "Beethoven," *The Dial*, 1841, p. 173.
[19] MARGARET BELL, *Margaret Fuller*, New York, 1930, p. 139.

Superior joys attentive souls confess,
The harmony which stars and suns obey,
Blesses our earth-bound state with visions
Of supernal day.[20]

She begins to dread the naked brutality of speech. "Oh, definition, definition, a deaf, unmusical creature" lamented the Jovian Herder. And Margaret Fuller: "O for the safe and natural Way of Intuition" . . . "The Ton-Kunst, the Ton-Welt, give me now more stimulus than the written Word, for music seems to contain everything in nature, unfolded into perfect harmony. In it the *all* and *each* are manifested in rapid transition; the spiral and undulatory movement of beautiful creation is felt throughout, and, as we listen, thought is most clearly, because most mystically, perceived." (*Memoirs.*) Like Moses Mendelssohn and Novalis, she unravels in pure, unadulterated melody and harmony remote decrees of fate, "the feeling of a destiny, casting its shadow from the very morning of thought." Like Wackenroder, she designates instrumental music as the only true art, a heaven gained by the renunciation of reality.

This faith Margaret transmits to Emerson and Hawthorne; she spreads it through her lectures and writings. Defining *Transcendentalism,* the *Dial* borrows all its ideals from the world of sounds, so "much beyond and above the deductions of logic and thoughts. Whence does the song of the early bird borrow its melody, and seems like audible tones of a universal harmony, echoing voices from that far land, where he has wandered in his so-called dreams?"

Music to Brook Farm is the only idiom which has not yet exhausted itself. Painting and architecture are doomed. But music is blossoming as never before. "The last hundred years have witnessed a succession of triumphs in this art, the removal of obstructions, the transcending of limits, and the opening of new realms of thought to an extent that makes the infinity of promise and hope very present with us." She alone is symbol of romantic progress, dynamism, the Infinite, free, world-permeating, ever-

[20] *The Dial*, 1841, p. 172.

shifting, Protean. Like the Gothic cathedral, music is "never finished, forever yearning and striving upwards, the beginning only of a boundless plan, whose consummation is in another world." [21]

To this heaven the *Dial* opposes the cheap contrivances of Russell, the "psalmody of the country choir and the dancing master's fiddle, *Jim Crow.*" How much more regal is music than the plebeian word, the definite, wingless creature, which is impotent to tell one even the life and the thoughts of a musician. Good music, true music "delivers us from our actual bondage; it buoys us up above our accidents and wafts us on waves of melody to the heart's ideal home." (*Concerts of the past Winter.*) No word can solve the mystery of intuition, the creative urge. Forever, it remains a marginal note, lacking the substance of genius. Who can explain why and to what end the creator of the *Fifth* is pure, simple, forceful, subtle, grand, grotesque, leonine, impetuous? Of melodies the unearthed ones are greatest; the *Ahnung* more magnificent than the realisation. [22]

Significant is the coincidence that the interest felt in Beethoven began simultaneously with the discovery of Emerson, "and notably in the same minds who found such quickening in his free and bracing utterance. It was to a great extent the great souls drawn to 'Transcendentalism' to escape spiritual starvation, who were most drawn also to the great deep music." [23]

Beethoven was liberation. Young men and women, "whom the new intellectual dayspring had made thoughtful, used to give themselves up completely to the influence of the sublime harmonies, that sank to their souls, enlarging and coloring thenceforth the whole horizon of their life" (Cooke, p. 66). No matter how crude the interpretation, the abstractions of Mozart and Beethoven were the predominant interests and mainsprings of those refreshing days. Music helped the democratic utopia.

---

[21] "Concerts of the Past Winter," *The Dial*, July, 1840, p. 126.
[22] M. FULLER, *Love-Letters*, New York, Appleton, 1903, p. 33.
[23] GEORGE WILLIS COOKE, *John Sullivan Dwight, Brook-Farmer, Editor, and Critic of Music,* Boston, 1898, p. 66.

Being innocent of creed and formula, it cared little for dogma. It cured the fatigued, gave courage to fight and to work. Unconscious of distance, the Brook Farmers would walk many miles singing and living the beautiful strains. From the first, instinctively, there existed in New England a true affinity between the great tone-poems and the great ideals of the human mind. Measure, order, harmony ruled here over the idle, the sensual, and vulgar, the products of " crude, swaggering civilization." " It was as if our social globe, charged with the electricity of new divine ideas and longings,—germs of a new era,—were beginning to be haunted by auroral gleams and flashes of strange melody and harmony " (Cooke, p. 66). People were forgetting how to think or talk: they felt!

What Herder and Novalis failed to accomplish for their own race, takes shape in the new Atlantis. Once more virtuosity becomes the means, not the goal. Thalberg, Chopin, Liszt, may be " rich, brilliant, wild, astonishing," they are exquisite and sweeping, but they have no rights of existence in the presence of Mozart.

> Oh nature's finest lyre! To Thee belong
> The deepest, softest tones of tenderness,
> Whose purity the listening angels bless,
> With silvery clearness of seraphic song.[24]

Instead of the vulgarities of opera and ballet, the last string *Quartets of Beethoven*; instead of minstrels—the Mendelssohn Quintet Club with its fine missionary work, instead of romantic philosophy endeavor, progress and betterment of taste, could Herder have asked for more? And rightly or wrongly, romanticism in American music still pursues its dynamic course.

---

[24] MARGARET FULLER, " Mozart," *The Dial*, 1841, p. 173.

ROMANTIC PHILOSOPHY IN AMERICA

by

George Boas

IF by "philosophy" we mean courses in universities, it is safe to say that philosophy was quite untouched by the Romantic movement in America. The professors went on their way teaching Scottish realism or what they thought was the philosophy of John Locke. At Princeton, which became the headquarters of American philosophy, President Witherspoon took it upon himself to stamp out what remained of the idealism of Bishop Berkeley and apparently succeeded before the end of the eighteenth century. His successors carried on the good work and, if we may judge at this distance, no young Princetonian was ever tempted to doubt the reality of the material world, the efficacy of common sense, or even the finality of authority.

But if we mean by "philosophy" the speculations of individuals outside universities, we may say that philosophy was reborn during this period and that, curiously enough, the two leading figures in the movement were not only deeply interested in philosophy but also productive of it. All the members of the Concord School based their art and directed their lives by philosophical teaching. And in the South Edgar Allan Poe even produced a philosophical prose poem.

There is so much that is clearly absurd in Bronson Alcott that it is none too easy to discover that which is profound. His extreme vegetarianism, for instance, which prevented his children from drinking milk and his garden from absorbing animal manures, is in itself enough to make the most sympathetic expositor of his ideas tremble. When one goes through the list of books in the library of Fruitlands, his ideal community, one finds translations of Confucius, of the Hermetic letters, of English and Hellenistic

Neoplatonists, of seventeenth century theologians, but not one book on agriculture. Yet this was to be a society which drew its sustenance entirely from the soil by its own efforts. When one reads his daughter's wry account of the experiment, "Transcendental Wild Oats," or the pages from his wife's journal in which she hopes that "the experiment will not bereave me of my mind,"[1] one finds it hard to sympathize with this man who was more Pythagoras than Christ, as Charles Lane put it.

Yet there was in spite of the naïvety, the gullibility, the downright childishness, a vein of poetry at least, a vein of independence of judgment, of religious insight, which America needed as much then as it does now. Like Emerson and Thoreau, Alcott was a staunch believer in the rights of the individual and in his duty to be true to himself. The individual had rights in the eighteenth century also, but those rights accrued to him as a human being and were no different from those of any other human being. This group of Yankee philosophers was interested in other rights, the right of the individual to be different from other human beings, the right—in fact the duty—of the individual not to conform. How important it was for such a right to be preached appears more clearly when one knows the story of Joseph Palmer.

Joseph Palmer came from an old New England family; his record for what was then called "respectability" was untarnished. He was refused communion, jailed, beaten, starved; in the words of a writer in the *Boston Daily Globe* in 1884, he "was persecuted, despised, jeered at, regarded almost as a fiend incarnate; . . . was known far and wide as a human monster . . . with whose name mothers used to frighten their children when they were unruly."[2] When one asks what hideous crime, or what revolting manner of life led to such treatment, one discovers that the

---

[1] See *The Journals of Bronson Alcott*, ed. by ODELL SHEPHARD, Boston, 1938, p. 149. In 1851 he had a copy of some of the Latin agricultural writers, but could not read Latin. See *Id.*, p. 253.

[2] Quoted in *Bronson Alcott's Fruitlands*, by CLARA ENDICOTT SEARS, Boston and New York, 1915, p. 56.

unhappy Palmer wore a beard and beards had not been worn in America for a full generation.

If men could be so treated because they anticipated the style of the coming generation, one can see that the preaching of what to us is a truism was in those days an important novelty.

But the right and duty of being an individual did not simply mean a policy of ethical *laissez-faire*. As Josiah Royce was to say seventy-five years later, one cannot express one's self unless one has a self to express. Alcott like Emerson believed strongly in the necessity of achieving a self, of building up a character which would be master of the world instead of its slave. The extreme asceticism which he practised was simply the means which he thought to be appropriate for conquering his world. The pioneers, the railroad builders, the great business men were beginning to conquer the world in a way which meant their own inevitable defeat. He saw clearly enough then what we are beginning to see now, that the conquest of material obstacles is in the long run surrender to them. " As to money," he wrote to his mother in 1839, " I take no second thoughts about it." That this won him a reputation of idler and sponge did not leave him cold, but his philosophy comforted him. " All because I had one set of gifts and not the other, and fell so obliquely on my time that none caught my point of view to comprehend the person I was. 'Tis as disastrous to leave body as soul out of our regards. Mind is not always a merchantable commodity; and here's the Pedlar, July 1850, the pack of metaphysic that he is, set bodily, mystically, down in the best market in the world. Athenian times, yet without customer for his handsome wares." [3] Had he been less of a metaphysical pack, it might have been better for his wife and daughters; but at the same time a voice decrying the pursuit of money was needed at that time in America as it is needed now.

The achievement of a character, however, was of religious importance to the Transcendentalists. For Alcott the primary fact in the universe was not its material but God. Matter was to him but the last manifestation, as he called it, of God. The basic

[3] *Journal*, p. 232.

metaphor of these men was that of Plotinus; the light whose beams spread out into darkness. As the darkness grows, matter becomes thicker and man's task in life is to return to the source of light, not to immerse himself in shadows. Men are situated in that realm which lies between the Heaven of ideals and the Earth of corporeal entanglements. Their life is a struggle to escape from the one into the freedom of the other. Whatever one may think of the truth of such a metaphysics, that its lessons were appropriate to American life between 1812 and 1860 can surely not be denied.

The most important effect of all this is to be seen in Alcott's theory and practice of education. As early as 1826 he was writing in his Journal what later became the doctrine of self-reliance, now associated with the name of Emerson.[4] He urged that men think for themselves, follow Reason and forsake authority, act rather than talk, and be willing to cleave to their own line. In dealing with children, and it was children's education which particularly interested him, he strove to " prepare the child to aid himself." That system of education which was associated with the name of Locke and which considered the child's mind as a tablet upon which the teacher wrote his message, was abandoned for one which considered the child to have his own incipient personality which had its own right to grow. " The Child is the Book," he wrote at the age of twenty eight.[5] The teacher's whole duty was to study that book, rather than those written by pedagogues. The various schools for children which he directed gave him an opportunity to carry out these principles and, though they all ended in financial failure and attracted a certain amount of ridicule, at the same time they made their mark upon American education and were respected by some of the best minds of the time. In them lay the whole theory of progressive education, as it is now called, and at a time when the equality of man was popularly considered to imply the equal gifts of all and the uniformity of human nature, the daring of Alcott's theory and practice was all the more remarkable.

[4] See *Journal*, p. 7.   [5] *Journal*, p. 12.

Alcott's fame has been overshadowed by that of his friend, Emerson. For Emerson not only did not go to the extremes of radical behaviour in which Alcott seemed perversely to delight but, what is more, Emerson had a literary style which eclipsed that of anyone alive at that time. It is questionable whether Emerson actually contributed anything new to Transcendentalism and whether he discovered any ideas which Alcott had not previously discovered. But, however that may be, he did have a genius for verbal expression and a personality which charmed his audiences. Curiously enough his style was more in keeping with Alcott's character than it was with his own; yet Alcott never achieved that kind of racy Yankee prose. He remained in the Johnsonian tradition of elegant English, and regretted it. He knew at the age of thirty-five that his thought was too abstract and his spirit lacked the gift of simple and concrete illustration.[6] More than that, it lacked the direct contact with experience. His inspiration was literary particularly in his youth, regardless of his theories. He did not look into his own soul and write nor did he look out to his own fields and write. His diary echoes the English Platonists and Thomas Taylor (the translator of Plato and Plotinus), Coleridge, the Germans. There is no ring of the New England farmer and pedlar in his phrases. If Emerson writes as Alcott might have been expected to write, it is because Emerson had been through Harvard, had preached sermons and delivered lectures, knew the literary tradition and evaluated it as worthless. Had Alcott written as he spoke, the world would have thought he knew no better; when Emerson wrote colloquially everyone knew it was not because he lacked polite learning. Emerson's essays are, as everyone knows, little more than strings of brilliant sentences. They have no unity or coherence. But each sentence is so good in itself that few readers care whether they are logically tied to those that precede and follow or not.

There are a few leading ideas in Emerson's essays which have become catch phrases: Self-reliance, the Law of Compensation, the

[6] Cf. ODELL SHEPHARD'S discussion of Alcott's style in the Introduction to his edition of the *Journal*, p. xvii f.

Oversoul. To give them precise and verifiable meaning is next to impossible. A moralist can learn perhaps without books, but a scientist would be paralysed without them. Shall we therefore give up science? Evil may be balanced by good, but is the existence of another's good or a later good a remedy for my present evil? Man may indeed be " a stream whose source is hidden "; but the stream flows through banks of mud which are only in part of its making.

Such a philosophy could say to men only this: Your problems are not real problems, turn your backs upon them. That is, to be sure, neither trivial nor cowardly but insufficient. For though the world may be One at heart, it is many as we know it in our daily life, and the conflicts, frustrations, and tragedies which arise from its multiplicity cannot be denied. The rat in the trap is hardly comforted, to say nothing of being released, by learning that other rats are not trapped or that only his body is trapped, or that for many days previously he himself had not been trapped. His immediate problem is escape.

On the other hand, it can never be strongly enough emphasized that in a country where competition was the rule, co-operation had to be preached; that in a country in which material gain was considered almost the unique prize and the testimony of successful living, integrity still had to be held aloft as worth something; that in a country where defeat was ruthless and physical weakness a crime, much was to be gained from learning that the Soul when given to God, " calls the light its own, and feels that the grass grows and the stone falls by a law inferior to, and dependent on, its nature." Who cared, hearing such messages, whether they made any sense or not? What was needed at that moment was inspiration to rise above railroad building and electioneering to those things which alone in the long run made life worth living. Many a young man and woman hearing such words must have found new courage and at least poetic justification for turning from the counter to the desk.

Meanwhile in Fordham the poet whom Emerson called " the jingle man " was composing a prose poem on cosmology. Poe's

Eureka, written in a state approaching madness, was one of the very few attempts made in this country before the Civil War to produce a system of philosophy. It is a work which has been sufficiently ridiculed to deserve something more than ridicule now. It must survive, however, as a curiosity only, for it had next to no influence in America.

That there was no love lost between the Transcendentalists and Poe requires no proof. Each thought the others beneath contempt. But there are curious similarities between them for all that. For instance, the notion that all theory commences with intuition, the notion that in order to know God we should have to be God, the insistence on Unity as the ultimate character of the Universe, the description of the heavenly bodies as first expanding from a centre and then moving back into that centre, all such ideas might have been found in Emerson. What could never have been found, however, was the knowledge of physical science and the systematizing skill. Much of the former is wrong and was wrong even in 1848. But Poe's interest in collecting and organizing the material was not wrong at all.

Briefly, Poe presents us with a universe in a constant state of expansion followed by contraction. This process, he thinks, is exemplified in the Newtonian law of gravitation. The various particles of matter, which both attract and repel each other, make for a universe of diversity through expansion and for one of unity by contraction. The power of attraction by which bodies are composed, is identified by Poe with Matter; the power of repulsion with Mind. There is thus no fundamental difference between them. Not only that, but since both forces are in God as well as in Man, there is a fundamental identity between the divine and the human. Finally, when cosmic history shall have run its course and the present diversity of suns and planets and satellites shall have been condensed into unity, then individual souls will also have ceased to exist. But if one lose his individual identity, says Poe in a final foot-note, all will become identical with God.

There can be no question that such a picture of the universal scheme can be riddled with objections. And critics have not been slow to profit by the occasion. But Poe himself wished it to be judged as a poem, not as a philosophic treatise and, one imagines, had he omitted some of the mathematical portions and written up the rest in stirring blank verse, no one would have thought of picking logical flaws in it. To judge it as a poem is to attempt to visualise the process of the primordial atom swelling into stars and planets until the universe is peopled with lights; and then to see these bodies falling together and condensing into greater and greater masses with a final material unity as their goal. Surely there is little that is prosaic in such a picture.

More interesting now than its truth is the fidelity it shows to the pattern of Poe's poetic genius. The Transcendentalists too were fond of dealing with God and the Soul and were even more familiar with mystery. But there was nothing of the Gothic in their makeup. Nature to them was the rural landscape, brooks, smiling fields, ponds, the New England woods. But to Poe the only landscape he cared for was that of the heavens, interstellar space; his ponds were dark tarns, his valleys those of shadow, his brook the " ghastly rapid river " of insane laughing ghosts. One can no more imagine Poe seeking the fresh rhodora in the woods than one can imagine Emerson wandering

> By a route obscure and lonely
> Haunted by ill angels only.

Alcott, for all the ridicule and misunderstanding he attracted, was like Emerson, a man surrounded by friends. Poe was essentially the lonely man; he had neither disciples nor friends. A few poor souls, as lonely as he, were kind to him, but what communion could there have been between so keen a mind as that which wrote his critical essays and a woman like Mrs. Clemm? The women who loved him, even Sarah Whitman, were pale copies of womanhood. There was no place in America for such a man. His whole life shows, detail after detail, the steady search for something to satisfy his hunger for both truth and beauty. His adventures in science were disappointing.

Hast thou not torn the Naiad from her flood,
The Elfin from the green grass, and from me
The summer dream beneath the tamarind-tree?

His attempts at poetry were equally disappointing. With the notable exception of Lowell, most American critics could see little in them worthy of praise. One ventures to suggest that had he been born in France, had he known men to talk with on his own terms, his achievement both as poet and as philosopher would have been greater. As things were, he resorted to the friends of all such men—drugs.

The curious rationalism which led to *Eureka* also influenced Poe's conception of art. His essay on poetic technique is a good example of it. Whereas Alcott maintained that the poets are the " most effectual teachers of morality," and Emerson that " poetry exists to speak the spiritual law," Poe was saying that poems have only " collateral relations " with the intellect or with the conscience, that except incidentally, they have " no concern whatever either with Duty or with Truth." Poetry, even in his youth, had pleasure only as its end. To produce a maximum of pleasure required the use of intelligence on the poet's part and, as he said in his famous essay on the *Philosophy of Composition,* neither accident nor intuition would take its place. Many commentators on this essay have seen in it merely an attempt on the author's part to be shocking, an end which he achieved, whether he wished to or not. As a matter of fact, however false it may be to the facts of his own composition, it accords pretty well with what evidence the manuscripts of poets have to provide. Even William Blake's manuscripts show erasures, revisions, hesitation, groping, and if any poet might be thought to have been inspired, it is Blake. It is, to be sure, questionable whether Poe himself or any other poet was quite so calculating as Poe claims to have been in composing *The Raven.* It was a poem greatly admired in its own day and Poe undoubtedly derived a certain pleasure from telling his contemporaries just how he had planned his emotional effects. He had a cruel streak in him and, much as he courted admiration, he enjoyed mystifying and puzzling his readers. At a time when people were talking about inspiration, he was amused to point out that in his most inspired poem he had proceeded to its completion "with the precision and rigid consequence of a mathematical problem." But at the same time he was laying down a principle which in France was to become a commonplace, that poetry is an art, that artistry demands thought, is a controlled way of doing things, is not random playing with words. His impatient comment on Novalis's words, "The artist belongs to his work, not the work to the artist," [7] accentuates the importance of artistic intelligence: "In the hands of the true artist the theme, or ' work,' is but a mass of clay, of which anything (within the compass of the mass and quality of the clay) may be fashioned at will, or according to the skill of the workman. The clay is, in fact, the slave of the artist. It belongs to him. His genius, to be sure, is manifested, very distinctively, in the choice of the clay. It should be neither fine nor coarse, abstractedly, but just so fine or so coarse, just so plastic or so rigid, as may best serve the purposes of the thing to be wrought, of the idea to be made out or, more exactly, of the impression to be conveyed." Can one imagine Emerson speaking of "the impression to be conveyed?" To him artistry was the filtering of natural beauty through the human mind; art was "the spirit creative." Can one imagine Poe saying, "The artist does not feel himself to be the parent of his work?" or, "Nature paints the best part of the picture, carves the best part of the statue, builds the best part of the house, and speaks the best part of the oration?" [8] On the contrary Poe asserts, "we can, at any time, double the true beauty of an actual landscape by half closing our eyes as we look at it." [9] Emerson could not look at anything with half-closed eyes. Similarly one can find paragraph after paragraph by Poe on rhetoric, punctuation, poetic technique, and not a word by either Alcott or Emerson. But the penalty which Poe paid for this was his contentless verse which to-day for the most part is songs without words, whereas the

[7] *Marginalia,* in the Stedman-Woodberry ed., VII, 276.
[8] From the essay called *Art* in *Society and Solitude.*
[9] *Marginalia,* edition cited, p. 277.

poetry of Emerson—if not of Alcott—seems as meaty as when it was written.

There are always at least two philosophies in a country: those implied in the way people live and those which are the results of meditation upon life and the universe. A struggle is likely to ensue to make the latter turn into the former. In that struggle Poe was of course wholly unsuccessful, whereas the Transcendentalists—witness Thoreau—had a certain measure of success. But it is a question whether Poe's dream of a universe in which all souls would eventually meet in one was not a clearer indication to those who had the eyes to see it of the problems of life in America than the optimistic sentences of Emerson. To this day Poe's most sympathetic biographer sees little more than madness in *Eureka*. The real critic of American life will someday ask precisely what it was that drove so fertile a mind to such a climax

If one were to label the essential difference between the Transcendentalists and Poe, one would probably find it in their theories of knowledge. The former saw the source of truth in some inner sense which could be called " intuition." The latter carried over from the eighteenth century the idea of reason as the force impelling us to truth. It would be absurd to pretend that either group were consistent or even clearly aware of what we are attributing to them. But their predominant interests lay in the directions we have indicated. But beside Poe's rationalism was a consuming sense of mystery; and beside the mysticism of the Transcendentalists was the sense of a clear and sunny landscape. Read Thoreau, Alcott, and Emerson from cover to cover and you find little bewilderment or anguish over the complexities and puzzles of the universe or of the life within it. Their pages are as candid as buttercups. They had a kind of faith in something which they called " Nature," a faith that was childlike and a little absurd, and, being simple men on the whole, able to control and deny their carnal appetites, their lives were at least outwardly serene. Poe, on the other hand, had read too much contemporary science, had been too much immersed in journalism, had fought daily and—when adult—alone for his bread and butter, to have that simple faith. He knew that wits counted for more than candor and if he invented and perfected the detective and mystery story, it was because the unravelling of puzzles—of his own invention—was his way of conquering life.

One who would arrange human spirits for himself, would have coupled Poe's rationalism with Emerson's naturalism, and Poe's love of mystery with Emerson's transcendentalism. Such coupling would have made for greater psychological simplicity and the historian of ideas would have had an easier task. But the very complexity and possible inconsistency of these tendencies is instructive; it shows us how America duplicated in its romanticism the strange complexity of the European movement. It is not our purpose here to do once more that task which Professor Lovejoy has done so thoroughly in his *Discrimination of Romanticisms.*[10] But it is worth our while to indicate that in this as in other ideas, there was a multiplicity of motives and purposes and an unsuspected interweaving of diverse arguments. This volume as a whole should illustrate such a state of affairs, and every essay in it should contribute to the illustration.

[10] See *PMLA,* xxxix (June 1924), pp. 229-53.

PLATE I

ASHER BROWN DURAND: KINDRED SPIRITS

PLATE II

THOMAS COLE: NORTH-WEST BAY, LAKE WINNEPESAUKEE, N. H.

PLATE III

Courtesy, Wadsworth Atheneum, Hartford, Conn.

THOMAS COLE: JOHN THE BAPTIST IN THE WILDERNESS

PLATE IV

THOMAS COLE: DESTRUCTION. FROM THE "COURSE OF EMPIRE"

PLATE V

THOMAS COLE: THE RETURN

PLATE VI

THOMAS COLE: THE VALLEY OF THE VAUCLUSE

PLATE VII

THOMAS COLE: CATSKILL CREEK

PLATE VIII

THOMAS COLE: THE VISION

Plate IX

Original Design by Davis for Glen Ellen.
Built in 1833-1834, for Robert Gilmor, Baltimore County, Maryland

PLATE X

a   *(Courtesy of Henry H. Crapo)*

BAY WINDOW (Ceiling Restored).

HOUSE FOR WILLIAM J. ROTCH, NEW BEDFORD

From Downing's " Country Houses," Fig. 186

b

INTERIOR IN THE " BRACKETED STYLE "

PLATE XI

From Downing's " Country Houses," Fig. 179

a

DRAWING ROOM AT KENWOOD, "GOTHIC STYLE"

(Courtesy of the Metropolitan Museum of Art)

b

DESIGN BY DAVIS FOR DINING ROOM IN THE PAULDING HOUSE, TARRYTOWN

PLATE XII

from a drawing by A. J. Davis for the *New York Mirror*, July 14, 1827

TRINITY CHURCH, NEW YORK.—SAMUEL BARD
1788-1791 (demolished 1839)

PLATE XIII

a

H. A. B. S. photograph 1936   b   Architect's drawing, Md. Hist. Soc.

CHAPEL OF ST. MARY'S SEMINARY, BALTIMORE.—MAXIMILIAN GODEFROY
1806-8

PLATE XIV

from a drawing by E. W. Clay for C. G. Childs's, *Views of Philadelphia*

a

SEDGELEY MANSION, PHILADELPHIA.—B. H. LATROBE
1799-1800 (demolished)

H. A. B. S. photograph 1937

b

OLD STATE HOUSE, MILLEDGEVILLE, GEORGIA.—JETT THOMAS
1804-7 and 1835-37

PLATE XV

EASTERN PENITENTIARY OF PENNSYLVANIA.—JOHN HAVILAND
1823-35

from a drawing by Wm. Mason for C. G. Child's *Views of Philadelphia*